# EQUAL COMPENSATION
## FOR WOMEN

# EQUAL COMPENSATION FOR WOMEN

## A GUIDE TO GETTING WHAT YOU'RE WORTH IN SALARY, BENEFITS, AND RESPECT

Dawn Bradley Berry

LOWELL HOUSE
LOS ANGELES
CONTEMPORARY BOOKS
CHICAGO

Library of Congress Cataloging-in-Publication Data
Berry, Dawn Bradley.
    Equal compensation for women : a guide to getting what you're worth / Dawn Bradley
Berry.
        p.   cm.
    Includes bibliographical references.
    ISBN 1-56565-217-7
    1. Pay equity.   I. Title
HD6061.B47 1994
331.4'2153—dc20

93-45971
CIP

Requests for such permissions should be addressed to:
Lowell House
2029 Century Park East, Suite 3290
Los Angeles, CA 90067

Publisher: Jack Artenstein
General Manager, Lowell House Adult: Bud Sperry
Text design: Hespenheide Design

Manufactured in the United States of America
10   9   8   7   6   5   4   3   2   1

# DEDICATION

For Mom and Willy

# CONTENTS

# ACKNOWLEDGMENTS

First and foremost, I owe an enormous debt of gratitude to the Lowell House team: especially to Janice Gallagher, whose vision brought this project to life; Bud Sperry, my eternally cheerful and patient editor; Derek Gallagher; Peter Hoffman; Alina Storek; Jack Artenstein; Dianne Woo; and author Carol Cassell, who initially put me in touch with the great folks at Lowell House. I am also deeply grateful to those friends and colleagues who generously shared their time, expertise, and insights, not to mention their sympathetic ears, clippings, and stories: Jean Bannon, Barbara Bovee, Lynn Peters, Patricia Murphy, Margaret Brown Riggert, Janet Wiederkehr, Lisa Danielson, Jana Edmondson, Laura Kirby, Mary Blick, Becky Ralston, Clarette Bradley (a.k.a. Mom), Jennifer Mayfield, Muriel Kraszewski, Gail Feldman, Samuel Roll, Guy Saperstein, and many others. Thanks also to the folks in my office building, who supplied space, technical assistance, and an audience for my deadline hysteria. Special thanks to Eric Sirotkin, who shared a wealth of material, information, ideas, and insights. Most of all, I am eternally grateful to my husband, Willy Berry, for his steadfast support, even though he did steal my Uppity Women Unite bumper sticker for his truck!

# INTRODUCTION

Women have made tremendous strides in the past 25 years toward winning full equality in the workplace. According to the U.S. Department of Labor, women now comprise almost 46% of the labor force, with 56 million female workers, and the numbers are growing. Two of every three new workers are women. Moreover, women are staying longer in the workforce and working in a wider range of occupations than ever before.

Yet the average working woman still makes only 70 cents for every dollar paid to her male counterpart. Women who have achieved a degree of success in the corporate, legal, or medical profession are barricaded from the top by a very thick, very real glass ceiling. Most women are still segregated into low-paying jobs in what is often called the "pink-collar ghetto."

How can this be, after all the time and effort spent by so many people? Women and the men who support them have been seriously pursuing equal rights for female workers, both individually and through collective efforts, since the 1840s. A complex system of laws has been developed to guarantee women's right to equal compensation and equal treatment in all aspects of our working lives. Yet the experiences of working women and their access to opportunities for advancement remain far different from those of men.

Change in this inequity is long overdue. I find myself a little amazed—and more than a little appalled—that there is still a need for a book like this at the end of the twentieth century. By now humanity should have progressed beyond the ignorant practice of judging a person's worth according to gender, race, age, nationality, or religion. Sadly, however, bigotry still exists.

This unfortunate fact is reflected sharply in the different rates of pay between men and women for the same or essentially the same work, the unequal opportunities for advancement, and other discrepancies in the way people are treated on the job. And this discrimination can be found at all levels of the job market.

Equal compensation for women is not a radical issue; it is among the most mainstream of our country's problems. It is not about competition between women and men. Equal compensation affects both women and men, as well as industry, the economy, and perhaps most important, families. We are talking about the most basic human right. We are talking about fairness, a right that every human being with any common sense supports. I believe the only people who oppose equal rights in this day and age are those who are afraid of fair competition in the workplace, those who depend on the status quo, who feel a need to keep as many people below them as possible so that their precious mediocrity isn't threatened by someone smarter and more competent.

Is equal compensation a feminist issue? Certainly, but *feminist* is one of those words that has been so distorted by extremists at both ends of the women's rights movement that its meaning is different to nearly every individual you ask. Gloria Steinem defines feminism as the equality and full humanity of women. According to that definition, few could disagree that equal compensation is both a feminist and a human goal.

As my husband would say, real men appreciate uppity women. They know that when women win in the workplace, we all win. Men win when their wives, mothers, daughters, and friends earn more, contribute more to the household income, and have the opportunity to fulfill their potential. Children win when their parents are able to choose the careers and lifestyles that make them content and better able to build a secure, stable family. Society wins when all of its members can live up to their potential and contribute to the common good. When women are paid and treated fairly, there are measurable benefits to all workers, their families, and the employers who have learned that fairness decreases turnover and helps keep valuable workers on the job.

Indeed, the laws that protect the right to equal compensation apply equally to men and women, and more and more men who are being denied equal rights on the job are turning to the courts. In a recent case, a male nurse filed a discrimination suit against his employer and won. So, although this book is primarily geared toward women—because they are victims of employment discrimination far more often than men—the principles apply to both sexes equally.

What can be done? Plenty, I believe. As a lawyer, I have seen tremendous growth in the areas of civil rights and employment law, with more to come. These laws and the people that help make them work can give women a foundation on which to build real equality in the workplace—if you know how to use these laws.

I have two goals in writing this book. First, I want to help you learn to understand your right to equal compensation and how the law protects that right. Second, I want to show you how you can use the law and other tools available to prevent or correct problems of unequal compensation. Every working woman has the responsibility to know her rights and insist on the fair treatment guaranteed by those rights. I believe one reason for the ongoing problem is that many women are not aware of their legal employment rights and their entitlement, both legal and moral, to equal compensation.

The laws that protect our rights to equal pay and other equal employment opportunities are like a box of tools. Different tools are used to fix different kinds of problems. Sometimes it takes more than one tool to get the job done. And there are some big hammers that can be used as formidable weapons, if that's what it takes.

In this book I want to help you become familiar with these tools, to know which ones to use and when to use them. I also want to give you an understanding of the different ways you may be able to approach a problem, whether it's a quick fix or a major project. You will learn whether 10 minutes of friendly conversation with your boss may solve the problem, or whether you need to literally make a federal case out of it.

Why so many different laws? Because even with all of the changes that have taken place over the past 50 years or so, an astonishing disparity exists between the settings in which women work, even within the same field. In addition to being a lawyer, I have worked at some 20 jobs since the age of 13 in a broad variety of areas. My experiences have ranged from appalling to enlightening, and I have seen the worst and best sides of the treatment of women on the job. I've learned that the way things should be are unfortunately not always the way things are.

I was raised in a fairly traditional home. My father went to work, and my mother quit her job to stay home when I was born—a choice more women had in the prosperous fifties. Our friends and neighbors included blacks, Mexicans, Catholics, Jews, and people with disabilities, as well as career women and single parents. In both my upbringing and my own mind, discrimination was both wrong and illogical.

As soon as I started attending school, I encountered racist and sexist attitudes. I was shocked. Seemingly normal people really thought this way? They really believed that the color of a person's skin, where they were born, or their gender made them more or less valuable as a person. Unbelievable.

I'm still shocked, but I'm no longer as naive, though I do remain a determined optimist. Even today as we approach the dawn of the twenty-first century, ignorance and hatred persist. The Ku Klux Klan and neo-Nazis carry on their ugly legacies of hate and brutality. We hear unbelievable terms like *ethnic cleansing* used to excuse genocide. It would be wonderful if these demons would simply vanish, but unfortunately that's not going to happen. It's going to take education, hard work, persistence, and, most of all, courageous people to stand up and say, "I will not accept discrimination." People like Rosa Parks, who began the modern civil rights movement when she refused to give up her seat on a bus just because she was black. People like Muriel Kraszewski, who, when she was denied a hard-earned promotion because she was a woman, helped create federal law that protects millions of women. People like you.

Above all, I want to show you that you do not ever have to put up with discrimination, that you always have choices. In any circumstance, we have three basic choices: to stay and accept the situation as it is, to try and change things whether we stay or go, or to leave and not look back. In this book I want to help you assess your situation and your options by understanding your rights and how to use them. I have included the stories of many women who have experienced discrimination on the job. Most of the names are real; a few have been changed to protect the privacy of the individuals and their families, friends, and co-workers. It is my hope that their stories and the other materials in my book will inspire you and empower you to take the steps you need to make your working life everything you want—and deserve—it to be.

Discrimination is never your fault, never justified, and never something you should allow. The end of discrimination is long overdue. Other people have worked hard and fought hard to establish laws that protect your rights. Insist on *your* rights, because you're worth it!

⚖

# CHAPTER 1

# WHY BOTHER TO INSIST ON EQUAL COMPENSATION?

Why go through all the trauma of insisting on equal pay and treatment? Maybe you resent that things aren't fair, but your situation isn't all that bad. You make enough to live on, and the job isn't unbearable. Isn't a little unfairness part of the game, part of this difficult business we call life?

No! Don't allow yourself to fall prey to cynicism and discouragement. You deserve fair and equal treatment. Everyone does. But if nobody insists on this right, discrimination will never end.

There are at least three good reasons why you must insist on your right to equal compensation. First and foremost, is for your own well-being. The law says you do not have to put up with unequal treatment, harassment, and unfair pay. You don't have to, and you shouldn't. Second, when you allow discrimination to continue, a unique opportunity to make a difference is lost. Third, every time one woman allows herself to be subjected to discrimination, a message is sent out to others that says this is the way it is, and nothing can be done about it. Those who perpetuate inequality learn they can get away with it. Other victims of discrimination get the message that they shouldn't bother to assert their rights. And perhaps worst of all, young men and women are told that no one else seems to care, so why should they bother to hope or try?

## For Your Own Good and the Good of Others: Building Self-Worth and Self-Esteem

Our society places a high value on one's ability to generate income, and those who earn less tend to have a lower sense of self-worth. In addition, our work itself is an important component of our self-esteem. Work gives our lives structure, group identity, financial stability, and our sense of who we are. For most of us in contemporary society, how we value ourselves is closely tied to both our sense of accomplishment and our earning power. Equal compensation can become a life-or-death issue. People have committed suicide or gone on a shooting rampage when their sense of human worth—their dignity—was destroyed. The personal cost of doing nothing involves much more than a leaner paycheck.

Divorced women face special problems, especially if they spent years making a home or working off and on for extra income instead of building a career. "A woman who marries at 18, becomes a homemaker, and then enters the workforce at 40 may have the work identity of an 18-year-old," explains Dr. Patricia Murphy, a vocational rehabilitation expert. Known as displaced homemakers, these women include those who never worked outside the home and those who worked in low-paying, part-time, or occasional jobs during the marriage. The personal and financial difficulties faced by these women are reflected sharply in economic statistics: On the average, men who get divorced raise their standard of living by more than 70%, while their wives experience a decrease in excess of 40%.

Psychologists who work with victims of job discrimination, particularly sexual harassment, often find that these women may consequently suffer from several problems that interfere with their ability to simply function at work, let alone succeed and progress. Dr. Gail Feldman, a psychologist who has worked with many victims of employment discrimination, explains that a person's work setting is similar to a family: "It can provide a greater sense of self-esteem, of feeling welcome, of having people around us that want us to continue to grow and become more competent in the area of work that we have chosen. It's of crucial importance to our mental health that the work environment feel like a supportive, healthy place, just as it's crucial to children's well-being to grow up in a family where they perceive that those who are in charge of them encourage their growth, their independence, their autonomy, and their decision-making skills."

Dr. Samuel Roll, a clinical psychologist and professor of psychology at the University of New Mexico, has seen posttraumatic stress disorder, as well as depression and other disorders, in people subjected to harassment and discrimination on the job. One of his patients was a professional woman with a healthy, normal background who suffered years of harassment and discrimination on the job. In her he diagnosed anxiety, depression, fear, and other problems that severely impaired her ability to simply live through each day and experience life in a normal way. She maintained normal functioning in a broad range of activities and remained in touch with reality. But she suffered enough anxiety and depression to interfere with her ability to carry on with a day's activities. Dr. Roll diagnosed posttraumatic stress disorder, a condition caused by an unusual, traumatic life experience—not the common difficult experiences, such as the death of a loved one, the breakup of a relationship, or a serious illness, but something outside the realm of everyday experience. Dr. Roll emphasized that relatively minor events can add up to trauma sufficient enough to produce a posttraumatic stress disorder. For example, a string of harassing or abusive experiences at work could become traumatic, as could years and years of abuse or neglect by a spouse. Because Dr. Roll's client had endured the workplace abuse for over a year, her condition was severe and chronic. Dr. Roll felt it would take two to three years of therapy to help her get well enough to continue in her career.

The longer a woman remains in a demeaning situation, the greater the risk to her health. Dr. Murphy has found that women suffering from the after-effects of any kind of abuse have a hard time taking risks, have a distorted perception of reality, feel they are not as valuable as others, and are at special risk for sexual harassment. "These people are fragile," she explains. "They are vulnerable to further abuse. Also, they often let opportunities to advance pass them by. They prefer to remain in a safe haven. They often have little hope for the future and don't expect to have a productive career, so why bother to plan or to try?" Needless to say, this can stop a career in its tracks.

## The Parallels Between Discrimination and Abuse

Without question, discrimination is a form of abuse. Virtually all victims of discrimination suffer damage to their dignity and sense of self-worth. Dr. Murphy sees a serious risk in putting up with any discriminatory situation, even for a short period of time. "It usually starts with verbal abuse," she notes. "Words are tools of power. When women in the workplace are verbally demeaned, it may lead to more serious abuse. Even if it never moves beyond the verbal, people who let themselves be subjected to this kind of treatment are risking severe damage to their psyche and to their self-esteem—their sense of value and self-worth."

She believes verbal abuse can be more damaging over the long run than physical abuse. "It's insidious. It doesn't seem that important at the time, but we take these statements in and play them over and over, like a tape recording. Eventually we begin to believe that we're stupid, worthless, incompetent."

Furthermore, one type of abuse often supports another. When a woman doesn't earn enough to support herself or her children, she is more likely to stay in an abusive relationship at home.

In researching this book, every expert I talked to—psychologists, lawyers, and vocational experts—emphasized that most people who have experienced discrimination on the job will benefit from some form of counseling. "Individuals mistreated on the job experience similar traits to sexual abuse victims," says Eric Sirotkin, an attorney and employment law counselor. "The sense of trust is shattered. They tend to have lowered self-esteem and have problems with issues of power." He describes how these painful feelings follow the employee to the next job and can affect interpersonal relationships in the new position. "Similar events," he says, "can trigger painful memories of abuse. Merely calling the employee into the office and closing the door can lead the employee to fear a termination or reenactment of the abuse."

The damage can continue off the job as well. Sirotkin also emphasizes the importance of recognizing the crucial role work plays in the life of each person. "Work is where most of us spend the greatest portion of our waking hours. We are continually learning on the job—not just how to do the work, but also about power over and the treatment of human beings. Abuse, violence, or other affronts to human respect in the workplace that are condoned by the employer are carried home into the lives of employees and their families." He adds, "The powerless employee who has been victimized at work may lash out at his or her family to hide frustration at work and in order to feel self-powered."

But there is a flip side to extensive self-examination. Whatever you do, never blame yourself or allow others to blame you for being a victim of discrimination. Look at your past and your present state of mind to see if there is something that needs work or healing. There is no longer a stigma associated with seeking counseling or other mental health services. These services are available to everyone through private counselors, group medical plans, churches, and mental health associations. Free or low-cost services are available to people with low incomes. But don't shift the focus from assessment to blame. Many women tend to look for fault in themselves first when things don't go right.

In one of her writings, feminist scholar Mary Joe Frug tells a story that illustrates the tendency to self-blame. A woman goes shopping with a male friend to help him pick out a suit. He tries one on and poses before the mirror. The suit is too short in the arms, too long in the legs, and too tight in the seat. His reaction? "This looks great. Send for the tailor." His female companion realizes that if she had been in his position, her reaction would have been, "This looks terrible! My arms are too long, my legs are too short, and my rear is too fat." This story seems to capture a frequent response among women. We look for something wrong in ourselves rather than looking outward for the cause of the problem and how it can be fixed.

## The Courage to Act

Fighting back against discrimination can be difficult and intimidating. But when we gain the courage to act, the rewards can be tremendous. Muriel Kraszewski sued a discriminating company and won more than $400,000 for herself plus a class action settlement that netted some $250 million for her co-workers. Of course, this took an enormous amount of time and energy. But the payoff from even a relatively small effort can be amazing. Many problems can be solved in weeks, days, or even minutes without going the full route. Solutions can be reached through agency intervention, mediation, grievance procedures, or simply asserting your rights directly and insisting that you are treated lawfully and with respect. If you do have to go the distance, remember that not only are you helping yourself, but you may also affect the lives of many, many others as well.

I experienced one of the most satisfying moments in my law practice when I learned that a decision in a civil rights case a partner and I had won was being used by another party to help them win their rights. I had "made law"—law that was being used to help others. The case had been long and difficult, but at that moment I knew that all the effort put in by me, my co-counsel, and especially our clients was truly worth it. The case never went to trial; it was decided in federal district court at the pretrial motion stage, then settled. But the pretrial work resulted in a judicial opinion that was published in one of the federal reporters that lawyers and judges use to build, argue, and decide a case. So even if you settle your case before trial, you can "make law" that will open doors for other women. The next woman who finds herself in a similar situation can use your case to win or settle her own.

Building the law is a little like building a house. Once the foundation is laid, the frame goes up, then the roof, then the finishing details like floors and windows. In the end, the structure is complete, and all that remains is to fill in chinks and maintain repairs. As explained by Nancy Davis, executive director of Equal Rights Advocates, a nonprofit public interest law firm in San Francisco, "The law has been very important in empowering women. Those who went before us courageously filed suits that the rest of us don't necessarily have to bring. So we can go after the more subtle and sophisticated techniques."

Even women who didn't win their cases in the legal sense are often satisfied in the final analysis. Christine Craft became famous 10 years ago when she was fired from her job as a television news anchor at a Kansas City station for reasons that became the title of her best-selling book: *Too Old, Too Ugly, and Not Deferential to Men*. She took her case to court and won in the lower court, but her victory was overturned on appeal. But Craft has no regrets. Now hosting a radio talk show and attending law school part-time, she says she had a great time with her case and her book and was thrilled to find her case in the first textbook on gender and the law, published in 1993.

When people make an effort, they make a change, even if they don't succeed in meeting their goal. As Amelia Earhart wrote to her husband on the eve of her last flight, in which she attempted to go around the world, "Please know that I am aware of all the hazards of this trip. I want to do it because I want to do it. Women must try to do things as men have tried. When they fail, their failure must be a challenge to others."

Lynn Peters recalls banding together with her co-workers to file a State Department of Labor complaint when the owner of the magazine where they worked refused to pay them over-time and provide other benefits they had earned. "We won our agency hearing, and he was ordered to pay us what he owed. But then he ended up declaring bankruptcy, and we never did get our money," she recalls. "But I'm glad we went ahead and tried. It showed the community what a snake he was, and it also brought us all closer together, so we helped each other find new jobs. That was over 10 years ago, and I still keep in touch with some of my friends from that job."

There are other rewards when you speak out against dis-crimination. Publicity is a powerful and frightening thing. Both the problems and the solutions, the heroes and the villains need to be thrust into the limelight as an example of what works, to show what you can and can't get away with, and to plant seeds in the minds of others. How do you do this? The answer is more simple than you might think. A lawsuit with juicy allega-tions often makes the newspaper the day it is filed. Media peo-ple are always looking for a good story, whether it comes out of a lawsuit or simply one person's experience. Trade journals, newsletters, and other industry publications hunger for tales of what's new, what's working, who's in big trouble, who's shaking things up. Think about what's going on in your workplace that might interest the writers, reporters, and other workers in your industry.

Positive publicity can bring about real changes for oth-ers, too. If someone in your company came up with an innova-tive solution to a problem that saved money or kept valuable employees on the job, others will want to know about it. As def-inite, measurable progress is made, and "radical" ideas like flex time and on-site day care become more commonplace—espe-cially if the advantage of implementing these ideas is reflected in the bottom line—change will happen. It already has.

But for change to occur, people must take action, whether it's fighting for your own right to equal compensation, standing with your fellow workers to demand an end to sex discrimination in your company, or making sure others know what has been done in the past and what they can do today. There are many ways that you can make a difference. In the next chapter I'll explain the history of unequal compensation. Many women and men have worked long and hard to get us where we are today, and their stories provide the inspiration we need to continue the battle toward complete equality for all.

# CHAPTER 2

## What Are Your Rights and Where Did They Come From?

### What Is Equal Compensation?

The law guarantees your right to equal compensation in your work, and that is a broad guarantee indeed. What is covered by the term *equal compensation*? It is your fundamental right to be compensated fairly for the value of your work, to be treated with respect and in the same way as other workers, and to be rewarded according to your skills and efforts. It is your right to have equal access to all jobs you are qualified to do. It is your right to pursue your goals and realize your potential.

The courts applying these laws have defined *compensation* to include not only your regular pay—wages, salary, commissions—but also all of the rewards you earn for your work, such as equal access to overtime work, bonuses, and premium pay for night or hazardous work. Compensation includes fringe benefits such as insurance, retirement benefits, employee-sponsored annuity programs, IRAs, and club memberships; special pay for sick days, vacation days, and severance; and noncash benefits including uniforms, housing, and transportation. It also includes the right to equal opportunity to be hired and to advance. In short, it's everything you receive from your employer.

Where does the "equal" come in? Equal compensation should be reflected in your paycheck, of course, but all other benefits must be given equally as well. For example, women cannot be required to pay more to a pension fund because insurance mortality tables show females to have a longer life expectancy. You can't be required to pay more for insurance coverage because you may have a claim for childbirth costs. And if one of the company perks is membership in an all-male health club, you're not getting equal compensation unless you are given something equivalent, such as membership in a similar club for women.

There is more to the idea of equal compensation. The way it should be, under the law, it involves a simple concept known as the blindfold test. From the first job interview, an employer is supposed to behave as if he or she is wearing a blindfold so that it is impossible to tell the sex, race, age, or any disability of the applicant. The interview and subsequent treatment on the job should be based only on qualification and performance.

Beyond equal pay and benefits for equal work, you also have other rights that make up your entitlement to truly equal treatment. This includes your right to equal consideration for promotion, your right to raise a family without losing the seniority and status you've earned, and your right to work in a setting in which your comfort and integrity are respected. Today, the law essentially guarantees your right to equality in all areas of your work life.

## A Look Back: The Struggle of Working Women

One of the best ways to understand where we are today in the quest for equal compensation is to look at the way things used to be and how the changes came about.

In the early days of our country, women had virtually no rights. Women could not own property in their own name, nor could they vote. Women were considered the property of their husbands or fathers, the same as a horse or a plough. This idea was so widely accepted by the seventeenth century that the first American slaveholders adopted the law regarding women to set the legal status of slaves!

In colonial America, women generally worked in the home, manufacturing the necessities for the large families that provided labor in the agricultural society. There are records of women working as publishers, seamstresses, teachers, tavern keepers, and store proprietors during the eighteenth century, but their numbers were few. The next century saw modest growth, but by 1870 only 14% of women over the age of 14 were employed outside the home. By 1900, the numbers had increased to 21%.

Most women who worked in the 1800s expected to work only until they got married. Nearly all textile mill workers employed before 1860 were under the age of 25. Shortly thereafter the shift to immigrant women began, as most American-born women married, entered educational academies, took easier jobs, or joined the movement west. In addition to being overworked and worn out from long hours and childbearing, many of the immigrant women were handicapped by a poor command of English and intimidated by a new, unfamiliar life. They had no energy to revolt, and poor conditions persisted.

Yet some women managed to push for change. Although these workers endured long hours in dreadful conditions—sometimes as much as 14 hours a day, 6 days a week—they still had the spunk to make things happen. In the 1840s, the women who worked in the mills at Lowell, Massachusetts, created a society that published its own magazine. Some of the earliest labor laws were the result of organized efforts by the mill workers in Lowell, who testified about wages and hours before the Committee of Manufacturers in 1844–45. The first protective labor laws were passed in the 1850s, primarily to limit the hours per day women could be required to work.

But there were few factory inspectors, and the laws often were not enforced. Then the unions began to push for both protective laws and equal pay requirements. Until 1890, the unions were the chief proponents of all labor laws. After that time, middle-class reform organizations got involved. Naturally, the different groups disagreed about what laws were needed and what should be given priority, and the laws themselves were often inconsistent. For example, Illinois passed one law in 1872 prohibiting women from working in the coal mines; another law was passed the same year declaring that no person should be barred from any occupation except military service on the basis of sex.

Yet as late as 1910, some women still worked as much as 18 hours a day in steam laundries, which was unhealthy, dangerous work. Conditions in these sweatshops were deplorable, with overcrowding and little concern for health or safety.

In 1911, a fire at the Triangle Shirtwaist Factory resulted in the death of more than a hundred workers due to overcrowding and inadequate safety conditions. This tragedy acted as a catalyst to spur protective legislation that not only restricted female employment in dangerous conditions but also set safety standards for all workers in hazardous occupations.

When the first protective laws were enacted, virtually all organized women's groups supported them. This is understandable, considering the ills that the laws were designed to remedy. But when women got the vote in 1920, opposition to some of the laws was raised for the first time. The women's groups were divided on the issue. Those in favor of the laws believed women still needed to be guarded from exploitation, while others opposed any law that required different treatment of women. Most of the laws persisted until the late 1930s, when courts began to hold that these laws violated the freedom to make contracts. Some were repealed, others remained intact. Although the purpose of these laws was noble, they were often used to exclude women from certain jobs and provide an excuse for employers to pay women a lower wage. Indirectly, they helped foster paternalistic attitudes toward women, suggesting that women were weaker and unable to handle demanding labor. They also had the practical effect of limiting the type and number of jobs available to women. Many laws enacted under the guise of protection were blatantly exclusionary, such as laws prohibiting women from tending bar unless they were the wives or daughters of the bar's owner.

In the 1960s, after the Equal Pay Act of 1963 and Title VII of the Civil Rights Act of 1964 were passed, federal courts began to rule that most of the remaining laws, such as California's wage, hour, and weight-lifting law, violated Title VII and could not stand. The Equal Employment Opportunity Commission (EEOC) endorsed these decisions. By the early 1970s, the remaining protective laws had been struck down as violating the right to equal protection under the law. This trend was especially beneficial to male workers, who now had to be afforded the same rights under the laws, such as minimum wage, maximum hours, rest periods, safe conditions, and overtime pay.

In addition to restrictive laws and dangerous working conditions, women who pursued careers in the nineteenth century faced great social opposition. As women moved into nontraditional jobs outside the home, they were often treated by the news media as quaint oddities. A newspaper photo from about 1890 showed "the only woman bank cashier in America, or possibly in the world." Women who dared make it big were often characterized as barracudas or worse. Hetty Green, a highly successful Wall Street financier in the early 1900s, was called the Witch of Wall Street (although historical accounts indicate that this label may have been earned more by her ruthless character than her daring business activities). Yet even women who were true heroines did not escape criticism. Clara Barton, who nursed the wounded and dying on the battlefield during the Civil War and later founded the American Red Cross, was criticized for being "unladylike." She once wrote to a friend: "If you chance to see that the positions I occupied were rough and unseemly for a woman, I can only reply that they were rough and unseemly for a man."

The suffragists of the late nineteenth century and early twentieth century gave our country its first lesson in what happens when women unite to achieve a goal. The suffrage movement began in the 1840s, and women's right to vote wasn't guaranteed nationwide until 1920. Often, people working for the abolition of slavery joined with the suffragists in a common effort toward equality for all people. As Frederick Douglass, the former slave who became a writer, publisher, and tireless advocate for human rights, said in a speech at a women's suffrage convention, "No man, however eloquent, can speak for woman as woman can for herself. Nevertheless, I hold that this cause is not altogether and exclusively woman's cause. It is the cause of human brotherhood as well as the cause of human sisterhood, and both must rise and fall together. Women cannot be elevated without elevating man, and man cannot be depressed without depressing woman also."

The suffragists' unflagging persistence is both admirable and educational, because these early warriors used every imaginable tactic in their 80 years of determined effort. Some of their methods were theatrical. The wives of well-known politicians deliberately got themselves arrested. Women chained themselves to the White House fence. Parades were staged in which miles of women in matching capes carried matching flowers. Other tactics were shrewd. Rallies and meetings were staged on the eve of important political affairs to take advantage of the reporters gathered for the scheduled event. Still others were simple, enduring acts of persuasion—humorous writings and cartoons, passive resistance at the polls, recruiting and gathering together. Aggressively or gently, the suffragists persevered in the face of charges that they were antifamily, mannish, unnatural, anti-God, and free-love advocates. One of the most common tactics through history has been to accuse women who assert their rights of being loose or immoral, and this still goes on today.

Women were immovable despite the insults and barriers. In 1920, Congress finally passed the Nineteenth Amendment to the Constitution, which established that the right to vote could not be abridged on account of sex. After that, change began to happen fast. The flappers of the 1920s openly indulged in such scandalous behavior as smoking, dancing, baring their knees, and sipping bootleg hooch. The decade marked the increased participation of women in the arts, and it became more common for young women to work at least until they were married.

But even as women began moving into the workforce in greater numbers and enjoying the increased social freedoms that marked the trends of the 1920s, they were far from welcomed as equals. Married women still could not own property in their own right. Single women had few career options and encountered many restrictions on the legal and cultural freedoms we now take for granted. Even the few professions open to women were severely limited. As late as 1920 in most states, for example, female teachers were prohibited by law from continuing to teach if they married.

World War I marked the first mass movement of women into jobs formerly held by men. In 1917 the War Labor Board ordered that wages ordinarily paid to men should not be lowered for women rendering the same service. The unions supported this rule both in the interest of equality and to protect the gains earned by union men. Yet the number of women working declined sharply after the war, and despite the progress made during the 1920s, by 1930 only 24% of the workforce was female. Nevertheless, slow, steady gains kept coming. With the passage of the Fair Labor Standards Act in 1938, equal pay for equal work by men and women was mandated by federal law for the first time in our nation's history.

The wartime equal pay rule was restored during World War II, and the War Labor Board regularly tried to enforce it. But in practice, wages for women were often reduced by as much as 30%. And though few could question that the labor of women was vital, both to win the war and to keep the economy up and running while so many men were away, women were often criticized, harassed, and stigmatized. Many competent female workers were fired after the war, not because a returning veteran wanted his job back, but because the employer had seen the woman as an "emergency" employee all along, even if she had been on the job three or four years.

But things were changing, and the value of women's labor got some long overdue recognition shortly after the war. The devastating effects of unemployment brought about by the depression, along with the contributions of the women who worked in virtually all jobs during World War II, led Congress to redefine the meaning of full employment in the Economic Act of 1946. The act defined the concept as "the employment of those who want to work, without regard to whether their employment is, by some definition, necessary. This goal applies equally to men and women."

After the war, women filled more jobs than ever before. While much of this growth can again be attributed to the war effort, which brought women into the factories in "Rosie the Riveter" roles, the 36% of women working in 1945 decreased only slightly to 34% in 1950. The overall figures rebounded to 38% by 1960, increasing to 43% by 1970 and up to 52% by 1980. The increase between 1950 and 1980 is even more dramatic when expressed in actual numbers. In 1950 18.4 million women were in the workforce, and 44.7 million women were working by 1980. Today there are 56 million women working outside the home in America.

These numbers tell only part of the story. There have always been significant differences in the numbers of working women based on race, social class, and marital status. The most dramatic increase in the various groups of working women has been among married white women, only 10% of whom worked in 1930, and 49% of whom worked in 1980.

These gains could not have been achieved without the changes in the law and social standards, as well as the efforts of women both alone and in groups. The Women's Bureau of the Department of Labor was established shortly after World War I and worked ceaselessly for equal pay legislation at both the federal and state levels. In 1952 the National Committee for Pay Equity, a nongovernment organization, was established to consolidate the activities of some 20 separate equality groups. It focused its activities on passage of federal laws. The women's movement of the 1960s and 1970s produced dozens of alliances, including the National Organization for Women

(NOW) and the Women's Rights Project of the American Civil Liberties Union, founded by Ruth Bader Ginsberg, now serving as the second female Justice on the U.S. Supreme Court.

Why has there been such slow, steady growth in the number of women working outside the home? Many explanations have been offered, but two reasons stand out as the greatest influences in increasing the participation of women in the workforce: technology and social/cultural changes.

First, advances in technology have greatly decreased the amount of labor required to maintain a home. The advent of affordable refrigerators, stoves, washing machines, microwave ovens, and other appliances has paralleled the dramatic increase in women in the labor force, especially since 1950. Also, more effective methods of birth control have given women more freedom to plan the timing and number of pregnancies.

But the most important reason women have filled a constantly increasing portion of the workforce has to be the change in social attitudes and in our own expectations, needs, and desires. Early in the century, mainstream viewpoints toward education and career opportunities for women discouraged women from working, particularly after marriage. During this time, relatively few women worked outside the home except out of economic necessity. Professional women were scorned as "unnatural," and the pursuit of a career almost guaranteed being labeled a misfit. Also, during tough economic times, some people feared that if women had equal access to jobs, they would be taking away a position from a man who needed it to support a family. As recently as 30 years ago, it was considered common wisdom that men were entitled to be paid more than women, even when performing the same jobs. This rationale was based on the belief that most households were headed by men, and more money should go to the family breadwinner. It is easy to see from our vantage point in the late twentieth century that this idea was both inaccurate and unfair. But for many years this was the predominant point of view.

Some people still buy into this idea, including, surprisingly, some women. Many of us tend to think that we don't deserve what we have earned, because we have been conditioned by our culture and upbringing to expect second best. We may say, "Oh well, I really didn't want that promotion anyway, and he probably needs the money more than I do." Wrong! This is unfair to us, unfair to other women, and even unfair to the supposedly deserving male who gets the promotion or raise we should have received. The person hired or promoted under such circumstances is seldom receiving a favor. He is entering a climate in which he is expected to show leadership and gain respect, yet the people he must work with resent him.

I once worked in a specialty store owned by a man who openly stated to a female assistant manager that he believed that the job of store manager required a man. This, despite the fact that the store sold women's clothing! Despite having two qualified supervisory-level women in line for the position, he wanted to hire a college friend who had little or no retail experience, let alone management training. I was getting ready to go back to school and was not in line for the job, otherwise I believe I would have fought this. I urged the other two qualified women (both supervisors) to talk to the EEOC, an attorney, or someone who could advise them of their rights, but both chose not to make waves.

The man that was hired was a nice guy, and the employees agreed that their anger and resentment should be directed to the store owner, not to him. They did their best to make it work. The new manager knew little about women's fashion, the retail sales business, and personnel management. He did surprisingly well under the circumstances, but he didn't last long. Before the year was up, he had decided to seek another job.

This illustrates one of the fundamental frustrations among women working at all levels of employment today: Although we are moving into the workforce in greater numbers than ever before, the gap in both wages and advancement opportunity has not kept pace. There is still a persistent chasm between what men and women earn. In 1915 women made 29 cents for every dollar paid to men. By 1930 that figure had risen to 55 cents. In the 1950s the gap actually widened as women entered the workforce in greater numbers during and after

World War II. Many of these women were taking unskilled positions, whereas the smaller number of women working before this time tended to be in the skilled, more highly paid professions such as teaching. Also, men with veterans' benefits were gaining higher levels of education at this time. This was only a temporary trend, however. The wage gap narrowed in the mid-1950s, and by 1978 the number of women entering college outnumbered the number of men. Yet this makes the problem all the more vexing. Women are catching up educationally yet stalling somewhere along the line.

## Where Are We Today and Why?

Despite all the gains and the vast numbers of women in the workforce, women are still paid less than men. The earning gap between men and women actually rose between 1955, when women made about 64 cents to every dollar earned by men, and 1980, when the figure dropped to 59 cents. But the news is getting better. The gender gap narrowed rapidly in the early 1980s, when women's earnings began to rise more rapidly than men's. The ratio rose from 59 to 68% between 1981 and 1989. Current figures place the gap at 70 to 74%. While some predict that it will take decades before we achieve true equality, others see the rapid changes of the past decade as a sign that we are moving swiftly toward closing the gap once and for all.

How much of the persistent wage gap can be blamed on discrimination? This is one of the toughest questions the analysts in all fields have grappled with. Discrimination cannot be measured directly or with any real accuracy. There is no question that it exists at all levels of employment and in all professions, and that it is widespread and ongoing. Too often, not even the victims are aware it exists at all, let alone how it impacts on wage disparity.

Many reasons other than discrimination have been offered to try and explain why the wage gap persists. Many women still choose professions traditionally attractive to female workers, such as teaching and nursing. These professions generally pay less than others that require similar training and effort, because they have been considered "women's work." Others suggest that it is simply a matter of time—that large numbers of women did not begin to enter the higher paying professions until 10 to 15 years ago, and those at the top of these fields take 20 or more years to get there. These factors undoubtedly account for some of the disparity, but it is equally undeniable that discrimination is one of the main culprits.

Today, 30 years after passage of the Equal Pay Act, the average female worker earns significantly less in nearly every profession. A recent study by the U.S. Department of Labor showed that women are still getting less pay virtually across the board. The study found only one occupation—mechanics and repairers—in which women's median earnings were 2.8% higher than men's. But women hold less than 4% of these jobs. The problem does not stop when women retire. Overall, women are less likely to have adequate retirement incomes because pensions are based on earnings, and women generally earn less.

What about affirmative action? Affirmative action is a controversial and widely misunderstood concept. It is often criticized as a form of reverse discrimination by its detractors. However, the goal of affirmative action is essentially to equalize the competition for jobs among all qualified individuals, regardless of race, sex, religion, or other discriminatory factors. Affirmative action refers to all of the various steps an employer can take to open up opportunities previously unavailable to women and minorities. Contrary to popular misunderstanding, affirmative action does not mean a quota system, although such goals as making a workplace 50% female have sometimes been stated.

For example, Executive Order 11246, which applies to most federal contractors and subcontractors, requires these employers to submit affirmative action plans to the Office of Federal Contract Compliance (OFCC). The plan is regulated by the Department of Labor and must include concrete goals and timetables to achieve them. These are not quotas but rather targets to ensure that qualified women and minorities are truly given an equal opportunity to compete in the workplace. Records showing hiring, job categories, salaries, and benefits are also required from these employers. The records serve several purposes, including proof that the employer has complied with the law, identification of problems, and in some cases, protection of the employer from claims of discrimination where none exists.

One of the most troubling ironies facing women today is that despite the many gains we have made, despite the opportunities, the legal advantages, the shifting view of society, women as a whole have less economic security than our mothers did in the 1950s. Part of the blame for this sad fact is economic, and part of it is due to demographic and social factors such as the higher divorce rate. Of course, we have far more freedom of choice than we did in the 1950s, but those choices are often tough, confusing, and unfair.

It's easy to see what a complicated problem we have in trying to figure out why inequities remain and what to do about them. With so many factors to consider, it is tremendously difficult to analyze the real causes of the persistent wage gap. Some of the blame certainly rests on discrimination, but other factors have played a part as well. While some of these factors can be measured, such as years of experience, education, and training, supply and demand in the market for a product or service, hours worked, and productivity, the others, such as reasons for job choices, social factors, distribution of skills, and discrimination, are nearly impossible to identify on a widespread, statistical basis.

## So Where Is the Good News?

One thing is sure: While the extent of discrimination is hard to see on a large scale, you, the worker, know when it's happening to you. And if every victim of discrimination stands up for her rights and says "Enough," this factor in the inequality equation can be eliminated. Every case in which a court says, "This is discrimination, and it is illegal, and you're going to pay," is another battle won, and another tool created for others to use.

One of the most heartening lessons in the history of women's struggle for equality in work is that once the door is broken down by a few women, others follow in droves. In 1973 American Airlines hired flight instructor Bonnie Tiburzi as the first female pilot for a major airline passenger service. Twenty years later, more than 900 women are pilots for major passenger carriers. Sally Ride was hired in 1978 as the first female astronaut and made her first trip into space in 1983. Today we are seeing more and more female astronauts. Elizabeth Blackwell, the nation's first woman doctor, had a long career that began in the mid-1800s. More than a century later, there are about 105,000 female doctors practicing in America. In 1912 Madame C. J. Walker, a descendant of slaves, became one of the first female self-made millionaires. She started life in the cotton fields and went on to build a hair products empire. Today there are more than 5 million businesses owned by women in America, and these companies employ more people than the *Fortune* 500. The U.S. Small Business Administration (SBA) predicts that women will own 40% of all small businesses in America by the turn of the century.

Women are making tremendous political strides, too— 54% of the American electorate is now female. Women hold numerous powerful political positions at all levels of government, including California and Texas, two states which not only are among the most populous but also have produced the most presidents. Political issues are rarely divided into "men's issues" and "women's issues" today, as there is a growing awareness that family concerns affect everyone. Perhaps most important, more and more men from all age groups are supporting equal rights for women in all phases of life.

Progress is also being made in many specific career areas. Among women with M.B.A. degrees working in financial fields, the wage gap is only 3.3%. Some believe that women have made more rapid gains in this type of profession because the results can be measured objectively in dollars and cents.

Also, there is evidence that the pink-collar ghetto is finally undergoing some much-needed urban renewal. In *Megatrends for Women,* authors Patricia Aburdene and John Naisbitt report heartening statistics showing sharp increases in the salaries of nurses, secretaries, and teachers through the late 1980s and early 1990s. These professions are gaining both respect and monetary rewards as supply dwindles and demand grows. According to Aburdene and Naisbitt, the average salary of a staff nurse in 1991 was $34,500, with specialists such as nurse-anesthetists earning up to $100,000—more than many doctors. Teacher's salaries also increased by 50% between 1987 and 1991. Secretaries, too, are making rapid strides. In New York City, a top executive secretary may earn $75,000 a year, and a salary of $50,000 a year is not unusual in other major cities.

It is also interesting that women are rapidly advancing in formerly male-dominated fields, as well as in taking the traditionally female skills into the marketplace. For example, high-tech science and math fields are welcoming and encouraging more women into their ranks, and both schools and private groups are actively encouraging girls to become interested in these fields early in their schooling. Forty percent of all law degrees and 33% of all medical degrees are now earned by women. Some law schools report that female applicants now outnumber the male applicants. California has started a program designed to bring more women into construction apprenticeships.

Women are making colossal gains in the arts as well. Producers of television shows have learned that showing a pregnant reporter or anchorwoman on the air—formerly taboo—can actually increase ratings. Although still rare overall, there has been a dramatic increase in the number of female directors, studio heads, and other important behind-the-scenes executives in Hollywood over the past few years. The last decade has also seen tremendous growth in the number of female fine artists moving into the forefront of their fields. Women have made enormous gains in the fields of advertising and publishing, too.

In the more traditional spheres, women with homemaking skills who recognize the needs of families are turning these talents into profits. One of the fastest-growing areas of women in business is food and nutrition. Women are leading the industry in areas such as natural food stores, restaurants, and specialty convenience foods that provide tasty, nutritious meals that cater to special needs. For example, one successful woman-owned company makes microwave meals for kids that are appealing, healthy, and easy for children to prepare. Female entrepreneurs are especially savvy in filling the unmet needs of other working women, from personal shopping to training seminars to delivery of hot evening meals.

One of the most promising signs is the progress being made in some of the last bastions of male superiority, such as the military. Early in 1993, U.S. Defense Secretary Les Aspin ordered all the services to lift restrictions prohibiting women from flying combat aircraft and stated that he would ask Congress to end the ban on women serving aboard warships at sea. The Air Force is actively recruiting women to apply for its fighter jet pilot training program. Two events appear to have helped spur these changes. The first was Operation Desert Storm, in which nearly 40,000 American women served as helicopter and cargo plane pilots, drivers, and technicians, as well as in various other hazardous combat positions. Ironically, the other event that helped spark change was the infamous Tailhook scandal, in which the assault and harassment of Navy women at the Tailhook convention filled national headlines. Although few would put Tailhook in a positive light, its exposure did help identify the need for change regarding equal rights for military women.

History has shown repeatedly the power of political pressure. Boycotts, strikes, exposure in the media—these tools and others have been used successfully for centuries to fight repression, from the individual who writes a letter urging the boycott of a company that treats its workers unfairly, to organized groups that implement national movements to bring about justice and change. Think about what you may be able to do, both on your own and with others. Learn about the political and special action groups in your area. Many national organizations have local affiliates. Check the *Encyclopedia of Associations* at your library, your local telephone directory, bulletin boards at the YWCA, universities, even private businesses such as women's bookstores. And don't forget—all of these groups were started by someone at the grassroots level. Dr Patricia Murphy believes such groups can be among the best tools for achieving change. This seems especially true today, when people are again feeling a sense of social responsibility. The greed, cynicism, and apathy of the 1980s has been replaced by a renewed sense that individuals, working alone and together, can and must take action to preserve, improve, and change what's wrong in the world.

In *Megatrends for Women,* authors Aburdene and Naisbitt identify three emerging themes as we move further into the 1990s: opportunity, leadership, and balance. They feel that opportunity is plentiful for young women, for all women making midcareer shifts, and that both leadership and balance are possible for women today. They also note that Superwoman is no longer our heroine, that the people who are the most successful tend to be dedicated but not workaholics. This is certainly good news for us all.

Fortunately, attitudes do seem to be changing throughout corporate America as well. A *Fortune* magazine poll conducted in 1992 found that 92% of CEOs reported that over the past five years, the number of women in middle management in their companies has increased, and 62% reported that the number of female officers rose as well.

Demographics are also helping women to advance. Younger men moving into the workplace today are more likely the product of homes in which both parents worked, and the overwhelming majority are married to, dating, or have friendships with career women. The two-career household has become the norm due to both social changes and economic necessity. Men whose wives are denied equal earning power are themselves harmed by the hardship this creates for their entire family. Some argue that young men entering established companies where the "old boy" mentality remains firmly in place will be groomed to adopt this attitude. This outlook ignores the power of other influences on such men—the influence of their wives, mothers, peers, and other young men with more modern views. Older men saw women primarily in the roles of wives, daughters, girlfriends, or secretaries. Today's men are becoming increasingly accustomed to seeing women as equals, as colleagues in the workplace. As the new generation of men and women ascends to power, things are bound to get better, because these people have experienced the challenges and rewards of a dual-career household.

Of course, obstacles still exist. But for most of us, our own efforts, combined with the women's movement, the laws protecting our rights, and various grassroots achievements of women working together, have given us tremendous gains throughout the past two decades. True, some studies show that even among men and women who are willing to work identical hours, travel, accept transfers, and put identical efforts into their career, women still earn less. But, as the researchers who conduct these studies point out, the time factor has to be taken into account. A dozen years ago, the number of women in these positions was so low that the surveys couldn't have been done. And it takes at least that long for most people in high-level corporate positions to reach those heights.

The tremendous gains made by women far, far outweigh the frustration of the persistent but slowly crumbling barriers. "If you say there are still obstacles, it creates an artificial air of discouragement for women," says Charlotte Beers, chairman of Ogilvy & Mather Worldwide, a multibillion-dollar advertising corporation. "I've been advantaged as a female in as many ways as I've been disadvantaged. Talent and the choices you make are more significant than gender."

The companies that are making women more welcome in the upper echelons may have some altruistic motives, but essentially the effort is based on the wisdom that diversity is in the best interests of the company. In a 1992 *Fortune* magazine article, Aetna Life & Casualty Company CEO Ronald Compton said it well: "I'm not doing this out of the goodness of my heart. I'm selfish. I want the very best people I can get. A lot of them happen to be women." Compton has practiced what he preaches; roughly half of the managers at Aetna are female, and the company recently made *Working Mother* magazine's list of the top 100 companies that support working families.

Money talks, and employment discrimination is extremely costly to employers. Courts award workers back pay, front pay, double and triple pay, out-of-pocket damages, noneconomic damages, legal fees, and punitive damages. These can add up to vast sums. When women are willing to fight discrimination, the unfair employers are the ones who pay. In 1979, Bechtel Corporation, the nation's largest private construction company, settled two sex discrimination suits, agreeing to pay a total of $1.4 million to its female employees. A pattern of discrimination against women cost State Farm Insurance Company approximately $250 million in 1988. In 1977 the city of Chicago had more than $100 million in revenue-sharing funds withheld due to the Chicago Police Department's racially and sexually discriminatory practices. Did these employers change their ways? You'd better believe it!

The point is, one person can make a difference just by pursuing her own potential and refusing to accept unequal compensation or other mistreatment. As I will explain throughout this book, there are many different ways to do this, and you have choices in almost all the situations you face. Very few of the questions or problems that confront us have only one right answer. A recent article in *Executive Female* magazine illustrated this. A hypothetical problem was given to several leaders in various fields. The question involved a woman who felt she was being treated unfairly on the job. She had prepared a memo outlining the reasons she believed this to be true. The experts were asked to tell her what she should do. Their answers were all over the board—from "Say nothing but keep gathering information," to "Send the memo at once," to "Don't send it but schedule a meeting to discuss your concerns." The only answer none of them gave was "Do nothing."

# CHAPTER 3

⚖

# WHERE DO I START IF I'M NOT GETTING EQUAL PAY?

S uppose you've landed the job you wanted. You enjoy the work, you like your colleagues, and the pay seems adequate. But something doesn't feel right. Maybe you've heard through the office grapevine that the men in your department are getting paid more for doing the same work you do. Or maybe you've noticed that all the clerical workers have the same duties, yet the women are called "secretaries" while the men are called "clerks," and the job of clerk pays a higher wage. Or perhaps you work for an insurance company, where there are separate departments and job classifications for claims representatives (females) and claims adjusters (males), although everyone seems to work equally hard, doing the same tasks to achieve the same results. Yet the claims adjusters are paid at a higher rate.

In each of these scenarios, a woman is being denied equal compensation. As one woman on the job, what can you do about it? Plenty, once you have a clear picture of what is going on and how to approach it. Each situation is going to be different in important ways that will influence your decision as to how to proceed.

31

# Understanding the Language

To begin with, you need to have a basic understanding of the terminology used in the legal and business fields to describe different types of equal pay problems. You also need to gain some knowledge of what your rights are and where they come from.

*Equal pay* and *pay equity* are broad terms that apply to any situation in which an employer pays different wages to workers of the opposite sex within the same workplace for equal work on jobs that require about the same skill, effort, and responsibility and are performed under similar working conditions. In the example described earlier, all three of the situations are equal pay problems.

Two categories of equal pay cases are generally recognized. The first situation described above is a same-job classification case, in which the discrimination is obvious. The latter two are "different-job classification" cases, in which an employer has created artificial distinctions between two jobs that are essentially the same by using different job titles or departments. As a general rule, the same laws, tests, and standards apply to both categories of equal pay discrimination, but the second case is more difficult to prove. Over the last 50 years, however, the law has developed to help women in this situation, and proving such a case is getting easier all the time.

## THE DIFFERENCES BETWEEN EQUAL PAY AND COMPARABLE WORTH

It is important to distinguish different-job classification cases from a related issue that has received a good deal of attention in recent years. *Comparable worth* is a term frequently used to describe another type of equal pay problem, one that is both tough to define and even tougher to control. The concept essentially involves a comparison of wages paid for jobs traditionally held by women (the so-called pink-collar jobs) with wages paid to workers in traditionally male jobs. For example, nurses' aides are usually paid less than iron workers, teachers are paid less than stockbrokers, and child-care workers are paid less than tree trimmers.

Statistics compiled by the U.S. Department of Labor show that women are still three times more likely than men to be hired for low-wage jobs, even when both share equal education, training, work experience, and skills. Six out of every 10 women work in sales, office staff positions, food service, health, and cleaning and personal services. These fields pay less than those that employ most men, including crafts, manufacturing, management, professional positions, and trucking.

It is easy to see the difficulty of trying to compare jobs involving totally different kinds of work. Terms like *worth* are highly subjective and can be applied in many ways—such as worth to the employer, worth to society, or comparative worth in the marketplace. As might be expected, progress toward equality has been slower in this area than in the basic equal pay field. Virtually all of the court cases in which women have tried to achieve equal pay on a comparable-worth basis have failed. There is widespread disagreement on whether a workable system can ever be developed to deal with this difficult problem. Most people—everyday folks and professionals alike—see any across-the-board attempt to require comparable worth by legislation or other government mandate as a bureaucratic nightmare, as well as an idea too socialistic for American sensibilities to accept.

Therefore, the best way to tackle this issue at the present time is through working for change within the system. One way to do this is through industry support groups, women's organizations, and efforts to change public attitudes about the value of woman-dominated professions.

Aburdene and Naisbitt, authors of *Megatrends for Women,* suggest that the way to eliminate the wage gap and achieve a system of comparable worth is through women's economic and political power. They recommend: (1) acknowledging the role market forces play, (2) isolating pure discrimination and going after it with the full force of women's political power; and (3) enacting comparable worth within each corporation.

Thus, the second effective way to move toward comparable worth is by changing one workplace at a time. Each time a step is taken toward a more fair system of compensation, we move that much closer to solving the problem for everyone.

## THE "SUBSTANTIALLY EQUAL" PRINCIPLE

Fortunately, there is *much* that can be done to gain equal pay in both same-job classification and different-job classification situations. One of the main principles that has emerged during the development of the law is that for work to be equal work, requiring equal pay, the job need not be identical but only "substantially equal." This involves a comparison of the skill, effort, and responsibility required for each job, as well as the working conditions under which they are performed. Does one job depend on some special skill, such as operating a particular machine, that the other does not? Is one more dangerous, or does it require more physical effort? Does one job carry a higher responsibility, such as final inspection of accounts, that the other does not? How significant are these differences? Small differences between the two jobs will not make the job unequal. Also, the labels an employer may give two different job classifications mean nothing.

In one well-known case, for example, flight attendants working for an airline challenged the company's policy of paying higher wages and providing better fringe benefits to male pursers, who did essentially the same work as the female stewardesses. The airline argued that the pursers had more supervisory duties. But the court found that these differences in duties were insignificant, and the jobs were declared "substantially equal." The situation was obviously unfair: in addition to more pay, the men were given such benefits as private hotel rooms, laundry allowances, and other travel perks the women did not receive. The stewardesses were awarded back pay, equal benefits, and money damages. Other cases have involved beauticians and barbers who worked for a large nursing home chain, male police patrol officers and female car markers, janitors and cleaning women, and prison guards and matrons. As these examples help illustrate, the key is not what a person is called on the job, but what she or he actually does on the job.

## Picking the Right Legal Tools

Over the past half century, a large body of complicated law has developed to try and achieve what should be a simple objective: equal pay for equal work. There is a great deal of overlap in the laws, and any type of equal pay claim may involve a number of different, complementary laws. But what do the laws really mean when you're trying to get fair and equal pay for your work? They mean you have tools to work with in constructing a better and more fair system of compensation for yourself and other women workers. You need to know how to choose the right tool, and you may need to use several to get the job done.

The laws work together to cover just about every employer and every type of job discrimination. In most situations more than one of the laws will apply, and different laws will allow for different remedies. For example, one law may require back pay, another may allow "out-of-pocket" damages, and another may allow you to recover your attorney's fees. Some laws require you to go through an administrative procedure first, such as filing a claim with the EEOC, before you can go to court. Others allow you to go ahead and file a case in court from the beginning.

How do you know how to find your way through this maze? The very best thing you can do is consult with an employment attorney who is knowledgeable about what the laws are, how to use them, and what strategy will work best for you. Although many problems can be solved without going to court, it is important to understand the law behind your rights in order to know whether you have a good equal pay claim and to understand how to proceed within a system that is set up to protect your rights. Then you will be prepared to take your claim as far as you need to go to get it resolved. This book provides a basic overview and is not intended to prepare you to represent yourself; rather, it familiarizes you with the laws that protect your rights so that you can assess your own individual circumstances.

# The Federal Laws

The following is a summary of the federal laws most often used to combat sex discrimination. The list is far from complete; there are many other federal laws that prohibit sex discrimination by particular employers, such as railroads and educational institutions that receive federal funds. You should also be aware that many of the agencies that enforce these laws have authority from Congress to make rules and regulations that are also a part of the law and are related to the main federal statute. These are found in the Code of Federal Regulations, or CFR. Since it would take a 10-volume treatise to list and explain all the laws, rules, and regulations that reach every worker, I've selected only those that cover the broadest number of people. Be certain to keep this in mind if you may have a claim for discrimination.

## THE FAIR LABOR STANDARDS ACT
(29 U.S.C. §§ 201–219)

**What it means:** The first big breakthrough in the struggle for equal pay took place in 1938. Since that time, federal law has prohibited unequal pay for equal work, plain and simple. The Fair Labor Standards Act of 1938 (FLSA) was passed as a part of President Franklin D. Roosevelt's efforts to end the depression and to prevent such a tragedy in the future. The FLSA provided nationwide standards for minimum wage, overtime pay, child labor, and equal pay, among other things. Today, the FLSA is the federal wage-hour law that sets the minimum wage and overtime pay. In 1963 the part of this law that requires equal pay was amended to make it stronger and more specific, and it is now discussed separately as the Equal Pay Act, explained below.

**Who it covers:** The FLSA covers all employees subject to the minimum wage law. It excludes casual babysitters; companions for elderly or infirm persons; executive, administrative, and professional employees; outside salespeople; employees of some small local retail or service establishments; family employees of family-owned businesses; and some agricultural workers. In addition, under certain conditions apprentices, students, and handicapped workers may be paid a different wage. Employees under 20 years of age in certain on-the-job training programs may be paid a training wage of at least 85% of the minimum wage for up to 90 days.

**Who enforces it:** The U.S. Department of Labor regulates and enforces the law and rules that govern wages, hours, and training programs. Private suits may be filed for violations of the FLSA by the Secretary of Labor or the individual employee. In some cases where there is an employment contract that provides for grievance procedures, these procedures must be exhausted first.

**Time limits:** Suit for violations of the FLSA must be filed within two years, unless the violation was willful (that is, the employer knew or should have known it was violating the law, such as by paying wages lower than the minimum wage). Suit for willful violations may be filed up to three years after the violation.

**Remedies:** An employer who violates the FLSA may be ordered to pay back wages, front wages, or double back pay as liquidated damages for willful actions. Attorney's fees may also be awarded.

**More on the FLSA:** The current minimum wage for the first 40 hours each week is $4.25 an hour. Most workers covered by the FLSA are entitled to one and a half times their regular rate of pay for work more than 40 hours a week. Exceptions to this rule are made for agricultural workers, live-in household workers, taxi drivers, and employees of motor carriers, trains, and airlines. Also, health-care centers and hospitals may adopt a different program of overtime pay based on 14-day periods if the employees agree and are paid at least time and a half for working more than 8 hours in a day or 80 hours in a 14-day period, whichever is greater.

The FLSA allows some benefits it terms *valuable accommodations,* such as room and board, to be considered as part of wages. For employees who regularly receive more than $30 in tips per month, the employer may take a specified tip credit toward their minimum wage obligation. Since April 1, 1991, the credit has been $2.12 (50% of $4.25). However, if the employee's average hourly tip earnings plus wages do not meet the minimum wage, the employer must make up the balance. No matter what, the employer must pay tipped employees at least half the minimum wage, regardless of how much the employees make in tips. Furthermore, the employer can only use the tip credit if the employees are informed of this provision of FLSA law. In 1977 a federal court of appeals found that a restaurant owned by the Marriott Corporation paid the difference only if employees' tips fell below the minimum wage, a violation of the FLSA. In addition, the court found that the employer's failure to inform the employees of the real tipping provisions of the FLSA was in bad faith and ordered it to pay back wages in the full amount of the minimum wage during the period of violation.

States may have their own minimum wage laws as well that set a higher minimum wage, set different standards for teenage workers, or cover workers not within the FLSA provisions (see discussion of state laws, below).

## THE EQUAL PAY ACT OF 1963 (29 U.S.C. § 206(d))

**What it means:** The Equal Pay Act (EPA) is part of the FLSA but is generally treated as a separate law. It prohibits employers from discriminating on the basis of sex in the payment of wages, in situations where the male and female employees perform substantially equal work under similar working conditions in the same establishment.

**Who it covers:** The EPA covers virtually all private employees, not only those covered by the FLSA, but also executive, salaried, administrative, professional and outside sales employees who are not covered by the minimum wage and overtime laws. Most government employees are also covered. Some employees of small retail and service establishments, seasonal workers, farm workers, and household employees are excluded. There need be only two employees, one male and one female, to support a claim under the EPA.

**Who enforces it:** The EPA can be enforced by the Equal Employment Opportunity Commission (EEOC), as well as through a private suit in the federal and sometimes state courts. Unlike a Title VII claim, discussed below, a worker who brings a claim for violation of the EPA is not required to go through the EEOC procedure before going to court.

**Time limits:** EPA suits must be filed within two years after the violation unless it was willful (the employer knew there was an EPA violation), in which case three years are allowed.

**Remedies:** A jury trial is available under the EPA. Actual damages in the form of back pay and liquidated damages in the form of double back pay may be awarded. Back wages include all overtime rates, bonuses, vacation and holiday pay, payment into insurance, retirement and pension plans, and other compensation the employee was wrongfully denied. Attorney's fees may also be awarded.

**More on the EPA:** When President John F. Kennedy signed the Equal Pay Act into law on June 10, 1963, he said that he hoped the bill would "call attention to the unconscionable practice of paying female employees less wages than male employees for the same job."

In essence, the EPA says that men and women in the same establishment, who are doing equal work on jobs that require equal skill, effort, and responsibility and are performed under similar working conditions, must be paid equal wages. *Skill* means the actual knowledge, training, and abilities that are required to do the job. For example, if you have a law degree but work as a jeweler, your degree does not entitle you to more pay than the other jewelers in your establishment. *Effort* means both physical and mental work and the actual work done on the job. Differences that are small or incidental (such as occasional lifting) or voluntarily taking on extra duties (such as staying late now and then) will not justify pay differences. *Responsibility* refers to the importance of the job, supervisory structure, and accountability— who is responsible if something goes wrong; who has to report to the boss. *Wages* includes all employment-related payments, including overtime, uniforms, travel, retirement plans, profit sharing, and fringe benefits. *Similar working conditions* refers to physical surroundings and job hazards. Hours of work (day versus night, unless night work is more dangerous) or minimal differences in conditions (such as working in an older building) won't create different conditions sufficient to justify different pay scales. Similar working conditions also means that the employees work in the same establishment. In general, *establishment* means one building. But one establishment may also be a business housed in a cluster of buildings (such as a big factory), or different locations under one central administration that hires, pays, and assigns employees, such as a group of schools.

In an EPA case, as in most cases, the burden of proof is on the plaintiff (you, the party who is bringing suit) to establish a prima facie case. The burden then shifts to the defendant, who must disprove it. What does this mean in plain English? First, you have to show that certain elements are present—that is, prove them by the evidence. To establish a prima facie case in an EPA action, a worker must show that at least two employees of the opposite sex are (1) located in the same establishment and (2) receiving unequal pay (3) on the basis of sex (4) for work that is equal.

If the employee proves this much, the employer can raise one of four defenses. An unequal wage can be justified if it is paid (1) according to seniority, (2) on a merit system, (3) according to quality or quantity of production, or (4) on a differential based on any factor other than sex. This final defense is the one most commonly raised by employers. It may apply if a male worker has completed some unbiased training program or has more education or experience related to this particular job. Another legitimate factor is payment at a "red circle" rate. This means a worker was reassigned to a job that ordinarily has a lower rate of pay than his former position, but he is allowed to keep working at the higher rate. Workers are often "red circled" when they become injured or disabled and have to move to a job with lighter duties.

Employers have tried some common defenses that *don't* work. These include the argument that "market rates" demand men be paid more; the old "head of household" argument that men, as primary breadwinners, need more money; and the "relative costs" claim that it is more expensive to employ women. In *EEOC v. First Citizens Bank of Billings,* a bank was paying different wages to male and female workers in three different jobs. First, a male teller was paid more than any female teller, even though all the women had more seniority and were more experienced. The bank claimed that he was a management trainee, but there was no real training program, no manual, and no managers conducted training sessions with him. The court said such a program has to be "more than an afterthought" to justify a different wage. Second, a male proof operator was paid more than the women who performed the same job, supposedly because he had more experience. While experience is a legitimate factor, testimony proved that it made little difference on this particular job. The main qualities necessary for a proof operator are speed and accuracy, and the female operators who were paid less were both faster and more accurate. This, too, was an EPA violation. Third, a male installment loan officer was hired at a salary higher than a female officer. The bank argued that a raise was given to the woman after the EEOC investigation began, but the court didn't buy it; the issue was the starting salary, not raises. Then the bank claimed that the man earned more because he had a college degree and the woman did not. But the court found that the degree was only marginally related to the position, and the female officer had had some college plus three years of experience in the department.

The employees in this case recovered back pay plus liquidated damages. The court explained that where the EPA is violated, and the employer fails to show that its violation was in good faith (that is, the employer had made an honest effort to understand and follow the EPA requirements and had reasonable grounds to believe that no violation took place), these extra damages must be awarded.

This case was easier than many because the workers were in the same positions, with the same job titles and duties. But under the EPA, as in all laws prohibiting sex discrimination, job titles are irrelevant.

One important thing to remember is that an employer may not remedy EPA violations by lowering the wage rate of the higher paid employees to eliminate the illegal pay difference. This is specifically prohibited under the act. Also, retaliation against a person who files a charge of equal pay discrimination, opposes an illegal pay practice, or cooperates in an investigation into such matters is also prohibited.

Here is how the EPA worked for one woman. When Maureen Bullock was hired by Pizza Hut of Louisiana as a unit manager, she started out in a management training program with a male trainee who was hired at the same time. Both were paid equally for the duration of the program, but when it ended, the male manager received a much higher raise than Bullock. The next round of raises did not even things out; the male manager still made more, despite the fact that Bullock was running one of the most profitable Pizza Huts in Louisiana. She filed a charge of discrimination with the EEOC. When the EEOC could not resolve the problem, she sued the company.

In federal court, Bullock proved that the two positions required substantially the same skill, effort, and responsibility in similar working conditions. She also proved, through the testimony of co-workers, that Pizza Hut's general manager believed that women should not hold managerial positions and should not make as much money as men. She presented evidence that company records on the race and sex of employees had been altered when they did not reflect compliance with EEOC standards. This, the court noted, was evidence of bad faith.

In its defense, Pizza Hut tried the old tactic of arguing sex stereotypes. It claimed that being female inhibited leadership qualities, so women in management could be paid less. The court considered such stereotyping "a clearly inappropriate factor under the law" and noted that the elimination of this kind of stereotyping was one of the goals of the EPA. Since Pizza Hut had deliberately and willfully denied Bullock equal pay for equal work—that is, they knew or should have known that they were doing something against the law—she was awarded double the amount of back pay she should have received (based on what her male colleague was paid) as liquidated damages, plus her attorney's fees.

The EPA does not allow class action lawsuits, but it does allow multiple-party suits. For example, if you work in a small establishment with 10 employees, 6 of whom are women who received unequal pay, you can join together to sue your employer under the EPA. But if you work for a giant company with thousands of employees, where it would be nearly impossible to discover the identities of all the people who have suffered from an unequal pay policy, you may need to file a class action suit. Title VII, explained below, does allow class action suits, and most violations of the EPA also violate Title VII.

In its first decade, the EPA was used by workers to recover $20 million a year in back pay and other awards, but in the 1980s, recovery for EPA violations dropped to less than $2 million annually. There are a number of possible reasons for this, including the overlap with Title VII, especially since the EEOC now enforces both laws. But the EPA is still a powerful law that should be given careful consideration in any pay discrimination case.

## TITLE VII OF THE CIVIL RIGHTS ACT OF 1964 (42 U.S.C. § 2000e)

**What it means:** Title VII prohibits employment discrimination of any kind based on sex, race, color, religion, or national origin. It prohibits discrimination in all *terms and conditions of employment.*

**Who it covers:** Private employers, state and local governments, and educational institutions with 15 or more employees as well as all private and public employment agencies, labor organizations, and joint labor-management committees for apprentice and training programs.

**Who enforces it:** The EEOC. In states that have their own Fair Employment Practices Agencies (FEPAs) to enforce parallel state laws, the EEOC usually refers the claim to the FEPA for investigation and enforcement under state laws. The FEPA may proceed until the problem is resolved or it may send the claim back to the EEOC. If the claim is not resolved by the EEOC or FEPA, or if a person wishes to bring a lawsuit on her or his own before the agency has completed its investigation, the EEOC or FEPA will issue a "right to sue" letter and the individual (or group of people) can file a lawsuit. Sometimes the EEOC files Title VII suits on behalf of people who file complaints, but more often the EEOC tries to resolve the problem through conciliation (similar to mediation) or allow the person to sue on her or his own. The Attorney General may also bring a Title VII suit if a "pattern or practice" of discrimination is alleged—that is, if an employer has an ongoing policy or habit of discriminating against workers who are female or are in one of the other groups protected from discrimination under this law. Class action suits are allowed under Title VII.

**Time limits:** A Title VII claim must be brought within 180 days after the last act of discrimination. There is an important exception to this rule: If you go through a state or local agency process first, then you have 300 days from the last act of discrimination to file your complaint with the EEOC.

Two additional points are important to remember. First, if the discrimination continues over time (such as paying a lower wage to a female employee for several years), this is a continuing violation as opposed to a "single, concrete act." In that case, you have to file within 180 days of the last date of the violation. For example, in *Calloway v. Partners National Health Plans,* a black secretary was paid less than either of the white secretaries who held the same job before the black secretary started and after she left. The company argued that there was only one violation, which occurred when it offered her a lower salary on the day she was hired. The court rejected this theory and emphasized that each week's paycheck that delivers less to a black person than a similarly situated white person is another wrong actionable under Title VII. The violation continues every day the person works.

The second point involves the single filing rule, another issue that came up in *Calloway*. If you join another person who is filing a charge; if that person's charge is filed on time and otherwise meets the requirements, and if the two claims involve the same or similar discrimination that happened in the same time frame, this satisfies the timing requirements and you don't have to file a separate charge.

**Remedies:** EEOC conciliation efforts, administrative proceedings, or litigation may result in a wide variety of remedies. These may include back pay, hiring, promotion, reinstating you in your old job, placing you in a better job you were denied because of your sex, front pay (future pay instead of sending you back to a job that now would be awkward), restoration of lost benefits, and compensatory damages for your economic and other losses. If the employer acted with malice (intentionally or with reckless indifference to your rights), you may receive punitive damages. Equitable relief may also be awarded, including injunctions that order the employer to stop the illegal practices. *Equity* is a catch-all phrase that covers the court's broad powers, beyond awarding money damages, to order whatever will correct the discrimination, compensate the victims, and stop the discrimination from happening again. For example, the court may order the employer to post a notice in the workplace advising employees that it has complied with orders to remedy discrimination and informing employees of their rights under the law. The court may also order the establishment of training programs to correct or prevent the discrimination from occurring again. Equity allows the court to be creative in fashioning a specific solution to each individual problem.

**More on Title VII:** Title VII is one of the most important laws affecting the struggle for equal pay and is probably the law that is now used more than any other to fight sex discrimination. It prohibits discrimination in *all* terms and conditions of employment, including hiring, recruiting (including job advertising), firing, compensation, assignment or classification of employees, testing, use of company facilities, transfer, promotion, layoff, recall, fringe benefits, pay, retirement plans, disability leaves, training and apprenticeship, and anything else relating to employment rights.

**Hiring and exclusion from certain jobs:** The protections of Title VII cover job applicants as well as employees. As many women are aware, an applicant is not supposed to be asked about her marital status, whether she has children, or if she plans to have children. In *King v. Trans World Airlines, Inc.,* a woman who applied for a job in the commissary was asked about her most recent pregnancy, her marital status, the nature of her relationship with another TWA employee, the number of children she had and whether they were illegitimate, her child-care arrangements, and her future child-bearing plans. The court found that all of these questions, except the one referring to child-care arrangements, violated Title VII according to the EEOC sex discrimination guidelines (published in 29 C.F.R. § 1604.7). The guidelines state, "Any pre-employment inquiry in connection with prospective employment which expresses directly or indirectly any limitation, specification or discrimination as to sex shall be unlawful unless based upon a bona fide occupational qualification." The court also explained that even if these questions did not so blatantly violate the law, Title VII also prohibits an employer from having one set of interview questions for women and another for men.

The only time hiring decisions may be based on sex is where sex is a "bona fide occupational qualification (BFOQ) reasonably necessary to the normal operation of that particular business." This is a very limited exception and applies only in situations where the job absolutely requires either a male or female (for example, a wet nurse, a sperm donor, an actor playing a male role, or a swimsuit model). Safety, moral, or societal concerns are almost never considered BFOQs, except in a few narrow cases. For example, certain jobs in obstetric or gynecological nursing may be limited to women because of legal requirements that a female nurse be present in some circumstances. Likewise, in 1978 the Supreme Court decided that women could be excluded from certain jobs as state prison counselors because the job required extensive physical contact with prisoners in an all-male maximum security prison. But these cases are very fact-specific, and courts are careful to apply them in a very narrow manner so that women are not excluded from other jobs.

The BFOQ exception does not apply to positions traditionally denied to females because they were strenuous, dangerous, or "unladylike." As one judge put it, "Title VII rejects this type of romantic paternalism as unduly Victorian and instead vests individuals with the power to decide whether or not to take on unromantic tasks."

**Types of discrimination prohibited:** Title VII recognizes two general categories of discrimination, which may occur during either the hiring process or on the job. The first is called disparate treatment. This involves intentional discrimination— when you are treated less favorably than other employees because you are female (or because of race, religion, and so forth).

To establish a prima facie case of disparate treatment discrimination under Title VII (again, this means proving enough elements that you will win your case if the employer can't establish a defense), you must show (1) that you are a member of the group protected by Title VII from discrimination (here, women); (2) that you were adversely affected by the employer's decision (for example, you were not promoted); (3) that another person not in the protected group received the benefit you sought (a man was promoted to the position you wanted); and (4) that you had comparably good job performance or you were as qualified as the other employee who got the job.

At this point the burden of proof shifts, and your employer must prove that the action (here, the man being promoted instead of you) was taken for a "legitimate, nondiscriminatory reason." For instance, your employer could show that the job required a person with extensive computer skills, and that you do not have these skills while the person who got the job does.

The other defense the employer can raise is the claim that sex is a BFOQ for the job you wanted. Again, just as in hiring, this claim cannot be based on sexual stereotypes or preferences. For example, an oil company in one case argued that only men were welcome to conduct business in the foreign countries in which the company traded. This argument failed. Discriminatory treatment of women is not justified by the biased preference of employers, customers, or clients.

If your employer does prove a valid defense, the show is not over yet. The "burden of persuasion" goes back to you, and you will have a chance to show that the employer's "legitimate, nondiscriminatory reason" was pretextual, a mere scam to cover up the motive to discriminate. Consider the example of the man's promotion into a management job that requires computer skills you don't have. Perhaps you could show that computer skills are not required. Others in the same job do not have any special computer skills; all they need to know is basic word processing, which you do quite well. You can also bring in circumstantial evidence that all the managers are men and that men less qualified than you have been promoted to manager, as well as any direct evidence of intent to discriminate, such as posting notices of openings in management where only male workers are likely to see them. The employer can still try to rebut your evidence and show that there is no discrimination, but if you've come this far, you usually have made your case.

**Disparate or adverse impact:** The second type of discrimination that Title VII prohibits is called disparate impact or adverse impact. This refers to a situation in which employment practices may appear to be perfectly fair, but the effect of the practice is to discriminate. This type of discrimination does not require proof of any *intent* to discriminate—it's the effect of the practice, not the motive behind it, that matters.

For this type of charge, you establish your prima facie case by proving that (1) your employer uses a particular employment practice that causes a different impact on female employees, and that (2) each of the employment practices you are challenging (or the practices in your workplace when viewed as a whole) causes a discriminatory effect. Together these factors must show that a "facially neutral employment practice" (one that seems O.K. at first glance) has a significant discriminatory impact. The main thing to remember is that the court looks at the *effect* of an action or program that may seem fair but in practice operates to exclude women.

Three types of evidence can be used to prove this kind of discrimination, and in many cases you may be able to use all three. *Comparative evidence* is proof that male workers in comparable positions are treated more favorably. *Statistical evidence,* while usually not enough by itself, can be very helpful. When the applicant pool is 50-50 male and female, but the workforce is 85% male, this is highly suspicious. *Direct evidence,* when available, is often the strongest. Derogatory remarks made about women by a plant manager, comments in performance evaluations, and similar negative actions directed toward women fall into this category.

Once you have shown these elements are present, the employer gets a chance to defend himself or herself. To defeat your case, the employer must show that (1) the challenged practice is job-related to the position, and that (2) the practice amounts to a *business necessity.* Then you will have a chance to show that the reason is a pretext—a mere excuse—or that alternative practices could be used with less disparate impact, but the employer refuses to adopt such a practice.

Here's an example. Suppose you work in a factory where workers on one line, who are paid more, have to lift steel plates that weigh about 25 pounds each. The employer requires all employees who want to work on this line to be able to lift 150 pounds, which is never actually required. The result is that no women have been able to work on the line. You challenge the lifting requirement as creating a disparate impact. The employer argues that being able to lift 150 pounds is necessary because employees need to be able to lift several plates at once during peak production times. You show that a line worker can keep up with top production speed by lifting one plate at a time, and that hand trucks are always available if heavier lifting is required. The 150-pound requirement is neither job related nor a business necessity.

Disparate impact is hard to prove but not impossible. Terms such as *business necessity* are subjective, but the courts have begun to list criteria to help decide whether an employer's justifications will fly. These criteria include requirements of safety, efficiency, whether the policy is closely related to getting the job done, and whether a less discriminatory alternative exists. The total process of selecting employees is considered, and if the percentage of those selected from available workers of a certain race, sex, or other group is considerably lower than the percentage of that group in the applicant pool, a closer look at the selection process will be taken.

One important difference between Equal Pay Act cases and Title VII cases is that there are no prelawsuit requirements to take your case to court under the EPA, whereas Title VII requires you to go through EEOC procedures first. Also, the EPA covers most employers of at least two people, whereas Title VII covers only employers of 15 or more workers. Like Title VII, a suit for violation of the EPA may be filed by a private individual or the EEOC. If the EEOC files, it may also bring the suit as a class action (unavailable under the EPA) if there are a large number of people who have been the victims of company-wide discrimination. Class actions are complex, and the law requires they be handled by a competent attorney.

**Title VII and sexual harassment:** Title VII also protects your right to be free from sexual harassment, which has been absolutely established as an unlawful employment practice since 1980. That year the EEOC published guidelines that included sexual harassment in its defined unlawful employment practices.

The definition was expanded in 1986, when the U.S. Supreme Court declared that not only direct harassment but also unwelcome sexual advances that create an offensive or hostile working environment violate Title VII. Since 1990, the number of complaints filed with the EEOC has more than doubled to about 12,000 in 1992. That same year, *Working Woman* magazine conducted a survey in which 60 percent of the readers responding said they had been harassed at work.

Sexual harassment has been a popular topic in the media over the last few years, and there has been a lot of confusion about what it means. According to the EEOC and court decisions that have interpreted the term, sexual harassment means:

1. Unwelcome sexual advances, requests for sexual favors, and other verbal or physical conduct of a sexual nature constitutes sexual harassment when:
   a. Submission to the request or conduct is made or suggested to be a term or condition of continued employment;
   b. Whether the person submits, or the way she reacts to the conduct is used as a basis for employment decisions;
   c. The conduct has the effect or purpose of unreasonably interfering with the person's work performance or creating an intimidating, hostile, or offensive work environment.

This covers two distinct kinds of sexual harassment. First, "quid pro quo" harassment occurs when submission to sexual acts is made a condition of advancement, keeping your job, or other employment benefits. The second is "hostile work environment" sexual harassment, in which sexual conduct (or nonsexual yet offensive behavior based on a person's sex) creates an abusive or hostile work environment and is severe enough that it alters the working conditions on the job. A 1993 decision by the U.S. Supreme Court helped clarify what is required to prove this type of sexual harassment. "Whether an environment is 'hostile' or 'abusive' can be determined only by looking at all the circumstances," Justice Sandra Day O'Conner wrote in the Court's opinion. "These may include the frequency of the discriminatory conduct; its severity; whether it is physically threatening or humiliating or a merely offensive utterance; and whether it unreasonably interferes with an employee's work performance." The decision also made it clear that while the behavior's effect on a worker's psychological health is relevant, a woman does not have to prove that she suffered psychological harm or was unable to perform her job.

Your employer may be held responsible for sexual harassment by supervisory employees at any time, or by one or more co-worker against another if the employer knows or should have known about the conduct. The employer has an obligation to take immediate and appropriate corrective action to stop such behavior. Your employer may also be held responsible if you are the victim of sexual harassment by clients or customers.

Sexual harassment is simply one more form of discrimination that violates Title VII, and the remedies available for other types of sex discrimination also apply here. Especially in cases where the harassment prevented the woman from getting a deserved promotion or drove her from the job, courts and EEOC administrators have ordered reinstatement with adjustment for seniority, back wages, bonuses, and benefits at the level the employee would be receiving if the discrimination had not occurred. A victim may also receive front pay (for loss of future income), a transfer, payment for counseling sessions if they are not fully covered by insurance, funds for finding another job if she does not want to stay in the workplace, and attorney's fees. Also, as explained below, a 1991 amendment to Title VII now allows other monetary damages for intentional discrimination in violation of Title VII, including sexual harassment. Courts or the EEOC may also issue orders requiring the employer to develop effective procedures to investigate harassment complaints, to educate workers about what sexual harassment is and why it will not be tolerated, and to discipline employees who harass subordinates or co-workers.

Sometimes a distinction is made for what is called sex-based harassment, which is based on sex but not sexual in nature. This includes physical aggression, intimidation, hostility, or other mistreatment because a woman is not welcome on the job. It involves any form of negative behavior that is targeted at you just because you are a woman and interferes with your work performance. For example, if your male co-workers damage your work equipment, steal your personal belongings, or keep you out of men-only buildings to make it hard for you to do your job because they don't want a woman around, this is indeed sexual harassment.

In March 1991, the EEOC issued a special instruction to its lawyers and investigators to target sexual harassment claims for quick investigation and, if required, court action. Charges of sexual harassment are supposed to be reviewed by the EEOC legal staff as soon as they are filed, and quickly investigated where appropriate. If harassment is found, the EEOC has a special procedure to bring the case quickly before the U.S. District Court and obtain a court order requiring the employer to stop the harassment immediately while investigation and conciliation efforts continue. A victim of sexual harassment may also have claims under both civil and criminal state laws or under the National Labor Relations Act. How to recognize and put a stop to sexual harassment is discussed in greater detail later in the book.

**Retaliation:** Like the EPA, Title VII prohibits retaliation against a person who files a charge of discrimination, helps with an investigation, or opposes an illegal employment practice. To win on a claim of retaliation (again, to establish your *prima facie case*), you must show that (1) you exercised your protected rights, (2) an adverse employment action occurred, and (3) the adverse action was caused by your protected activities. For example, you may have spoken out against illegal activities going on in the freight-shipping company where you work as a receiving clerk. After you spoke out, you were transferred to a less desirable location. Once this is shown, your boss will have a chance to prove that there was another legitimate, or "nonretaliatory" reason for the decision. For example, your employer could claim that the company departments were being restructured, and all the receiving people were being transferred. You then have another chance to refute this reason by showing that it is a mere pretext. For instance, the others were moved because their building was sold, while you could have easily stayed where you were because receiving work is still being done at that location.

## AMENDMENTS TO TITLE VII

### *The 1978 Federal Pregnancy Discrimination Act*
**What it means:** Your employer cannot discriminate against you in hiring, placement, promotion, leave policies, or benefits because you are or may become pregnant.

**Who it covers:** All employers and employees covered by Title VII.

**Who enforces it:** The EEOC or your state FEPA, and the appropriate court after the agency action is completed.

**Remedies:** The same as other Title VII remedies listed above.

**Time limits:** The same as other Title VII claims.

In 1978 Congress expanded the existing law protecting women in the workplace by passing an amendment to Title VII specifically prohibiting discrimination based on pregnancy. Employers cannot refuse to hire a pregnant woman, fire her because she is pregnant, force her to go on leave at some arbitrary point in her pregnancy, require that she take a set amount of time off after the baby is born, or penalize her by reducing the benefits she has earned, such as credit for previous service, accrued retirement benefits, and accumulated seniority.

There are a few exceptions to these requirements. A pregnant woman may only be denied employment due to pregnancy when it would prevent her from doing her job. For example, a female airline pilot close to term could endanger the safety of the passengers if she went into labor during a flight, so the airlines may make reasonable restrictions related to safety such as requiring a pregnant pilot to stop flying at a set time prior to her due date.

This law does not require an employer to give the employee any specific amount of time off for maternity leave, nor does it require the employer to establish any special benefits for other workers where none exist (these issues are now covered for many workers by the Family and Medical Leave Act of 1993 and some state laws, discussed below). Under the 1978 act, however, women who are pregnant or have recently given birth must be treated the same as other "temporarily disabled" employees for all employment-related purposes, including fringe benefits and insurance. Also, an employer may not fire or refuse to hire a woman because she has exercised her right to have an abortion.

If you work with industrial substances that may be hazardous to your baby, you may also have the right to be temporarily reassigned to a job in which this risk is not present. Many states have their own laws relating to pregnancy, childbirth, and parental leave for workers, as discussed below.

### The Civil Rights Act of 1991

**What it means:** This 1991 amendment to Title VII made several important changes to expand its existing power and advance the rights of working women.

**Who it covers:** All employers and employees covered by Title VII.

**Who enforces it:** The EEOC, your state FEPA, and the appropriate court after agency procedures are completed.

**Remedies:** The Civil Rights Act enhanced the remedies available under Title VII. Now, when employment discrimination is intentional, a worker may get a jury trial and recover money damages in addition to back and front pay and the other remedies formerly allowed. The award may include damages for future financial losses, emotional pain, suffering, mental anguish, counseling costs, loss of enjoyment of life, and other compensation for losses beyond actual money out of pocket.

The amount of these damages is limited according to the size of the employer's workforce. Employers with 15 to 100 employees can be ordered to pay up to $50,000 per individual complaint; employees with 101 to 200 employees, up to $100,000; employers with 201 to 500 employees, up to $200,000; and employers with more than 500 employees, up to $300,000. These amounts do not include any recovery for back pay, which is not considered damages but a different type of compensation. You may get back or front pay plus damages.

In addition, punitive damages may be ordered if the employee can show that the employer engaged in one or more discriminatory practices "with malice or with reckless indifference to the federally protected rights of an aggrieved individual." That is, the employer knew or should have known that what was happening was illegal and deliberately continued or just didn't care.

**Time limits:** The same as other Title VII claims.

**More on the Civil Rights Act of 1991:** In addition to expanding the remedies available under Title VII, the 1991 amendment clarified the law regarding disparate impact. The Supreme Court issued rulings on a number of cases in 1989 that Congress believed were incorrect and left the law in a state of confusion. In effect, the amendment restored the law to follow *Griggs v. Duke Power Co.,* a landmark 1971 class action suit by black employees against the North Carolina power company where they worked. *Griggs* established the standard for proving "disparate impact," as explained above. It involved a high school completion requirement and testing practice that appeared fair in form yet was discriminatory in operation. The tests measured academic aptitude and mechanical comprehension and required scores at approximately a median high school level. At this time, North Carolina census statistics showed that while 34% of white males had completed high school, only 12% of black males had done so. The Court held the requirements were not related to job performance and not a business necessity.

The third major impact the act has for women in the workplace is found in Title II of the Act, known as the Glass Ceiling Act of 1991. Title II recognizes that women and minorities are underrepresented in management and decision-making positions in business, and that artificial barriers exist to their advancement in the workplace. Among other things, it set up a "Glass Ceiling Commission" to conduct a study of these and related problems and to make recommendations on how to solve them.

Also, the 1991 act specifically stated Congress's finding that "additional remedies under Federal law are needed to deter unlawful harassment and intentional discrimination in the workplace" and stated that one purpose of the Act was "to provide appropriate remedies for intentional discrimination and unlawful harassment in the workplace."

### The U.S. Constitution

**What it means:** That certain fundamental rights are guaranteed to all Americans.

**Who it covers:** All American citizens and others legally in the country, including resident aliens.

**Who enforces it:** The federal and state courts. Private organizations such as the American Civil Liberties Union (ACLU) also monitor violations and sometimes represent people who have been denied their constitutional rights.

**Time limits:** It depends on what other law is involved, as explained below.

**Remedies:** Remedies for violations of constitutional rights can include equitable relief (in which the court orders someone to do or not do something), compensatory damages, and punitive damages. Attorney's fees are also available in some cases, depending on what other law is involved.

## TOOLS FOR PROTECTING CONSTITUTIONAL RIGHTS: THE RECONSTRUCTION CIVIL RIGHTS LAWS

Following the Civil War, Congress passed a group of laws to protect all U.S. citizens, particularly former slaves, from violations of their civil rights. These laws are now used by citizens in assorted ways to protect them from unlawful actions by governments or others under the control of the government, including state-run hospitals, schools, or government subdivisions such as zoning boards. In a few situations these laws can be used to sue private persons as well. Some are narrow and cover only certain situations, but they can be powerful weapons if they are compatible with your circumstances.

### 42 U.S.C. Section 1983
**What it means:** This law, 42 U.S.C. Section 1983, gives citizens the right to bring a civil lawsuit against any "person," including the states and their subdivisions (counties and municipalities), who acts "under color of state law," in violation of the constitutional or other federal rights of another. This law is one of the most powerful tools in enforcing citizens' civil rights. It provides a wide range of remedies for violations of "rights, privileges, or immunities secured by the Constitution and laws."

**Who it covers:** The main limitation to Section 1983 is that it applies only to employers acting "under color of state law," so private employers are not covered. However, this has a broader range than you might expect. State hospitals, universities, libraries, municipal governments, state highway commissions, local police and fire departments, and many other entities fall within these boundaries.

**Who enforces it:** The federal and state courts. There is no agency to enforce Section 1983; the only way to use it is by filing a private lawsuit. The U.S. Commission on Civil Rights is authorized to investigate complaints that citizens are being deprived of their civil rights, and many private civil rights organizations listed in the Appendix (such as the ACLU) can provide information, referrals to qualified lawyers, and in some cases direct legal representation.

**Time limits:** Section 1983 actions are considered personal injury actions for purposes of calculating the statute of limitations. Therefore, you must look at the law in the state where the violation took place to find out how long you have to file.

**Remedies:** Damage awards in Section 1983 cases can include all compensatory damages, punitive damages, and attorney's fees.

**More on Section 1983:** The fifth and fourteenth amendments to the Constitution are commonly involved in cases of employment discrimination. The right to a job has been recognized as property within the meaning of the Constitution, which says that you cannot be deprived of property without due process of law. This means two things. First, you cannot have your job taken away without receiving notice of why you are about to lose your job; you are also entitled to a hearing in which you can tell your side of the story. This is called *procedural due process*. Second, you cannot have your job taken away for reasons that are "arbitrary and capricious." There must be a good, legitimate reason, backed up by facts. This is called *substantive due process*.

People who are not fired outright but are forced off the job because their working conditions are made intolerable are often able to show that they were deprived of their job through *constructive discharge*. Constructive discharge from your job occurs when working conditions become so miserable that any reasonable person would find them intolerable and feel compelled to resign. This is a violation of your property rights and will support a Section 1983 claim for a due process violation.

If your employer retaliates against you for criticizing the employer, reporting to an agency, filing a lawsuit or union grievance, or taking other steps to assert your rights to equal compensation, you may file a Section 1983 claim for violation of your First Amendment right to exercise free speech. The speech must be on a matter of "public concern," but this term has a broad interpretation. Sex discrimination is illegal and undoubtedly a matter of public concern, so if you complain about unequal pay, harassment, or other discrimination and you are penalized, this is retaliation against protected speech. In cases that aren't so clear, the court will look at whether your speech involved a purely personal issue or included a matter of public concern. For example, in one case, an employee of a public housing authority complained that she did not have a sufficient staff to inspect the apartments and arrange for repairs. As a result of the understaffing, housing that did not meet the minimum standards for human habitation was being rented anyway. She lost her job and sued. The court explained that this was much more than just a worker wanting more help, it was a matter of serious public concern.

Retaliation can include anything that makes your job harder or more unpleasant, such as demotion, transfer, lowering of salary, loss of benefits, or other actions that alter your employment conditions. Retaliation also occurs when your employer requires you to give up your First Amendment rights (essentially, "Shut up and get back to work") in order to keep your job or favorable conditions such as your current title.

Retaliation claims are frequently brought by men who speak out against discrimination in support of female co-workers and then suffer the wrath of the employer. The person claiming retaliation must prove that his speech (or other protected activity, such as the right to freely associate with others to engage in speech and other activities protected by the First Amendment) was the main motivating factor that made the employer decide to take action against him.

*Marshall v. Allen* was a suit brought by a male attorney who worked for the Chicago Housing Authority (CHA). The attorney, Cornelius Marshall, supported four female attorneys who filed complaints with the EEOC about unequal pay and working conditions in the CHA legal department. Marshall was later fired, and he proved that working with his colleagues to support their claims caused his discharge. Both speech and association were involved in this case, because Marshall got together with the female lawyers to speak, assemble, and work for the redress of grievances. The court emphasized that the freedom to associate in order to promote and advance one's beliefs and ideas is a constitutionally protected activity.

Discrimination will often involve several constitutional violations. In *Keenan v. City of Philadelphia*, Karen Keenan, a female police detective, was excluded from much of the important work assigned to the male detectives because, in the words of the captain who supervised her, these tasks were "no job for a woman." Several of her male colleagues saw how unfair this was and stood up for her. As a result, Keenan and four of her fellow officers were transferred and targeted for bogus internal investigations. Keenan sued for sex discrimination in violation of her right to equal protection under the law. She and the male officers joined together in filing claims for violation of their right to free speech and association. The court looked at the evidence and ruled that the transfers and other actions amounted to impermissible discipline in violation of constitutional rights.

Proof of retaliation is a powerful tool because it makes judges and juries mad. It's bad enough when discrimination occurs in the first place, but when someone is penalized for trying to win his or her rights or help a co-worker, it becomes a constitutional double-whammy. Punitive damages can be awarded in Section 1983 actions where the defendants acted deliberately, with reckless or callous disregard of or indifference to the rights or safety of others. Retaliation is a good way to prove deliberate action. Large punitive damage awards seem to be more common when retaliation is proven than in any other type of civil rights case.

Equal protection claims like Keenan's are also common under Section 1983. The employee must prove intentional discrimination, also called purposeful discrimination. This means that she must prove she was treated differently than other employees in similar circumstances because of her gender. She must show either overt discrimination or disparate treatment. The "adverse impact" theory of Title VII (as explained above) won't work here. In Keenan's case, she had little difficulty showing that she was deliberately treated in a much different manner than her male colleagues.

Sexual harassment cases have also been brought under Section 1983 as a violation of a woman's right to equal protection under the law. The courts have declared that the government has an interest in allowing women to have access to equal employment opportunities and nontraditional employment. In several cases, courts have ruled that sexual harassment of a public employee violated the equal protection clause. This type of claim can be brought along with a claim under Title VII.

Any time an employee of a state, city, county, or an agent thereof (such as a state-run university, hospital or prison) is the victim of pay or other sex discrimination, Section 1983 should be considered as a valuable option. A word of caution: This is an extremely complex area of the law, involving sovereign immunity, difficult entanglement with state law, and enormous potential to ruin a good case. Make sure your lawyer is well versed in civil rights law.

### Bivens Actions

While federal employers are not covered by Section 1983, a similar type of lawsuit, called a *Bivens* action, named for the court case that first made it into law, can be brought against individuals who work for the federal government, such as the armed services, the Postal Service, the IRS. Thus, if you work for the FBI, for example, and your employer discriminates against you, you may be able to sue him or her in a *Bivens* action. You may also have a claim against the United States under the Federal Tort Claims Act, which allows you to sue the government for certain "torts," or legal wrongs, as described in the next chapter. Federal employers also have a special relationship with the EEOC, which enforces Title VII, the EPA, and other laws. Again, all of these laws and the way they work together are complicated, and it is best to talk to an experienced civil rights attorney if you believe you may have any kind of constitutional claim.

### 42 U.S.C. Section 1985

Section 1985 is another of the reconstruction civil rights laws. It prohibits two or more persons from acting in a conspiracy to deprive a person of his or her constitutional rights. In some cases, state action is not required—that is, private citizens may be liable for violating this law if they act together to take away someone's rights—but most of the time, in practice, a connection with the state is necessary. This statute is not used nearly as often as Section 1983, but it has come up in some sex discrimination cases. If you have a Section 1983 claim and suspect a possible conspiracy in which several people acted together to discriminate, you might want to discuss Section 1985 with your lawyer as another possible claim.

### The Family and Medical Leave Act of 1993

**What it does:** The Family and Medical Leave Act guarantees that eligible employees shall be entitled to a total of 12 work weeks of unpaid leave, during any 12-month period, for the birth or adoption of a child, to care for a spouse, child, or parent with a serious illness, or because the employee is seriously ill and unable to work. An employee who takes this leave is entitled to return to her former position or an equivalent position with equivalent pay, benefits, and other terms and conditions of employment. Group health benefits will be maintained during the employee's leave. It is important to note that seniority will not accumulate while you're off, but you cannot lose what you have earned.

**Who is covered:** Most people who have been on the job for at least one year and work for an employer with 50 or more employees, including public employers. Special provisions apply to civil service employees, congressional employees, and teachers and other school district employees who work on academic term schedules. Some "highly compensated employees" in the top 10% salary range in their workplace may be denied restoration after leave under certain conditions in which it is necessary to "prevent substantial and grievous injury to the operations of the employer."

**Time limits:** A suit may be filed within two years after the last event in violation of the act, or within three years if the violation is willful. As with most of the federal employment laws, retaliation is specifically prohibited.

**Agency enforcement:** The act is enforced by the U.S. Department of Labor through local and regional offices. The Department of Labor can receive complaints and conduct investigations in the same manner as is provided for complaints under the FLSA and may bring suit on behalf of the employee. If suit is filed by the Secretary of Labor, the employee cannot then bring a private suit. Otherwise, an employee can sue on her own.

**Remedies:** The act allows an employee to bring a private lawsuit to recover any wages or salary lost because of the violation, or other actual money lost up to the equivalent of 12 weeks' wages or salary, plus interest. Liquidated damages may be awarded in the form of double these damages if the employer did not act in good faith. Equitable relief may also be ordered, including reinstatement, employment, and promotion. A group of employees may sue together, or a class action may be brought. A successful plaintiff may recover attorney's fees.

**More on the act:** It will take some time to see how the act works in practice, but it is well written and represents a milestone in both employee rights and recognition of the importance of a worker's family. Two of the findings set out at the beginning of the act state: "(2) it is important for the development of children and the family unit that fathers and mothers be able to participate in early childrearing and the care of family members who have serious health conditions; [and] (3) the lack of employment policies to accommodate working parents can force individuals to choose between job security and parenting." You wouldn't think such obvious principles would need to be stated by an act of Congress, but it's fortunate, at long last, that they have.

### Executive Order 11246 (3 C.F.R. 339 [1964–65] reprinted as amended in 42 U.S.C. § 2000e note)

**What it means:** Executive Order 11246 is a special law enacted in 1965 that applies to federal contractors and subcontractors, as well as private contractors who hold federal or federally assisted construction contracts exceeding $10,000. Employers who are covered may include state or local agencies participating in federal contract work. It prohibits these contractors from employment discrimination based on sex, race, color, religion, or national origin and requires the contractor to take affirmative action to assure equal employment opportunity. The affirmative action provision is not a quota system, but it requires that special attention be paid to equality in recruitment, job advertising, hiring, upgrading, demotion, transfer, layoff, termination, pay rates and other compensation, and selection for training, including apprenticeship. Such contractors include state or local agencies participating in federal contract work.

**Who it covers:** All employees of the employers described above.

**Who enforces it:** Executive Order 11246 is enforced by the Office of Federal Contract Compliance Programs (OFCCP) of the U.S. Department of Labor. This agency sets policy and regulations relating to the order and checks to see that federal contractors comply with the regulations, mainly through compliance reviews. If an employee or group files a complaint with the OFCCP charging discrimination, the OFCCP will investigate in a manner very similar to that of the EEOC. If it appears there are violations of the executive order, the OFCCP will try to reach a conciliation agreement with the employer. If the efforts to settle are not successful, the administrative process continues with a formal hearing. The agency may refer you to the EEOC or FEPA on an individual complaint. The Department of Justice may, in some cases, file suit in federal court on behalf of the Department of Labor for violations of Executive Order 11246. An employee may not file his or her own private suit for violation of the order; the agency must enforce this law.

**Time limits:** The complaint must be filed within 180 days of the discrimination, in person or by letter, at a local or regional OFCCP office. It should include a description of what happened, the names and addresses of the contractor and of the workers who were discriminated against, and any other information that might help the OFCCP investigation.

**Remedies:** If a federal contractor discriminates, the contractor may be ordered to give the affected employees back pay, seniority credit, promotions, or equitable relief. The OFCCP may also recommend that the Secretary of Labor impose sanctions, which may include cancellation of a government contract or banning the company from applying for any government contracts in the future.

**More on Executive Order 11246:** The OFCCP guidelines state that contractors may not state a preference for one sex or the other when advertising for employees unless sex is a BFOQ for the job, nor may contractors base seniority lists on sex, deny a person a job because of state protective labor laws, or make distinctions between married or unmarried persons of one sex only. In a 1971 court case brought under Executive Order 11246, the Supreme Court held that the employer could not refuse an assembly trainee job to a woman because she had preschool-age children when the same restriction was not applied to male trainees with young children.

Many companies do federal contracting work and are therefore subject to Executive Order 11246. Find out if your employer is covered by this law, because it is a powerful weapon in the arsenal against discrimination. Since all federally assisted construction contracts over $10,000 are included, many small companies fall within the scope of the order, as well as the giants such as Martin Marietta. An individual cannot privately sue a company for violating the order, but she may file a complaint of discrimination against her employer by phone, letter, or a visit to one of OFCCP's offices (see Appendix).

The OFCCP is most concerned about practices that affect an entire segment of the employer's workforce. Complaints involving discrimination against only one individual will be referred to the EEOC. However, one person may file on behalf of all persons in the workplace affected by the discriminatory conduct. Organizations may also file a complaint.

Contractors who refuse to comply with the orders of the OFCCP can lose their lucrative government contracts, have payments on those contracts withheld, or become ineligible to receive future federal contract work. For the many companies that depend on government contracts for a large part of their profits, Executive Order 11246 is a strong motivator to avoid discrimination.

## OTHER FEDERAL LAWS:

There are a number of other federal laws that protect workers in specific occupations or against specific forms of discrimination. Some of these laws include:

1. Title IX of the Education Act of 1972 (20 U.S.C. § 1681 *et. seq.*) prohibits sex discrimination by educational institutions receiving federal funds in hiring, on the job, and in all educational programs.
2. The Occupational Safety and Health Act (OSHA) (29 U.S.C. § 660) protects workers from health and safety hazards on the job, and prohibits retaliation for complaining about unsafe conditions. Many states have their own OSHAs that provide similar and additional protection for workers.
3. The Age Discrimination in Employment Act of 1967 (ADEA) (29 U.S.C. § 621 *et. seq.*) prohibits employers with more than 20 employees from discrimination based on age against people over 40. It is enforced by

the EEOC. Like OSHA, many states have their own laws prohibiting age discrimination.

4. The Employment Retirement Income Security Act (ERISA) (29 U.S.C. § 1140) prohibits employers from discharging an employee in an effort to deprive the employee of retirement benefits—for example, when someone is fired just before the retirement plan vests.

5. Consolidation Omnibus Budget Reconciliation Act of 1985 (COBRA). Employers with more than 20 employees must continue group health insurance for employees who leave (unless they are fired for gross misconduct) for 18 months at a cost of no more than 10% of the group cost.

6. The Americans with Disabilities Act (ADA) (42 U.S.C. § 12101 *et. seq.*) prohibits discrimination against people with disabilities in employment, telecommunications, public service, public transportation, and public accommodations.

7. The National Labor Relations Act (NLRA) (29 U.S.C. § 129, 141 *et. seq.*) guarantees employees the right to form, join, or assist recruiting for labor unions, to engage in collective bargaining through union representatives, and to engage in related activities such as striking and comparing wages between workers. It also prohibits discrimination and unfair activities by unions. Complaints must be received by the National Labor Relations Board (NLRB) within 180 days after the violation. The NLRB can investigate and conduct hearings on charges of unfair labor practices and can order employers to cease and desist from the unfair practice, reinstate employees, and provide back pay. It can also order the employer to make reports to show it is complying with orders. The NLRB can file its orders with the U.S. district court and ask the court to enforce them and to issue an injunction to stop an unfair practice. The orders of the board can also be appealed to the court.

The NLRA has also been applied in at least one case to prohibit sexual harassment. When a group of seamstresses complained to a "consulting" plant manager about being sexually harassed by the regular plant manager, they were fired. A U.S. Court of Appeals held that freedom from sexual harassment is a working condition that employees may organize to protect according to the NLRA. It upheld the finding of the NLRB that firing these workers violated the act's prohibition of employers from interfering with, restraining, or coercing employees in the exercise of their rights under the act.

There are many other laws that forbid discrimination or retaliation, such as environmental laws that prohibit discharge of employees who report violations, instigate charges, or testify at hearings on their employer's illegal activities. Check with your personnel, EEO, or human resources manager, your professional organization, your lawyer, or others in your profession to learn whether additional laws may protect your rights.

# CHAPTER 4

## STATE AND LOCAL LAWS

All states have their own laws related to the rights of workers. These laws exist to complement the federal laws by dealing with areas the federal laws do not cover, or in some cases by adding additional protections. State laws often help fill the gaps in the federal laws—for example, by protecting workers in small establishments with less than the 15 employees required to be under the umbrella of Title VII.

The general rule is that a state may make its own laws to govern the rights of workers in the state as long as those laws do not conflict with federal laws. State laws that do conflict will be repealed, or, if they remain on the books, they are of no effect and cannot be enforced. For example, some states still have old protective laws that set different work hours for women or restrict female employees from certain occupations perceived to be dangerous or morally improper. These laws conflict with Title VII, so they cannot be enforced or used as a defense by an employer who discriminates.

States often have minimum wage laws that expand on what is covered by the FLSA. A state may not set a minimum wage lower than that set by the FLSA, except for types of work not covered by the FLSA at all. Most states have wage payment laws that are enforced by the state Department of Labor. These

71

laws specify how often you are to be paid and how long you must be paid after termination, among other things. Some states also have laws limiting the number of days a week an employee can be required to work, regulating work on Sundays or other Sabbath days and holidays, and mandating rest periods.

The vast majority of the states now have their own laws requiring equal pay and prohibiting discrimination. FEPAs enforce state equal pay laws and also act as representatives for the federal EEOC by taking the first shot at resolving employment discrimination complaints and starting an investigation. State procedures are usually very similar to EEOC procedures. Once your charge is filed, the agency will investigate and, if there appears to be discrimination, try to reach a settlement. If this is not successful, an administrative hearing will be scheduled, which is something like an informal court proceeding, in which the employer will have to answer to the charges and evidence will be heard by a hearing officer. If the hearing officer finds in your favor, he or she will issue an order telling the employer what must be done and indicating damages to be paid. If the employer does not comply, the order can be enforced by the district court, or either party may appeal. A list of the main FEPA offices is provided in the Appendix.

Many states also have parental leave laws that require employers to allow new parents a specific amount of time off for the birth or adoption of a child, and subsequent reinstatement to the same or a similar job after the leave. Some states have maternity disability laws for recovery after childbirth; others provide leave when the employee, her child, or another family member is ill. Some require the employer to continue providing health insurance while the worker is on leave. Some states provide such provisions only for state government employees. Others provide temporary disability insurance for pregnancy and childbirth. The Family and Medical Leave Act of 1993 now covers most of these topics, but this law only applies to workers in places with 50 or more employees and has other exclusions as well.

Although Congress has not yet passed an equal rights amendment (ERA) to the U.S. Constitution, many states have passed equal rights amendments to their own constitutions. For example, in 1972 New Mexico passed an ERA that states "equality of rights under the law shall not be denied on account of the sex of any person. Any part of a state or local law that does not meet this requirement cannot be enforced."

In New Mexico the passage of the ERA resulted in changes to the community property law, which now gives a husband and wife equal rights to manage their common property. It also resulted in the eligibility of women to enroll at all public schools, including the New Mexico Military Institute, that was previously all male. Many states have special commissions or other groups that help citizens understand and enforce their rights under such laws; for example, the New Mexico Commission on the Status of Women. These commissions offer a variety of free pamphlets to help you understand the laws that protect your rights. Additional information on such laws in your state can be provided by your state Department of Labor, Civil Rights Commission, or Human Rights Agency (see Appendix).

## Workers' Compensation Laws

Every state has a system of laws designed to compensate workers who are injured on the job. These laws require employers to carry insurance that will pay injured workers a percentage of their wages while they are unable to work. They also provide income for workers who have been permanently disabled on the job. The laws vary a great deal from state to state. If you are hurt on the job, consult with a lawyer who is very familiar with your state's laws.

Workers' compensation laws cover only sickness or injuries that happen as a "normal part of employment activity." Sex discrimination is against the law, so it is not a normal part of employment activity. Therefore, if you suffer physical, emotional, or psychological injury on the job due to discrimination (including sexual harassment), you probably can't bring a claim for workers' compensation.

This sounds like a disadvantage, and it may be in some cases. But you can usually bring a better case, with more remedies, under the other laws I've been describing. And workers' compensation is an exclusive remedy: If your injury fits into the worker's compensation statute, you must file suit according to that law. Yet if you file a claim under these statutes, that's it—you can't bring any other claim. Employers have tried to use this against employees, but the courts won't buy it. For example, in a California case, *Accardi v. Superior Court (Simi Valley)*, a female police officer suffered continuous harassment because of her sex; including threats, damaging rumors, unfavorable work assignments, unfounded complaints, lewd statements, and double work assignments without adequate assistance. She endured this hostile work environment for close to 10 years before suffering severe emotional and psychological damage. Her employer tried to say that her only remedy should be a workers' compensation claim, since she was injured at work. The court soundly rejected this, explaining that if an employee suffers such problems because of a legitimate demotion, criticism of work practices, or some other normal part of the employment environment, she would have go through the workers' compensation system. But the court stressed that "discrimination in employment is *not* a normal condition of employment."

## Protective Laws

As explained in chapter 2, most protective laws limiting the hours or kinds of work open to women have either been struck down as discriminatory or amended so their protections extend to all workers, male and female alike. Today, protective laws take the form of wage and hour laws that guarantee all workers the right to timely payment of wages, overtime, and minimum wages provided by state law. These laws are generally enforced by state labor departments or labor commissions.

Other forms of protective laws are the occupational safety and health laws, which exist at both state and federal levels; and state unemployment compensation laws, administered by the Labor Department. State criminal statutes also protect employees from assault, fraud, battery, and blacklisting.

## Common Law

The term common law, or case law, refers to law made by the courts. When a higher court decides a case, it becomes precedent—that is, a binding decision that must be followed by the lower courts in the same jurisdiction. These decisions are persuasive in other jurisdictions, too—that is, other courts often choose to follow them, especially if there is no case law explaining what happens in that particular situation in their own jurisdiction. In state law, the jurisdiction is generally the state, and in federal law it is the district or circuit. Decisions of the U.S. Supreme Court must be followed by all the courts of the United States and its territories.

Most common law is state law, and the federal court will generally apply the state common law of the state in which it is located. However, in some fields there is such a thing as federal common law, including employment law.

Common law may involve principles that have been accepted and understood for centuries but never became a part of the collection of written laws, or "statutes," passed by a legislature (such as what it takes to make a contract), or it may involve a court's interpretation of what the written statutes mean. Both versions often will be involved in a court's decision, especially in a field like employment law, where so many written statutes and common law principles can apply to the same set of facts. For example, pay discrimination by an employer may involve violations of the Equal Pay Act, Title VII, and state common law breach of contract. Courts use other cases similar to yours to decide whether the facts of your case fit within the laws you claim are violated, and whether the elements of your common law claim are all present and valid.

There are quite a number of common law claims that may be available to a victim of employment discrimination. Remember, the law varies from state to state, but the following are the basic principles most states apply.

## BREACH OF CONTRACT

If you have a written employment contract that sets out your rights and responsibilities on the job, you are in a lucky minority. If your employer violates the terms of the contract, you can sue, and vice versa.

Unfortunately, written employment contracts are the exception rather than the rule. However, you don't necessarily need a formal written document in order to have a contract. Basically, any time two people enter into an agreement in which one makes an offer, the other accepts the offer, money (or any consideration, namely something of value) is exchanged, and both people understand they have struck a deal, there is a contract. Of course, this is subject to a million exceptions, but in the employment context courts are becoming more lenient in finding contracts between worker and boss. The main obstacle is proof. Your employer may have specifically promised you a raise after six months, a promotion in a year, and a company car. Unless you can prove this, it will often be the classic swearing match—the word of one person against that of another.

However, there are other ways to make a binding contract. If your employer gave you a personnel manual that you were required to follow, and this manual guaranteed certain rights, you may have an implied contract. This type of contract can be made when the people involved don't bargain for any specific deal, but something such as a manual shows a clear understanding that there was an agreement between them. For instance, many personnel manuals describe reviews, benefits, set times for wage increases, and procedures for announcing advancement opportunities. You and your employer agree to these terms when you take the job. If your employer goes against these rules, it may be in breach of an implied contract.

In some cases implied contracts can also be formed by several informal written documents, such as memos, schedules, or notes. For this reason, it is always a good idea to send your boss a memo or letter stating your understanding of any promises or policies that you discuss, with a request that he or she let you know if your understanding is incorrect. Even handwritten notes on scratch paper can be important evidence that an implied contract was made.

Unfortunately, in most places, unless you can prove that some kind of contract existed, you can be fired for any reason or for no reason at all, provided that this does not violate one of the established laws. This outdated system is called employment at will and is based on the idea of a "master and servant" relationship between employers and employees. If you work for the government, however, civil rights laws protect you from arbitrary firing. In addition, a few states have begun to require that employment decisions be objectively reasonable, based on an implied duty of good faith and fair dealing among all those who do business together, including employers and workers, although relatively few states have well-developed law on this point.

## TORTS

The next group of common law principles falls under the heading of torts. A tort is a wrongful action by one person against another that gives the victim the right to sue and receive financial compensation for damages. Most people are familiar with such torts as battery, trespass, and negligence.

*Wrongful discharge.* Wrongful discharge is a tort that is based on public policy interests. In most states it is considered wrongful discharge to fire a worker for refusing to do something illegal or to retaliate against her for asserting a right, such as the right to equal pay. A worker who proves wrongful discharge can get damages for lost wages and other injuries caused by being unfairly fired, including pain, suffering, and damage to reputation. If the worker was fired maliciously as punishment for doing something encouraged by public policy—such as reporting discrimination in the workplace—she may be able to recover punitive damages as well. Retaliatory discharge is sometimes considered a separate tort, another species of wrongful discharge. As discussed, the Constitution and many of the federal laws strictly prohibit an employer from firing or otherwise punishing an employee who speaks out against discrimination or other unlawful practices. Retaliation can also support this common law tort action. The employee must prove that she took a legal action, that she was then punished, and that the punishment was caused by her taking the action.

*Constructive discharge.* This tort is a form of common law protection against discrimination. The standard for constructive discharge is that the employer's illegal acts of discrimination or retaliation created a climate in the workplace that would force a reasonable person to resign. The worker must show that the employer deliberately made working conditions intolerable for her because she was a woman. The employee is not required to show that her boss intended to make her quit, only that his actions or the overall climate of the workplace became so unbearable that the average person in her position would be forced to quit, and she suffered damage as a result.

In a Washington state case, *Hill v. GTE Directories Sales Corp.,* a female sales representative showed that she was assigned to a sales unit that did not want a woman but was forced to take her; that she was expected to compete with her male counterparts but not given equivalent training; that she was not paid the same salary as the male employees; that she was assigned accounts that her employer knew would not be renewed or increased; and that she was expected to meet unrealistic sales quotas. She went to court claiming sex discrimination and constructive discharge and won damages of $19,000 for lost income, plus noneconomic damages (for proving she suffered emotional distress and had to seek medical help for stress-related problems) of $125,000.

*Intentional infliction of emotional distress.* This tort commonly occurs when an employee is forced out of a job or subjected to continuous harassment. Intentional infliction of emotional distress occurs when (1) a person does something either intentionally or recklessly (2) that is considered by most to amount to extreme or outrageous conduct and (3) causes the other person to suffer severe emotional distress. One act is enough if it is truly outrageous; however, continuous badgering by a series of small but annoying acts can add up to intentional infliction of emotional distress. This tort often accompanies charges of retaliation or constructive discharge in which an employer tries to force a worker to resign.

*Defamation.* Defamation occurs when someone makes a false statement of fact about a person to at least one other person, and that statement is understood to be damaging to the person's reputation. A defamatory statement is essentially a rotten, untrue thing to say about another person, such as accusing them of committing a crime. Defamation includes slander (spoken statements) and libel (written statements). Note that the statement must involve facts, not opinions. We're all entitled to our opinions about someone, but we're not entitled to say things that will be taken as true and hurt her or his reputation. Defamation sometimes occurs when an employee is fired or demoted for a pretextual reason—for example, she is falsely accused of stealing or being drunk on the job—and her boss tells others this is the reason she was let go.

*Fraud.* The tort of fraud includes actual fraud, constructive fraud, and misrepresentation. The main difference is the intent of the wrongdoer. Actual fraud requires that the person has an intent to deceive the other. In any kind of fraud, person A makes a false or deceptive statement that person B relies on, and person B is hurt as a result. For example, an employer may tell someone she is being hired for a desirable position at a good wage. Then, when she quits her old job and shows up for work, she is placed in another job at a lower wage instead. Or, the employer may tell the person that she will be next in line for manager, which may be technically true, but no management positions exist in the plant where she works.

***Tortuous interference with contractual, business, or economic relationships.*** These business torts involve deliberately interfering with the ability of another person to carry on his or her business or enter into contracts. Essentially, it means taking unfair action to harm another person's livelihood or ability to make a living. The wrongdoer must have this motive and do improper things expressly to harm the other person, with the result of actually harming the other person's business interests. For instance, a former employer "blackballs" you by telling others in the industry that you are a troublemaker. As a result, you are unable to get another job. Or suppose you leave a job and start your own competing business, and your former boss bribes your customers not to do business with you or tells them lies to make your business seem undesirable. Be aware that fair competition is not prohibited. There must be deliberate and unfair interference with your ability to do business or make contracts.

***Assault.*** Assault often accompanies harassment. Assault occurs when one person intends to touch another in a way that is harmful or offensive or makes the person apprehensive that she will be harmed. The threat of harm has to be immediate and usually requires more than just words. There has to be some gesture or action that puts the victim in apprehension of imminent harm. If one co-worker corners another in a dark hallway and waves his fist in her face, telling her that she had better stay out of his way, this is an assault.

***Battery.*** Battery requires the same proof as assault, with one more requirement: Harmful or offensive touching must actually take place. Any touching that would offend a reasonable sense of personal dignity will suffice. There is no requirement that the person be injured. Slapping or spitting on someone, unwelcome sexual fondling, or throwing things that hit a person have all been found to amount to battery. It is easy to see how many cases of sexual harassment will also support common law battery claims.

***Invasion of privacy.*** There are four separate kinds of invasion of privacy, but the one that most often occurs in employment cases is called "false light before the public." This happens when an employer spreads rumors or otherwise makes statements that place the worker in a false light in the eyes of the public, in a way that would be highly offensive to the average reasonable person. The statements are often based on facts but are twisted or distorted so they become false. For example, suppose an employer fires a worker for violating a rule against dating clients. Then he publicly states that she was disrupting the workplace by having sex with numerous co-workers and clients. As a result of these statements, she is humiliated and embarrassed and has trouble finding another job. This is false light invasion of privacy.

Two other forms of this tort occasionally crop up in the employment context. "Intrusion upon seclusion" occurs when one person snoops into another's private business by offensive acts such as opening private mail or listening to personal conversations or messages. "Publicity to private matters" occurs when a person publicizes information that would be highly offensive to a reasonable person and is not of legitimate concern to the public. For example, an employer prints an article in a widely distributed company newsletter detailing an adulterous affair between co-workers.

## Damages, Defenses, and Combined Common Law Claims

In each of these tort claims, the plaintiff must show some kind of damages; some harm she suffered as a result of the actions of the defendant. This need not be physical harm. Injury to your dignity and feelings can be enough.

Also bear in mind that the person accused of committing a tort will have a chance to raise any number of defenses to his or her actions, just as is the case in the statutory law. For example, self-defense is a defense to battery, provided the force used is reasonable. If you start slapping a co-worker who made a rude remark, then he shoves you away and you fall, he will probably have a defense to battery. Truth, while not an absolute defense, is usually a defense against defamation and the other "spreading lies" group of torts.

State common law may give a worker several different claims based on one incident or set of circumstances. In one case I worked on, a pharmacist was fired after being falsely accused of stealing from the company and using drugs or alcohol on the job. These accusations were written into his personnel records, which were made available to other companies at which he applied for work. This also threatened his professional license. He was able to file claims for defamation (slander or libel), invasion of privacy, interference with contractual relations, and wrongful discharge.

Another advantage to including common law claims, if they are available, is that they may provide more remedies. In addition to compensatory money damages and punitive damages in some cases, courts can fashion equitable remedies to fit the situation. The court may order an injunction, which requires the employer to engage in or refrain from engaging in a particular behavior. Courts have also been known to order wrongdoers to retract statements or make official apologies.

A word on punitive damages: People get very enthused when they hear about big awards of punitive damages. It's important to realize, however, that punitive damages are hard to recover and even harder to hang on to. Nevertheless, it's always a good idea to request punitive damages if the facts of your case support them. While the enormous awards are rare, they do happen, and smaller awards of a few thousand dollars are not uncommon. To recover punitive damages on most common law claims, you must generally prove that the defendant acted with legal malice. This is not the same as malice in the everyday sense of deliberately trying to hurt someone. It only requires that you prove the defendant's actions were done in bad faith, recklessly, or in a grossly negligent manner. In short, they should have known better, or they did know better and didn't care.

Many torts are also crimes. Virtually all states have criminal laws against assault, battery, and fraud. Many also prohibit defamation and blackballing. Talk to a police officer or district attorney if you have been the victim of an act that may be criminal. If someone has hurt you physically, you should always make a prompt report to the police.

Why are there so many complicated, confusing laws that seem to say the same thing? The main reason is that each law added something to the laws already on the books. After a period of time had passed and people saw that the laws were not enough, something more was necessary to achieve the goal of guaranteeing equal pay under all circumstances. At least one law now covers nearly all workers in all fields and jobs.

## Making the Most of the Laws: Combined Claims

The same actions that violate one law often violate others as well, both federal and state. When you file a complaint with several counts, this can give you a much stronger case.

One important thing to remember is that if you bring a suit in federal court, for example, a Title VII suit, you will not lose your right to bring your state claims at the same time. This is called pendant or supplemental jurisdiction. As you may recall in *Marshall v. Allen,* a male lawyer employed by the Chicago Housing Authority sued after he was fired in retaliation for helping a group of female attorneys file a sex discrimination claim. His complaint raised federal claims of Title VII, the FLSA, Section 1983, and state common law claims of breach of contract and intentional infliction of emotional distress. The more laws that apply to your unique situation, the more ammunition you have to win your rights and all the available remedies, and the more you'll be able to scare your opponent. You may be able to gain remedies that will help your co-workers as well. This kind of strategy can be vital in negotiating an early, fair settlement of your case.

What if you do have to go forward with litigation? Should you file a "kitchen sink" complaint that includes all the claims you can possibly bring? Opinions on this are varied. Most lawyers believe that all potential claims should be stated in the initial letter to the employer that states the employee's position. Since the goal at this point is to try to settle without litigation, it's best to use as much leverage as possible, for both practical and political reasons. An employer may be horrified at the thought of seeing the company's and managers' names in the local newspaper accompanied by charges not only of discrimination and harassment but of assault and battery as well. And believe me, when a juicy complaint full of such charges is filed, the news media won't miss a chance to sensationalize it.

But other matters need to be considered once you're actually on your way to court. Most lawyers I know believe that all strong claims certainly should be made. This keeps the pressure on to settle, allows broader discovery of facts, and gives the judge or jury more choices in deciding the case. It also covers more bases, since different kinds of claims brought under different laws allow different damages. But beware of the weaker claims. If they sound shaky, think carefully about the value of including them. And never, ever include a claim you know is no good, because the court can make you pay the fees and costs your opponents incur in defending any claim that is not supported by the facts or the law or that is imposed for improper purposes.

Bear in mind that some laws, most notably Title VII, require you to try to resolve the case at the administrative agency level first. Also, laws such as Section 1983 limit *who* you can sue as well. This is another vital consideration. In general, when you file a complaint, you should name all of the defendants who are responsible for the wrongdoing—both those directly involved in the actions and others indirectly responsible, such as supervisors and the company as a whole—those who had a duty to supervise the wrongdoer or who knew about the problems and did nothing. Sometimes there are limits, however, such as when you sue the government and encounter immunity issues. Also, principles of state common law often apply to these issues as well. In *Lehmann v. Toys 'R' Us, Inc.*, a former employee sued her employer, supervisor, and personnel director for hostile work environment sexual harassment in violation of the state law against sex discrimination. The court looked at the common law of agency (governing the work hierarchy and when an employer will be held responsible for an employee's behavior) to determine who should have to answer for the misconduct.

Your lawyer will also have to figure out issues of jurisdiction (which courts have authority to hear your case and bring in all the people or companies involved) and venue (the geographic location of the courts). The best bet is to tell your lawyer about everyone you think may be involved, where the people and companies are located or headquartered, then let him or her sort it out.

Public employees frequently combine Title VII and Section 1983. The process begins with the EEOC administrative effort, then goes to court if not resolved at the agency level. Women have won back pay, compensatory damages, and punitive damages. In *Sorlucco v. New York City Police Department*, 971 F.2d 864 (2nd Cir. 1992), a female police officer was raped by a fellow officer, then treated appallingly by her employer and eventually fired. She brought suit for gender discrimination in violation of her constitutional right to equal protection under Section 1983, along with a claim for violation of Title VII. The court found that by proving one (violation of equal protection) she had proven both. Common law claims can also be brought by government workers, of course.

The tricky part of combining the laws is the wide variation in what procedures and time limits each of them requires. Never assume that because you start a procedure under one of the laws, you will be excused from meeting the deadline to file under another law. The requirements are independent, and all of them must be followed. Where there is overlap, you should still be vigilant. While the agencies usually do the best job they can, many are overworked and underfunded. Don't rely on them to meet your deadlines or advise you on other claims you might have. Even if you are sure you want to proceed under only one law, with one agency, and feel totally confident in handling everything yourself, you should talk to a qualified employment lawyer as soon as you believe you may have any kind of discrimination claim. Notice I say *talk to,* not necessarily *hire or retain.* You may spend an hour with a lawyer just to learn your options and get advice on how to proceed on your own. If you establish a relationship with a lawyer early on, you have someone to call if you have questions or problems or later decide to sue.

Many of your rights under the laws are precarious. If you miss a deadline, your claim is gone forever. And this has happened because people weren't aware of how these claims are calculated. In one such case, a female police officer was fired for violating a department rule that said male and female officers couldn't socialize. The male officer was merely disciplined with a brief suspension. She knew she may have a Title VII claim and began counting her days to file with the EEOC according to her last day on the payroll, rather than the day she was discharged. Her case was dismissed as untimely, because under the correct method of calculation, the charge was filed six days late.

Many other factors can affect the choice of which claims to file. Certain areas like Section 1983 are so extremely complex that even attorneys with years of experience in this area and dozens of cases under their belts approach each new case with grave trepidation. The law changes constantly and gets more complicated as each new decision is handed down. I've been actively involved in civil rights cases for three years, yet I still feel like a babe in the woods. I would never consider taking a Section 1983 case alone without associating with more experienced counsel.

There are other pitfalls in trying to sort out the claims you may have on your own. If you pursue some claims but not others, you may lose the ones you didn't raise the first time around. You may have a wonderful claim that is not mentioned in this book because you are in a unique job situation that provides other legal remedies. State laws may impose additional restrictions, such as statutes of limitation, that are shorter than the deadlines for the federal laws. These limitations can prevent you from bringing a great state common law claim if you wait until the last minute to file your federal claim. Last week I was discussing a heartbreaking case with a colleague in which the family of a woman killed by a drunk driver—who had full insurance and money of his own—waited too long to seek legal advice. The statute of limitations had passed, and the thousands of dollars that would have almost certainly been recovered for the woman's children were lost.

This has happened countless times in employment cases in which someone who could have used several laws combined to make a stronger case lost all or some of the claims. Make sure you understand the deadlines and have competent advice so that you don't end up missing out on what could have been an outstanding case.

⚖

# CHAPTER 5

# THE AGENCIES THAT EXPLAIN AND ENFORCE THE LAWS

Fortunately, the vast body of law that has developed to protect your rights on the job has spawned numerous agencies with hundreds of field offices, so that sources of guidance and assistance are available almost everywhere.

Unfortunately, however, with so many agencies sharing the responsibilities of enforcing the various laws, deciding which is the right one to contact can be a daunting task. Even lawyers—myself included—frequently have to make several calls before reaching the right person to deal with a particular question or problem. If the labyrinthian bureaucracy is enough to confuse even lawyers, how can the average working woman use the resources available to her? How do you know where to begin and which number to call?

In one sense the confusion itself has given rise to its own solution. Because there are so many agencies, the people staffing them, especially at the intake level, are usually well trained to determine whether you are in the right place and where you need to go if you are not. Also, there is considerable overlap in what the agencies do, and they frequently work together. For example, the EEOC field offices, state FEPA agencies, local human rights offices, and in some cases equal opportunity offices on your job site all handle the types of problems under the jurisdiction of the EEOC.

Whichever agency you plan to approach, call first to ask about the filing procedure. Be sure to ask the following:

1. Am I in the right place, or should I go to another agency first or instead?
2. What is the time limit in which I must file?
3. Where do I go to file, and who should I ask for?
4. What will happen once I file?
5. Do you have a written description of the process, and may I have a copy?
6. Do you recommend I contact a lawyer?
7. If I file with you, do I lose any other rights? For example, the right to bring my case in court?
8. What can I do to help you expedite my claim?
9. When will my employer be contacted and what will he or she be told?
10. When can I expect to hear from you next?

I'll say it again: It's always best to meet with a lawyer for advice and consultation before you start the agency process, to be sure you understand what other claims you may have and the deadlines or other restrictions for acting on those rights.

What if you can't afford a lawyer or can't find one who can help you? Unfortunately, there is little funding and few programs, public or private, to provide lawyers to represent victims of employment discrimination. However, it's still advisable to call your local Legal Aid Society or a legal services group in your area. These agencies occasionally represent eligible people (generally those earning less than 125% of the current federal poverty level income) on this type of claim, and even if they won't take your case, they may be able to recommend a private attorney who takes employment discrimination cases on a pro bono or contingency basis.

The National Employment Lawyers Association (NELA) is working toward establishing employment law centers in which employment lawyers supervise trained paralegals who can help clients with counseling, investigation, negotiation, and referral services at moderate prices. These centers can help educate clients as to their rights and options, refer them to other professionals for related needs, assist them in dealing with agencies, help match clients with legal counsel, and help lawyers who are not employment experts learn to better represent clients. Also, check with law schools in your area. Some have legal clinics or other programs that can provide assistance. There are also a number of private organizations such as the ACLU that provide assistance and referrals to employment lawyers. Some of the leading groups are listed in the Appendix.

One word of caution: Never take legal advice (as opposed to help in filing your claim or following other procedures) from anyone but an attorney or someone working under the direct supervision of an attorney. Sometimes people with little or no training hold themselves out as paralegals and offer to help and advise you—for a fee, of course. Most of the groups mentioned above, except lawyers or law centers, do not charge. There is never a fee to file a complaint with an agency. If someone gives you reason to be suspicious, check them out before handing over any money.

## The Equal Employment Opportunity Commission and State Fair Employment Practices Agencies

The EEOC enforces Title VII of the Civil Rights Act of 1964 and its amendments, including the 1978 Pregnancy Discrimination Act, the Civil Rights Act of 1991; as well as the Equal Pay Act of 1963. In most cases of pay or other sex discrimination on the job, the EEOC will be the agency to contact. However, if you live in a deferral state (see Appendix), your complaint will generally be handled by the state FEPA, whether you file it with that agency or with the EEOC. Most major cities also have local ordinances prohibiting sex discrimination, enforced by such agencies as a city Human Rights Commission.

If you live in a deferral state and go to the EEOC first, you may be told to go to the FEPA office, or the EEOC may conduct an intake (compiling basic information about you, your employer, and your problem) and help you fill out a complaint, which will then be forwarded to the FEPA. In most cases the initial paperwork will find its way to the FEPA. Unless the FEPA waives its right to proceed and sends your complaint back to the EEOC, the FEPA will handle your case according to state law for the first 60 days after you file it. If there is no resolution by the state agency within this time period, the EEOC takes over. You won't always be informed of what is going on or when, so be sure to make an effort to keep in touch with the agent assigned to your case.

If you believe you have a claim under Title VII and you work for the federal government, or if you are in the military, you have to follow grievance procedures established by the Civil Service Commission. This usually begins with a complaint to a special EEO officer appointed to handle violations in your workplace. Federal employers are required by law (29 C.F.R. § 1613.204) to have an in-house EEO counselor to assure the workplace is free of discrimination and to deal with disputes when they arise. Certain other institutions or companies, such as state universities and other employers receiving federal financial assistance, may also have an EEO office to receive complaints on behalf of the EEOC.

A federal employee who believes a federal agency has discriminated against her must consult with one of the agency's counselors. The EEO counselors will do preliminary investigation and try and resolve the dispute. If this does not work, the employee can file a formal complaint, which the agency investigates in greater depth, then accepts or rejects. If the complaint is rejected or if the employee is not satisfied with the agency's determination, she can appeal to the EEOC. As always, you should talk to a qualified employment lawyer before going too far with this process, because you may have or lose other rights if you go through the appeal process and end up in court. Also, be aware that a complaint *must* be filed with an EEO officer within 90 days of the alleged discrimination. Many state employers have similar requirements. If you are in a union, it may have grievance procedures you must follow. No matter where you work, pay careful attention to the time limits.

Complaints are usually filed by individuals but may also be filed by groups of workers who have all suffered discrimination on the same job, or by organizations such as the National Committee for Pay Equity that represent the rights of workers.

The form of the complaint is not subject to any strict requirements, although the preferred method is to use the form supplied by the EEOC. You can contact the EEOC to obtain the form (see Appendix). FEPA forms are similar. Some cases have held that letters, intake forms, or even oral notice may be sufficient when time limits are at issue. These laws were enacted for your benefit, and the rules for filing are to be "liberally construed," meaning that every effort will be made to allow you to file your claim, even if you do not follow all the technicalities to a T. As the late Justice Thurgood Marshall explained in a Supreme Court case, Title VII is a remedial scheme "in which laypersons rather than lawyers are expected to initiate the process."

Although time limits do tend to be enforced more strictly than some of the other requirements, most court cases apply flexible standards. This is especially true if you can show circumstances beyond your control that somehow kept you from meeting the deadline. For example, if your employer, an EEOC or state officer, or another person gives you the wrong information, deliberately misleads you, or prevents you from getting your complaint filed on time, this can excuse a late filing. Also, where there is a continuing violation, such as a companywide policy that discriminates or a series of continued acts against one individual, this will affect how the time limit is calculated.

When you meet with an agency officer, you should bring as much evidence as possible to prove your complaint, including written materials you have prepared, company manuals and other literature, and lists of witnesses or others who have information to back your charges or who have agreed to help. Make copies of all these materials and keep a set for your files. Be prepared to tell the officer absolutely everything you can think of that indicates discrimination in your workplace, including other instances of discrimination based on sex, race, religion, disability, or otherwise. If you think of more later, call the officer and inform her or him. The more information, the better. In chapter 7 I will outline an easy way you can prepare and organize your information.

For complaints made under the Equal Pay Act (EPA), there is no formal procedure for filing. You just need to contact the nearest EEOC office. You may complain by mail, by telephone, or in person. There is no formal time limit, but there is a statute of limitations if you file a lawsuit. This limitation is two years for a nonwillful violation, and three years for a willful (reckless or deliberate) violation.

Because most acts of discrimination that violate the EPA also violate Title VII, it's best to follow the guidelines for filing a Title VII charge when you're pursuing an EPA claim. The EEOC enforces both statutes, so this is the practical place to start. One advantage to filing only under the EPA is that you can do it anonymously, and the EEOC will not disclose your identity to the employer. If you proceed under both acts or Title VII only, your name as charging party will be given to your employer.

Are you thoroughly confused? I don't blame you. I guess what all this boils down to is that if you think you have a cause to complain, tell somebody quick. Talk to someone at your local EEOC office, your FEPA, or both. EEOC publications recommend beginning the filing process by contacting the nearest EEOC office. If there is no EEOC office near you, call toll free 1-800-669-4000 (voice) or 1-800-800-3302 (TDD) for more information.

## Filing a Complaint

Whether you're dealing with the EEOC, your state FEPA, or one of the other agencies, many of the filing procedures are similar. I've decided to describe the EEOC process for investigating a Title VII claim, since this is one of the most common procedures. Check the sections on each law in chapter 2, or the law itself, to determine what will be different if you work with another agency.

First, an EEOC officer will interview you to learn as much as possible about what happened and get the details on the alleged discrimination. You will either be referred to your state agency or proceed with the EEOC process. A charge will be drafted by the officer and the investigation process explained to you.

Second, the EEOC will then notify your employer about the charge and begin investigating. This will include getting information from your employer about the issues that affect you, as well as things that may affect other employees in your workplace. The EEOC has very broad powers in conducting the investigation. Any witnesses with knowledge of the acts of discrimination you have charged will be interviewed, and if they do not want to testify voluntarily, the EEOC can get a subpoena (an order of the court that the persons give testimony or be held in contempt of court, which can mean a fine or even jail). The EEOC can also subpoena records and documents in the same kind of pretrial discovery that is done in a lawsuit.

Third, if the EEOC investigator believes the evidence gathered in the investigation does not show reasonable cause to believe discrimination took place, you and your employer will be notified, and you will be given a right-to-sue letter. The agency process ends, and you may then proceed to bring your claim in court. You will have 90 days after getting this letter to file your lawsuit.

If the EEOC investigator finds there is reasonable cause to believe discrimination occurred, EEOC representatives will hold conciliation meetings or take other steps to try and persuade the employer to voluntarily stop the discriminatory practices and remedy the situation. Conciliation is similar to mediation. You, your employer, and the officer will sit down and try to reach a solution to the problem. Many claims end here. If not, the EEOC can hold an administrative hearing, which is similar to a less formal court proceeding and involves an administrative judge. This proceeding can result in orders that must be followed by your employer. If the employer does not obey the orders, you can go to court to have them enforced.

If it doesn't end here, the EEOC will consider litigation on your behalf. If litigation is approved by the commission, the EEOC will file suit in federal district court on behalf of you or your group of employees. The EEOC has a Statement of Enforcement Policy that requires it to give careful consideration of each case in which the EEOC found reasonable cause to believe there was discrimination but could not make an informal conciliation work. The EEOC then decides whether to go to court. Most charges are conciliated or settled, so a trial is not necessary.

The EEOC's policy is to seek full and effective relief for each and every victim of employment discrimination. However, the EEOC is grossly overworked most of the time and short on staff and money. Do not count on the EEOC taking the suit on your behalf, even if you have the world's greatest claim. Have a lawyer lined up well before you get your right-to-sue letter.

Throughout this process the EEOC officer will probably ask for more information. You *must* follow the agency's instructions and rules and share the work. Cooperation is more than a matter of courtesy in this kind of case. From a practical standpoint, the agents are always overburdened and must have your help.

Your assistance is also a legal requirement. In one case, *Pack v. Marsh,* a civilian employee of the Army brought a discrimination complaint with the Army's EEO counselor. But she did not provide the additional information that the investigating agent needed, nor did she sign essential documents. She made several appeals through the EEOC, the federal district court, and finally the federal appellate court. When all was said and done, the court found that she had refused or failed to make use of the administrative process and had failed to prosecute her claim. Therefore, she did not exhaust her administrative remedies, and her case was lost.

## Deciding to Sue

If the EEOC determines that there is probable cause to believe there was discrimination against you, but it does not decide to litigate for you, it will give you a right-to-sue letter stating that you may file a lawsuit on your own, again, within 90 days. You may also request a right-to-sue letter if the EEOC has had your case for 180 days without resolving it and you're ready to sue on your own. Sometimes there are special requirements. For example, if your employer received federal funding, you may need to have the right-to-sue letter issued by the Department of Justice. Check with your lawyer and make sure you are aware of all these rules. You need to have a lawyer who can represent you before you get your right-to-sue letter.

Whatever the outcome of the agency investigation, you will be able to use the agency's files and the evidence that was gathered if you file a private suit. This can be very helpful and save you a lot of money. Discovery and investigation are expensive if you have to pay for them yourself. Nearly all lawyers will want you to cover these costs, even if they are taking the case on a contingency basis.

If you do end up suing on your own, you are usually limited to the charges you made in your initial complaint, although there are some exceptions to this rule. For instance, if there is continuing discrimination in your workplace or if something new has happened since you filed the first charge, this may be added, of course.

Although you are legally entitled to represent yourself, to try and do so in this type of complex case is sheer insanity. Even many attorneys who are well qualified generally are not capable of adequately handling an employment discrimination case. If you are going to invest the time, cost, and emotional expense of taking your case to court, it is absolutely essential that you be well represented. This is so important that I have devoted a separate section to choosing an attorney.

A word of caution: Although most EEOC offices and state FEPA agencies try to give you the best possible assistance, some are reported to be underfunded and inefficient. I have been told of one EEOC officer being assigned a hundred cases to investigate at once, and of one case that took five years to resolve! There have been rumblings in the media that some EEOC offices have stopped looking for violations and are encouraging people *not* to file complaints. Even if this is not true in your local EEOC office, there are traps in the administrative process, delays that can seem endless, and important deadlines that must be met. It is best to meet with your own attorney early on, even if you feel confident in the agency officials you are working with. If you choose not to get an attorney, make sure you are fully aware of the time limits and other requirements and keep abreast of what is going on with your claim.

## State and Local Agencies

Sometimes it is best to begin at the state or local level. Many cities have local ordinances prohibiting job discrimination, such as the Albuquerque Human Rights Ordinance, which is enforced by the Albuquerque Human Rights Office. This ordinance prohibits the same practices covered by the state Human Rights Act but covers all employers, employment agencies, and labor organizations that operate within the city limits. Check the City Government pages in your telephone directory or call your state FEPA to learn whether your city has such an ordinance.

Some claims, such as those involving wage and hour disputes or violations of the Family and Medical Leave Act of 1993, must be filed with your state or local U.S. Department of Labor office. The procedures followed by these agencies vary a great deal from state to state. Check the Appendix for the address of your state's labor department headquarters. Inquire as to what local branch you should contact, and what services they offer.

## The Agency Process in General

All government agencies seem to be chronically short on funds and staff. Agents want to settle as many cases as they can, or quickly evaluate them and issue right-to-sue-letters so that the burden of moving forward is shifted back to you. It's very rare these days for an agency at the federal level to take your case and represent you directly. This may be different at the state and local level, depending on where you are. The local level is often the best place to start. These offices tend to be less over-burdened and the officers there can explain how the interaction between the local, state, and federal agencies work. Again, these are very general statements, and staffing, funding, and quality of assistance vary greatly from one office to another. Sometimes your best bet will be to visit every agency that might become involved in your claim and see which seems to be the best equipped to work with you.

I've been told by employment attorneys that the agency officer often will not fully appreciate the value of a claim. It's easy to understand how this can happen. An agency officer is responsible only for knowing the law that his or her own agency enforces. There may be other claims—strong claims that could give you other kinds of damages—that the officer won't know about. The agents simply aren't required to be educated in the other avenues you might be able to explore. In short, don't count on the agencies for advice on your other options.

One more thing to keep in mind: If you get your EEOC right-to-sue letter, you may notice a sentence in fine print that reads, "If you can't afford a lawyer, the court may appoint one to represent you." This is virtually unheard of. Our federal court system, as well as most other courts in the nation, is essentially broke. It can barely afford to pay jury fees, staff salaries, and keep enough attorneys on the payroll to represent criminal defendants who must have counsel appointed by law. Until this changes, the chances of having an attorney appointed to represent you in an employment discrimination case are virtually nil.

In many cases the agency route can lead to a relatively quick and satisfactory solution. The following is a real-life example of how the agency process worked for one woman in a situation where the men in her department, with the same job classification, were being paid more.

Carolyn Patterson worked as a graphic artist for a large chemical manufacturing corporation. She was the only woman in a department of six artists. About seven months into the job, she learned through casual conversation with her co-workers that all of the men were paid more than she was; this despite the fact that two of the men had started on the job after she did, and the other three had less education and experience.

She began by compiling all the information she could, then asked her boss for a raise. When he turned her down, explaining that raises were not given until a new employee had been with the company for a year, she asked him point-blank why all the men in the department were making more than she was, even though several were less qualified. Her boss cut her off with the remark that all salary information was supposed to be confidential, and even if the men were paid more, there were "things she didn't know" that justified the company's decisions on compensation. Essentially, she was told to mind her own business and get back to work.

Patterson continued to collect information, then went to her state FEPA office. The officer reviewed her information, asked her more questions to complete the intake process, and began an investigation. A conciliation conference was scheduled. At the conference, Patterson's boss and the company personnel director tried to explain the higher pay to males by claiming that their jobs involved lifting supplies and equipment, moving heavy tables and boards, and other physical labor. But the investigator found that these tasks were only occasionally required, and that Patterson, too, did some heavy lifting on the job. In short, the differences were not significant enough to justify the unequal pay. Her employer did not want a court battle, especially since his chances of winning were by now obviously slim. The company was also concerned with the inevitable damaging publicity. By the end of the conference, the company representatives had signed an agreement that gave Patterson a salary adjustment and back pay.

She felt some trepidation about returning to the job after "making waves" but found the morale at work had actually improved. Several male co-workers expressed admiration for her spunk, and she received another raise at her annual review.

Patterson's experience shows that while the complaint process can be intimidating, especially for the employee who stays on the job, for the woman with the gumption to see it through the rewards are well worth the effort. Given all the alternative routes to equal pay, the many sources of assistance, and the probability of success, there is no reason why any woman should settle for less than what her work is worth.

## Unions and Other Labor Support Organizations

A union is any group of workers who have organized together to reach common goals and promote common interests. Most unions are formally organized as legal entities; some are simply groups of workers banded together for their mutual benefit. Trade unions or labor unions are run by workers to promote the interests of workers, to negotiate fair wages, benefits, and working conditions, and to regulate relations between employers and workers. Some unions are national organizations with millions of members, while others are local groups that are either affiliated with a larger organization or independent.

Some of the earliest efforts to gain equal pay for women workers were pioneered by unions. In 1866 the National Labor Union, an organization of numerous trade unions, adopted the principle of equal pay for equal work. The Noble Order of the

Knights of Labor followed suit in 1869 by adopting the slogan of "equal pay for equal work" and establishing a women's department. In 1886 Leonora Barry was appointed general investigator for the Knights of Labor and traveled throughout the United States to document the industrial exploitation of women and children. Since then unions have grown to the point where nearly all workers in some industries, such as automobile manufacturing, are represented by a union.

The method generally used by unions to negotiate a contract between union members (workers) and management is called collective bargaining. In this process union representatives deal with company management to negotiate the terms of the workers' employment, which will then be set down in a written contract. A contract is generally made for each "bargaining unit." This term is flexible and may consist of a group of workers in one plant, in an entire company with several plants, or only the workers in one craft or department within a company or plant.

Unions come in many sizes, from the powerful American Federation of Labor–Congress of Industrial Organizations (AFL-CIO), which is actually a federation of many affiliated unions, to huge, independent (non-AFL-CIO) unions such as the Teamsters and the United Auto Workers, which represent millions of workers, to small local unions with a handful of members. A national or international union often sets up chartered units, called "locals," which includes workers in a particular craft or industry within a geographical area.

Most of the law governing unions and the activities of organized labor are federal laws, including the National Labor Relations Act of 1935 (the NLRA, which established the National Labor Relations Board [NLRB]). The NLRB governs labor unions. One of its main requirements is that unions and employers bargain collectively in good faith and make reasonable efforts to reach an agreement reflected in a contract.

Unions can be one of the most powerful means of protecting the rights of workers. Unfortunately, women in unions tend to be underrepresented in leadership positions, and their special problems often fail to get priority in organizations that may be bureaucratic and mired in "old boy" tradition. A recent study by the National Association of Female Executives (NAFE) showed that the executive board of the AFL-CIO currently has only one woman among 33 members.

However, more and more unions are beginning to address the special needs of women workers, and union contracts now commonly contain an antidiscrimination clause prohibiting unequal treatment of workers based on race, religion, sex, nationality, or union membership. Some contracts contain affirmative action clauses as well. Problems such as sexual harassment and child care are also becoming more common subjects in union contracts.

Union contracts are similar to other employment contracts in that they cover wages, hours, pay increases, and other terms of employment. One advantage to a union contract over an individual contract is the watchdog and enforcement function of the union. When a worker with an individual contract is faced with a breach of contract or a need to renegotiate, she must hire an attorney or represent herself. A union contract is enforced through the union. Most union contracts contain provisions for grievance procedures to try to resolve employment disputes.

Also, unions were among the first to use mediation (in which a neutral person or team of people tries to assist opposed groups or parties to reach an agreement satisfactory to both) and arbitration (in which one or more third parties hear the claims of both sides, then reach a final, binding decision, as a judge would) to resolve disputes without involving the courts. If disputes between management and workers cannot be negotiated, the union may organize a strike. Strikes are controversial and generally regarded as an extreme measure. But their strength as a bargaining tactic cannot be denied.

How can individual workers become part of a union? If a majority of workers want to unionize their workplace, several options are available. The first step should be contacting the NLRB, which can advise you of the laws affecting union organization and activities and provide guidance on how to get started. Other labor organizations of particular interest to women are listed in the Appendix.

# CHAPTER 6

⚖

# PREVENTING PROBLEMS BEFORE THEY HAPPEN

Your right to equal treatment begins well before you start a job. As discussed in chapter 2, Title VII is the law protecting workers from discrimination in virtually all areas of employment, including hiring, classifying, referring, assigning, training, apprenticeships, or any other terms, conditions, or privileges of employment. So any discrimination in hiring practices is likely to be covered by Title VII and, in many cases, other laws as well. The term *hiring practices* includes a broad range of things, from advertising to taking applications to interviewing to the decision to hire.

## Be Prepared before You Apply

It is always to your advantage to know as much about a new or potential employer as possible. Ask questions, study the company structure, and learn what positions are available. Your best tool is information. Know yourself and your real interests and ambitions. Know the market and what jobs are available and where. Know what skills you have, including skills informally acquired through homemaking, hobbies, and so forth, and how they may be useful. Know what kind of training you do and do not need, where to get it, and what it costs.

Research pay scales in your field and know what you're worth. Learn about the salary ranges in this industry, in this region, and for your qualifications. Information on your business can be found in publications of the U.S. Department of Labor, industry publications, business groups, and from other people in the business. Most industries have both national and state organizations with their own publications. Public libraries have a wealth of information you may not know about; I discover new resources every time I peruse the shelves. Ask the reference librarian. University libraries and placement offices also have extensive collections of material on different occupations and major employers.

Also, many public and private career counseling organizations are available to help and advise. Organizations such as the YWCA provide these services, as do special agencies providing services for people of specific racial or ethnic backgrounds, older workers, students, or workers with disabilities. Check adult education catalogs in your area. You may be surprised by the number of courses in preparatory job skills, such as interviewing, career change, and career planning offered in addition to specific training for particular jobs.

If you have children that will need to be placed in a care program before you start a new job, it is tremendously helpful to get this squared away long before you begin your job search. Many of my friends with youngsters tell me that this can be a real problem. Caretakers and facilities often have waiting lists of a year or more. One friend who intended to return to her job six weeks after her baby was born started making inquiries as soon as she learned she was pregnant, and says she is glad she did. One good caretaker in her area had an opening coming up about the time her baby was due, and this was the only opening she located. Check with other parents you know, local caregiving facilities, your church, the local YWCA, the United Way, and area colleges. If you have a low income, you may qualify for some of the subsidy programs offered by your state or local Human Services Department. Peruse the telephone book and any local parenting publications. Many cities have referral services that can help you locate qualified providers.

# First Things First: Prehiring Legal Protections

A company's obligation to be fair in its hiring practices begins long before you walk in the door to fill out an application or drop off a résumé. Employers are required to be fair in the processes they use to select potential employees, called the applicant pool.

Advertising jobs as male only or female only is almost always illegal (unless sex is a bona fide occupational qualification) and almost never seen anymore. But there are other practices that, while not always illegal, can result in unlawful "adverse impact" discrimination.

One of the most common of these methods is word-of-mouth hiring. If the workforce in a company is predominantly white and male, relying on current employees to recruit others has, in some cases, been shown to result in the exclusion of nearly everyone but additional white males. Related methods include hiring relatives of current workers and enforcing no-spouse rules, which exclude women married to men already working for the employer. If the labor force on a job is predominantly one sex and/or race, and these are the hiring methods used, this is powerful evidence of discrimination.

The most common way that employers get new employees is through direct or walk-in application. This is generally acceptable unless there are practices in the process that tend to exclude applicants of one sex or race (such as accepting applications from men who come to the job site, but requiring women to apply at the central office in another city). Some of the most insidious discrimination practices can be hard to prove. I knew a young man who had worked in a store near a college campus. All the employees were students who applied on a walk-in basis. He told me that the manager had instructed her employees to put a small star at the top of all applications filled out by African-Americans. Those applicants with a star would not be called back for an interview. The applications were discarded after the jobs were filled, so it was hard to prove discrimination unless the employees testified. I was delighted to learn that this business went bankrupt a short time after I heard this story.

Employers may also subtly discourage a certain group of applicants in various ways. Some companies have been notorious for presenting certain images to the public, such as showing all males and using only male pronouns in company brochures. Other methods include discouraging women from applying for certain positions by making them seem undesirable in the view of the applicant, or giving female applicants incorrect or misleading information about the position. It all depends on the overall process used to get an applicant pool.

# Employee Selection:
## The Application and the Interview

What can you be asked on an application or in an interview? As with many legal questions, the answer is, "It depends." Generally speaking, Title VII says that an employer cannot ask you anything that will result in the rejection of a disproportionate number of women. Nor can an employer have one set of interview questions for men and another for women. Questions are supposed to stay in the bounds of job related matters and relate to the employer's business goals. Naturally, this will depend on the nature of the job.

Employers are not supposed to ask you about your family, number of children, marital status, or if or when you plan to have children. However, interviewers often get to these matters indirectly, through the initial icebreaking phase or the "tell-me-about-yourself" inquiry. This puts you in an awkward position. On one hand, if you refuse to answer or point out that the questions are improper, you might offend the interviewer. On the other hand, you shouldn't have to answer illegal questions. Perhaps the best thing to do is sidestep the question as gracefully as possible, then complain later if you like. One woman I know simply replies, "I'm lucky to have a very supportive family who wants to see me get a great job." Then she changes the subject.

An employer is allowed to use subjective criteria in making hiring decisions. Subjective criteria include the applicant's attitude, personality, ability to communicate, and similar judgments. This is naturally a sticky area, with few guiding rules. One thing that will be relevant is the importance of these criteria to the particular job. For example, a salesperson needs enthusiasm and good communication skills. These traits may be less important in a bricklayer.

I remember the applications I used to fill out during high school when I was searching for part-time jobs. The questions were often personal or irrelevant, but I didn't pay much attention to these forms or to the interview questions I was asked, until one time when I applied for a part-time job in a jewelry store. Not only was I interrogated on every aspect of my personal life, health, hobbies, habits, and future plans, but I was asked to take a polygraph exam in which I would be asked a panoply of questions covering every conceivable form of childhood mischief, deviant behavior, and popular vice, and whether I had ever done any of these things. Today, nearly all polygraph tests for preemployment screening are barred by a federal law enacted in 1988.

What really amazed me was what I encountered when I began interviewing for law clerk jobs during my second year of law school, in 1986–87. Nearly every interviewer—themselves lawyers—asked me at least one illegal question. The most common were questions about my husband, my marriage, and whether we had children or planned to. Other women in my class also reported hearing these questions on a routine basis. We were encouraged by the placement office to report improper interviewing techniques, but we were all so hungry for a job that few of us did, I'm sorry to say.

## Agencies That Can Help

How can a job seeker maximize her chances of getting the job she wants and still protect her legal rights? There are a number of services offered by agencies of the federal government that many people are not aware of. These agencies and offices help protect job seekers and workers from policies and practices that are discriminatory, as well as assisting people in finding jobs.

Similar services are available in many states, and some state agencies work in partnership with the federal offices.

One such agency is the U.S. Employment Service. This agency works with state-operated employment services, called Job Service in most states, to provide free counseling, testing, and job placement through a national network of public employment offices that follow federal guidelines. These offices provide listings of job vacancies in the area and channel applicants into various training programs. You local Job Service or Employment Service office is listed in your telephone directory in the State Government listings, and the main office in each state is listed in the Appendix.

The Job Training Partnership Act (JTPA) was enacted in 1982 to work with states, local governments, and private industry councils in planning and implementing job training programs to assist people with below poverty-level incomes, teenage parents, displaced homemakers, and other people with crucial employment needs. Their services include job search assistance, training programs that include on-the-job training, and, in some places, such support services as child care, transportation, and referrals to other sources of help for the individual's special needs. One division of this system is Job Corps, a program that helps disadvantaged young people ages 16 to 21 prepare for employment and further education or job training.

The JTPA has been amended by two recent acts geared especially toward female workers. The Displaced Homemakers Self-Sufficiency Assistance Act was enacted in 1990 to address the special needs of women who have spent the bulk of their lives as homemakers and now need to enter the workforce with little experience or formal job training. This act authorizes the award of federal grants to supplement training and support services by state programs and nonprofit organizations. The Non-Traditional Employment for Women Act was enacted in 1991 to encourage a wider range of training and job opportunities for women in occupations traditionally held by men. Your state Department of Labor, Human Resources, or Job Service office, as well as local private industry councils can provide more information on programs available under the JTPA. Each state's primary Job Training office, which acts as a liaison for JTPA programs, is listed in the Appendix.

Vocational education programs are also available through the Carl C. Perkins Vocational and Applied Technology Education Act of 1990. This act provides funding and support for state training programs that emphasize the skills needed to work in high-technology occupations. Some of this grant money is especially earmarked for displaced homemakers, single parents, and expectant mothers, and to career guidance and counseling programs to eliminate sex stereotyping and encourage women to enter high-tech professions. Each state is required to hire a "sex equity coordinator" to administer both the homemakers and equality programs and to make sure that vocational education programs do not discriminate, especially against young women ages 14 to 25. These coordinators work within each state Department of Education, which can provide information about the programs available in your state.

A national apprenticeship system has also been established under the National Apprentice Act. Apprenticeship, a method of teaching skilled trades through a combination of on-the-job training and classroom instruction, has been used for centuries in some trades and is currently becoming more popular in a variety of fields. In 1989 the U.S. Department of Labor set up the Office of Work-Based Learning to expand apprenticeship programs into a broader range of industries and occupations. One big advantage of apprenticeship is the opportunity to earn while you learn, with wages for apprentices generally about half of what a fully trained worker in the craft will earn. State and national standards govern apprenticeship programs and set standards for the type of work and pay and the scope and length of training. After completing the apprenticeship, an apprentice receives a special certification and becomes a journeyworker in the trade.

Sources of information about apprenticeship programs include the U.S. Department of Labor's Bureau of Apprenticeship Training, various state apprenticeship agencies, trade unions, and employers who have apprenticeship programs in their companies. Check your local telephone directory, national directories at your library, and trade publications. You may also get information from your state Department of Labor and local or regional office of the U.S. Department of Labor, listed in the Appendix.

Also, any of the educational endeavors you undertake on your own are required to be free from discrimination. Your right to equal compensation depends on your right to equal access to the educational opportunities that prepare you for entry and advancement in the field of your choice. Title IX of the 1972 amendments of the Education Act prohibits all educational institutions that receive federal funds (virtually all public schools, plus many private schools) from discriminating in admission, services, educational programs, fees, benefits (such as housing and insurance), rules, programs and activities, and guidance. Sexual harassment is also illegal in educational settings. Title IX also prohibits sex discrimination against instructors and other employees. Additional information is available from the U.S. Department of Education, which has local and regional offices. Major offices are listed in the Appendix.

The good news is that there has been a sharp drop in educational discrimination over the past several years, with the major topic of controversy today involving private educational institutions. Parents, teachers, and young women have demanded change, with encouraging results, including textbooks that show women and girls working in science, math, and other technical positions. But it wasn't that long ago that truly outrageous practices were commonplace. When I was in high school, one of my friends was considering a career in forestry. She wrote to a university known for its forestry program to inquire about admission. After writing twice and receiving no reply, she became suspicious. She wrote again using her brother's name. A package of information arrived almost immediately, extolling the virtues of a career in forestry for an ambitious man . . . an outdoorsman . . . a man who loves the wilderness. We were outraged. She wrote them a scathing letter, to which, predictably, she received no reply.

This sort of exclusionary tactic was illegal then, under Title IX, but it has taken years to develop the law to the point where even this type of blatant discrimination is rarely seen. More subtle forms of discrimination prevail. Some studies have shown harassment and discrimination against female students as early as kindergarten. Many women still report sexist behavior in the classroom, advisers or professors who discourage them from entering traditionally male fields, and preference shown to male students in educational opportunities ranging from participation in class discussions to hiring for assistantships.

If you have been the victim of discrimination in education or as an employee of an educational institution covered by Title IX, you should learn what procedures your school has set up to address these problems. Most larger institutions have a number of organizations that can offer assistance, including an affirmative action or EEO office, dean of students, women's center, women's studies office, or offices specially geared toward equal opportunity. If the inappropriate behavior comes from a professor, contact the department chair. As in most situations, informal grievances may solve the problem. If not, you can file a formal complaint under Title IX. Contact either the U.S. Department of Health and Human Services, Department of Education, or your local Affirmative Action Office. (See the Appendix for these and other organizations that can help.) There is a 90-day time limit after the violation occurred within which you must file.

## Starting a New Job

There are a number of things you can do as you settle into a new position to increase your chance of success and decrease the likelihood that you will be the victim of discrimination.

First, learn everything you can about your workplace, both the official policies and the human aspect. Make sure you are given copies of all manuals and procedures that govern your job, and read them carefully. Become familiar with the dynamics of your workplace. Be sure your immediate supervisor and others who could influence your compensation and advancement are aware of your commitment, your competence, and your contributions to the company. Learn how promotion and training opportunities are announced, both formally and informally. Ask women in high-level positions with your company how fast they rose through the ranks, and if they can offer you any advice on how to succeed in the company.

Get to know your co-workers and supervisors as human beings. If you have a good relationship with your co-workers, both male and female, you're less likely to face problems of discrimination, and if you do, you will be better prepared to summon support. Your credibility will be stronger if your colleagues like and respect you, plus the work environment will be more pleasant. This kind of rapport can be particularly important if a problem comes up and you need the support of your co-workers.

## MENTORING

One of the most valuable forms of association can be mentoring. A mentor relationship can be established both formally, through programs within professional organizations designed to pair individuals with others willing to guide them, or informally, simply by asking a more experienced colleague to share advice and ideas. Mentors can be anyone willing and able to help you. They can be retirees or middle managers, men or women, people in your field or in another. You can have one mentor or several.

It's best to have at least one mentor who does not work at your company. You need to have someone you can speak with candidly about problems on the job, about your company and its practices. While I believe the only stupid question is the one that doesn't get asked, there may be matters you don't want to bring up with your boss or someone who could influence your progress in the company, even if your concerns are perfectly legitimate. It's better to have a mentor who will never have a say in your advancement or evaluations so you won't be intimidated by the specter of future judgment. This person can also serve as a sounding board for problems at your job and advise you on how to deal with difficulties you might not want to reveal to your co-workers, such as whether a supervisor's behavior amounts to sexual harassment.

## THE OLD BOYS' CLUB

In my experience one of the best ways to break down the door of the old boys' club is to elbow your way in and join the party. It's no secret that male co-workers frequently use social events to conduct business and form bonds that help lead to advancement. This is an important part of the culture of the workplace and is often underestimated. Informal settings frequently involve the exchange of information and a forum for decision making. Males often simply don't think about inviting female colleagues to join in these events, but in my experience, if you make it known that you'd like to be included—even by going so far as inviting yourself along—you'll be welcomed. Not only can this be an effective way to assert your status as a member of the team, it can also be an enjoyable way to get to know your colleagues as human beings, and to make sure they see you that way, too. It will be a lot more difficult for your co-workers to harass you or your supervisor to give you an unfair review if, instead of Sally Something, that woman in receiving, they know you as Sally Smith from receiving who is a rabid Bears fan and likes to sail and makes a mean lasagna and has a collie. It's a lot more difficult to be suspicious of someone you know and like, so find a common ground.

Does this mean you have to take a crash course in every sport that's ever been played, memorize each issue of *Popular Mechanics,* and subscribe to *Golf Digest?* Hardly. It's as much a stereotype to assume men talk about nothing except sports and cars as it is to presume women know nothing except cooking and babies. You will probably discover you have more in common with your co-workers than you think. Everyone eats, has a family, has friends and pets, and does something on the weekend. Talk about the sports and hobbies you enjoy. Ask about their vacations. Of course you can discuss work, though sometimes it's better to sit back and just listen. You can learn a great deal about the power structure, the cliques, the rivalries, and other dynamics of the workplace.

What goes on at social gatherings can be just as important as what goes on at work. Be careful not to complain too much, and keep your wits about you. More than once, I have seen people make serious social blunders that caused severe damage to their careers. One in particular sticks in my mind. A woman I worked with in a professional, corporate job was extremely sensitive to any joking that she perceived (often unreasonably) as demeaning to women. One evening, as a group of us sat at a local watering hole, a young man made an innocent remark that she interpreted to be sexist. The chip thundered off her shoulder as she launched a tirade at the poor guy, then stomped out. Needless to say, the topic of conversation the rest of the evening, and the hot gossip for several days thereafter, was what had happened and how unreasonable she had been. There is no doubt that this hurt her chances at the company.

This does not mean, of course, that you have to put up with offensive behavior. But think before you holler, and if you feel that you have to say something, you can get your point across in more appropriate ways. I've responded to jokes that did go a bit too far with such comments as, "Pretty tacky, boys," or "You guys are pigs. Have a good wallow, I'm outta here." I've also responded to a bad joke about women with a bad joke about men (then added that I learned the joke from a male). A carefully chosen retort will send the message that you don't approve without alienating people who may not realize they're being offensive. Many are just trying to be funny and establish their own place in the crowd. Most important, they may be colleagues you need to get along with five days a week.

What about drinking? Some say you should never have more than one drink at a gathering, but I believe this rule is too strict. I say drink the way you usually drink with your friends. If you don't drink at all, have something nonalcoholic. If you enjoy two or three drinks, then have them. Just be sure to use your judgment and know your limits. You don't want to drink so much that you let your guard down. It may be hilarious after six or eight beers to refer to the boss as "that bald-headed old geezer with more hair in his nose than brains in his head," but if one of the guys doesn't like the idea of a woman in the crowd, your colorful commentary could very well find its way into the old geezer's ear. Always keep your wits about you. I've heard a lot of men comment that they respect a woman who can hold her liquor, but remember, the key word is *hold*.

What if your co-workers' activities don't appeal to you? Give it a good-natured try anyway. So what if you don't care a whit for football? Go to a game now and then and enjoy the people-watching. If you loathe playing golf or are the world's worst tennis player, show up for the tournaments and cheer. This raises an important point. Men tend to be more competitive than women, and while most are able to separate the rivalry on the playing field from their relationships at work, it can carry over. On one hand, if you are terrible at a game and your male colleagues always beat you, this can cast you in an inferior light. On the other hand, if you're the club racquetball champ and your boss is only mediocre, beating the pants off him every time you play is not the greatest way to enhance your opportunities. Play hard and play fair, but also play politics.

## YOUR ATTITUDE ON THE JOB

What if you find yourself in a work environment that makes you wary or makes you feel that women just aren't all that welcome? Perhaps you're trying to break down the barriers but having little luck. What can you do to maximize your chance of succeeding in a difficult situation and protect yourself from potential discrimination?

The most important thing is to adopt an attitude that says, "I'm here to work, I'm here to stay, and I'm not about to be a victim." If you have ever taken a class in self-defense, you know that one of the first rules of protecting yourself is to act as though you're not afraid, that you belong here, you have confidence, and you know your direction. Hold your head high and proceed in an assertive manner. Assertive does not mean aggressive; it means straightforward and direct.

Sometimes this requires the courage to develop behavior that doesn't come naturally. One of the main problems reported among women in middle-level management positions—and likely one reason there are so few women in upper executive slots—is that they are not heard at key meetings. Many women find that their opinions are not taken seriously, their presentations are cut short, or their statements are interrupted. How you react has to depend on the situation, but the important thing to remember is to react—don't just meekly sit down and close your folder. If some clown is rude enough to interrupt, interrupt back. Look him in the eye and say, "Excuse me. I wasn't finished."

Does this mean you have to change, to alter the fundamental nature of who you are? Of course not. You shouldn't have to. All it means is that you might have to develop your natural talents as well as learn some new skills for the job, just as you learn to use a new machine or speak a new language.

## Men and Women at Work: Different Styles That Can Work Together

A great deal has been written lately about the different ways in which men and women work, communicate, and travel through life. In her excellent book *Hardball for Women,* Pat Heim, with coauthor Susan Golant, explains the classic male-oriented corporate structure as business that is conducted as a sport, a game of hardball that a woman must understand in order to compete. By getting a handle on things that seem peculiar to most women because of the differences in male and female culture, women can thrive in the workplace while remaining true to their real selves. These differences include men's ability to be ruthless opponents by day and drinking buddies by night, and the emphasis on being a team player.

Heim points out that most young girls play dolls, house, and school, usually with small groups of one or two other girls. From this we learn interpersonal skills, negotiation, intimacy, cooperation, and an equal power structure, without definite winners and losers. Even when girls play competitive games, there is a tendency to trade off leadership and emphasize fairness. Heim believes that even girls who are the most rampant tomboys are barraged by messages from other sources—parents, media, teachers, and peers—that reinforce the more traditional roles.

Boys tend to play cops and robbers, baseball, super-heroes, and war, usually in larger groups with a definite leader and hierarchy. This teaches boys aggression, competition, team skills, how to take orders, and the ability to separate the game from the friendship—expectations that are carried into the workplace. Thus men see business as an aggressive team sport, while women view it as a series of personal encounters and seek cooperation and intimacy.

Where does all this leave women? Do we have to learn to "act like a man" yet "behave like a woman" to get equal compensation and succeed in the workplace? Most say no. There is a growing recognition among top managers, male and female alike, that different work styles suit different industries, different individuals, and different systems. Many women with very different perspectives and management styles have traveled far in a wide variety of fields. Among them are Anita Roddick of the Body Shop, who runs an international empire of 750 boutiques and believes in business practices guided by love, intuition, and social responsibility; and Bernadine P. Healy, M.D., director of the National Institutes of Health, who shook the bureaucracy in her quest to instill a corporate mentality and has been dubbed "She Who Must Be Obeyed." These women have shown that what it takes is a willingness to do things in a way true to yourself, with passion, enthusiasm, and guts, through methods that come naturally to you.

Also, the trend toward the cookie-cutter workplace is changing. Many top executives have learned that diversity is a great benefit to a company. As stated by Alice Lusk, corporate vice president of EDS, a multibillion-dollar corporation, "Diversity is a positive thing in business. It means there are complementary strengths among all players on a team."

Many executives today, both men and women, agree that certain traits we tend to think of as "female," including compassion, openness, and flexibility, can be extremely beneficial in business, especially when a tired company is looking for a new lease on life. Women in business tend to welcome innovation and creativity, which can be threatening to the status quo an old boys' club may be working hard to preserve. Most women in management speak favorably of mentoring and encourage those at the top to reach down and offer a helping hand to those on the way up. Perhaps most significant is the fact that women tend to appreciate diversity in personal work styles and realize that there is no one right way to get things done—that each individual is different, and this can have a positive effect.

Patricia Aburdene and John Naisbitt, authors of *Megatrends for Women,* agree that change is in the wind. Women are bringing in a fresh style of leadership, replacing the old pyramid design with a network or web in which command and control from the top is replaced by a cooperative approach that balances objectivity with a positive, encouraging, open exchange of information. The new style appreciates individuality, rewards input and creativity, and has the goal of empowerment, giving each individual the confidence to act on his or her own authority. They believe that we are currently in a state of transition, in which the new "female" approach is blending with the old, and the new style is rapidly becoming the dominant leadership model.

Some of the most successful companies are finding ways to integrate both approaches. Men, too, have expressed appreciation for the opportunity to escape the rigid and demanding traditional structure. Employers are learning that they can mesh the two styles into a kind of "best of both possible worlds" approach. For example, a hierarchy can make the power structure clear but also treat each employee as a valuable source of ideas.

The new style also seems to blend more effectively with the emerging social trend, which idealizes neither work nor family as the be-all and end-all of existence, but rather strives for balance. The era in which men with full-time homemaker wives set the standards has ended. The new status symbol is leisure. In one study, 70% of the people surveyed who made $30,000 a year or more said that they would sacrifice a day's pay for an extra day off each week. People today want job satisfaction without having to forfeit the rest of their lives to the corporation. A greater concern for the quality of life is one key not only to making the workplace more pleasant, but to ending discrimination as well.

Employment attorney and legal counselor Eric Sirotkin believes that the solution to problems in the workplace must involve making human rights and dignity our number-one priority. He argues that "The current power structure among most employers and workers, reflected in the law of 'master and servant,' has created the myth and the mentality that the employer's power gives them the right to mistreat employees." Sirotkin believes that instead of looking to apply labels like "discrimination," the focus should be on fairness—whether there is objectively reasonable cause for employment decisions. This involves breaking down the myths of blindly supporting managers or mistrusting employees and replacing them with strong internal company methods of dispute resolution that allow fairness to be the determining factor in employment decisions.

One of the greatest shortcomings of the existing body of law is that there is nothing to prevent an employer from mistreating a worker unless the mistreatment falls into one of the categories such as discrimination or breach of contract. White males often find themselves treated in a demeaning, humiliating manner, but because the treatment is not based on age, sex, race, or disability, they have no legal recourse. This type of abuse actually gives an employer a defense in some cases. For example, employers have won sex discrimination cases by proving they treated everyone horribly, male and female alike. This is sometimes called the "S.O.B. defense."

It's interesting to see the changes that *are* taking place in American companies, as executives learn that greater attention to their employees' overall satisfaction will be reflected in profits. More and more business experts are taking note of the shift in management and leadership trends from a traditional style to a "facilitation" style without mentioning gender at all. The facilitation style focuses on teamwork, quality of work, innovation, communication and input from workers at all levels, openness and trust instead of threats and intimidation, consensus rather than unilateral decisions, and motivation by praise and involvement rather than strictly by money and promotion. In short, the shift in leadership style amounts to acceptance of exactly the methods some have labeled a "female" style of management. Many male executives undoubtedly are more likely to accept an approach called "facilitation" than "female."

## If Your Own Style Isn't Welcomed

Despite the emerging changes, some companies are still stuck in the Stone Age, and women continue to encounter attitudes ranging from discomfort to open hostility. Vocational expert Dr. Patricia Murphy believes that in many workplaces the previously excluded groups, including women, minorities, and those with disabilities, will never have truly equal status until management takes active steps to train workers to support and appreciate the richness and benefit of a diverse workplace. Dr. Murphy believes that management can and must prepare workers for change. When companies ignore the importance of helping workers cope with transition, the results can range from discomfort to tragedy.

Dr. Murphy described one case in which neither the women nor existing male workers were prepared in any way for a policy change. A group of women was thrown into a previously all-male department in a male-dominated profession, with tragic results. The men made the women feel unwelcome, and there were several incidents of harassment. Two women filed complaints with the EEOC. The work atmosphere became perpetually tense, and the power structure broke down. One worker became so confused that he hesitated to call a vehicle's brake problem to the attention of a female worker who was responsible for the vehicle. The brakes failed, causing a crash in which several people died. Dr. Murphy believes that if management had prepared the workers for the changes ahead, this tragedy could have been prevented. It is unconscionable to

expect workers to simply get along with no training or preparation for drastic and combustible change.

If there are persistent problems in the attitudes of your
co-workers, suggest to management—probably upper management rather than your immediate supervisor—that some kind of
training program should be considered. This is one of the solutions often ordered by the EEOC or the court when a pattern of
discrimination is shown. Many large companies are instituting
such programs. Standardized tapes, classes, training kits, and
even board games are widely available to ease companies into a
more diverse workplace where the talents of all can be appreci-
ated without some workers feeling threatened. When Du Pont's
own in-house four-hour workshop, "A Matter of Respect,"
won high praise from inside and outside the company, Du Pont
decided to start a new venture to teach others. It now produces
a training package that it markets to other companies. Some
sources of diversity training programs and materials are listed in
the Appendix.

## Getting Credit for Your Achievements

How do you make sure you get credit for your ideas? First,
make your presence in the company known in a general way. Be
visible and let people know what you're doing for the company.
Put what you're doing in writing, even if it's not required. A
short memo can serve to remind others of where an idea came
from and provide a good record of your achievement. Be sure to
keep copies of all the records that show your accomplishments
on the job—letters of commendation, company publications
praising your work, awards, production reports.

One of the most effective ways to be assured of getting
what you're worth is making sure your employer knows what
you expect and what you are achieving. Many women are shy
about tooting their own horns, but in business it's essential.
Becky Ralston had been working in the sales end of the printing
industry for a number of years before she decided to move into

a position as a print buyer for a medium-sized advertising company. "In sales," she explains, "it's easy to make sure you're getting fairly rewarded, because your commissions and other compensation are based on numbers that your employer sees every day. But in the buying end it's not so obvious. You have to take an active role in making sure the right people see what you're doing for the company."

Ralston also discovered that those key people included many others besides her direct supervisor. Her job involved both internal work, in which she was required to coordinate the artists in her department to be sure they worked efficiently to complete projects, and external work, in which she engaged in competitive bidding and negotiations.

As for the internal work, she made sure her supervisors as well as the company owners were kept up to date on what was being accomplished in her department, and what her role had been in the process. "You have to talk about what you've been doing, both directly and indirectly, as a part of the office routine," she advises.

The outside work was equally important in Ralston's job, but her supervisors were not as directly involved in this facet of the job as the account executives were. Ralston believes that her communication and rapport with these people was a large part of her success on the job: "The AEs are interested in keeping their clients happy. I made sure they knew how much money I saved for their clients, and how I negotiated to get the clients more for their money." The AEs reported to the company's owners, and their satisfaction with Ralston's work gave her a real plus in the view of the top people. They received a constant flow of information from various sources about what she was doing for the company. This kind of contribution is not forgotten. Ralston left the company when she moved to another city, then later returned to the area. The advertising firm offered her the chance to return to her old job, with a 25% raise.

Don't be afraid to brainstorm, to envision how the company could be more successful, to listen to your instincts, and then to speak out. If you know you have a good idea, push it! Persistence will be rewarded. If your idea is especially innova-tive, you may want to build a coalition among co-workers at your own level to support you before presenting the idea to those above you. This is also an effective way to hone a good idea into a great one, and to spot any bugs that need to be worked out. Get the help and enthusiasm of co-workers, fine tune your idea, then share the credit. This is sometimes called tin-cupping—as though you're collecting pennies of support and help with your co-workers, who will know they can count on you when their time comes. Again, since most women have been taught to work in a cooperative rather than competitive mode, this system comes naturally to most of us.

## Other Common Problems

You will often encounter behavior by co-workers that doesn't seem terribly serious, but it may be annoying, and you need to deal with before it escalates into something serious. You also need to demonstrate to others in the workplace that while you can be personable, you're not a pushover. Becky Ralston learned that it helps to be flexible, especially in a job that involves working with many different people. Again, it's important to appreciate the diversity of the workplace and move toward harmony rather than hostility. "I don't think I have a chip on my shoulder," Ralston comments. "I didn't worry about it if one of the workers in the plant called me 'honey,' especially one of the older men whose sense of what is appropriate was formed in a different era. Why make someone I have to work with uncomfortable if I'm not offended and there's no benefit in doing so? On the other hand, if someone was consistently doing or saying something I didn't like, I tried to take a gentle, humorous approach to get my point across, and it usually worked without getting anyone upset."

I've heard many women say that one effective way to stop the use of inappropriate language—especially when the other person may not be aware how they sound—is to toss a parallel version right back at them. For example, if you're the only woman in a staff meeting of department managers and one of them asks you, "Would you get us some coffee, honey?" you can reply, "Sorry, sugar, I've got a meeting to run." Or if your supervisor strolls into your area and asks, "How are you girls today?" you might reply, "Just fine, and how are you boys?" The point is made without making waves.

While an employee who suffers discrimination should never blame herself, neither should she allow it to continue or accept poor treatment. While no one wants to work in a sanitized, lifeless environment in which people have to walk on eggshells for fear of being offensive, it's important to speak up when fun and games cross the line and aren't amusing anymore. Allowing the behavior to continue, instead of insisting on a climate where fun doesn't cross the line of dignity, may seriously hurt your case if things deteriorate into real trouble.

Employment attorney Jean Bannon recalls an especially distasteful case in which she represented the employer. "It was just a very unprofessional work environment," she explains. "Yes, our clients, who ran a hotel, made inappropriate remarks to the employees. They told tacky jokes, and they did stupid things like throw the waitresses from the hotel restaurant in the pool. But the workers participated willingly and behaved just as badly. They actively took part in the sexual innuendo and constantly teased and flirted with their bosses. When one employee was fired for poor performance, she filed a sexual harassment suit. She had more than enough examples of bad behavior by the management to make us want to settle, even though her own conduct was more offensive than that of the managers. We were lucky to resolve it with a reasonably fair outcome through mediation. But it really was a problem created and perpetuated by everyone on the job site."

## The New Way to Dress for Success

Whether we like it or not, there can be no doubt that how we dress plays an important part in how our supervisors and colleagues perceive us. We tend to form a lasting impression of a person in the first 30 seconds we meet them, and the bulk of what we notice is overall appearance. Does this mean you have to forgo all sense of personal flair and assume the corporate uniform? Not anymore. The "corporate clone" uniform of the early 1980s is dead, thank goodness.

The key word today is *appropriate*. In most jobs, overtly sexy clothing is not a good idea. It tends to reinforce the image of sex object as opposed to worker. But this doesn't mean you can't wear attractive, flattering clothes that reflect your personal style. In fact, most executives today shun the 1980s dress-for-success look of dull, boxy suits and believe that a distinctive look helps set you apart.

Alice Lusk, EDS corporate vice president, has always rejected the mannish uniform of dark suit, light shirt, and bow tie. "Style is really important for any executive," she says. "But it's easier for men to tell what's appropriate dress. Women, by default, often end up wearing something very similar to men's suits. I enjoy color and fashion, and I've taken time to build a wardrobe that I feel is appropriate in the business environment—not sexy by any stretch of the imagination, but appropriate. What you decide to wear is an expression of your self-confidence. Who you are is how you present yourself." Lusk was profiled in *Executive Female* magazine. In a photograph accompanying the article, she is shown wearing a turtleneck cranberry knit dress with bold golden accessories and black hosiery. It's a look that is feminine and stylish yet leaves no doubt that she is a serious professional.

Of course, what's appropriate depends on the workplace, the season, and the job requirements. When I was the manager of display in a department store, I had to climb ladders, haul mannequins up and down stairs, and crawl around on the floor hammering nails. Jeans or other sturdy trousers were the only practical choice. But I still had to remember I was working in the fashion industry, and I was a manager. It wasn't always easy, but we were at least expected to dress in a style that was funky and fun. I took advantage of the looks that could be adapted—canvas baggies, parachute pants, and brightly colored carpenter jeans were trendy then—and kept a neutral blazer handy for staff meetings in which I wanted to project a more professional image.

Consider what is appropriate for your particular job, and be aware of the image you're projecting. Some women advise looking at what the women in the positions just above you are wearing, and adopting a similar version that fits your own style and budget.

## To Date or Not to Date?

How does romance in the workplace fit into the overall scheme of things? I cannot agree with those who say never date co-workers. (I can hardly accept that point of view when my parents met on the job!) Work can be a great place to meet men. By working together you already share something in common, and if you happen to meet the man who may be your soulmate, is it wise or even sane to back away from something so rare in the name of protocol?

As a hopeless romantic, I say no way! The law generally agrees. Rules against husband and wife in the same workplace have been struck down as discriminatory, especially when the woman is forced to leave. Also, rules that prohibit fraternizing or are designed to prevent co-workers from dating have received varying verdicts in the courts, but may violate the First Amendment right to freedom of association. It is not up to your company or your boss to regulate any behavior off the job unless it has a definite impact on your performance at work.

At the same time, however, there is no denying that workplace relationships can be tough, especially if there is a painful breakup and you have to see your former lover every day. There are also the risks of gossip and petty jealousy that can make your work less pleasant. But living, as opposed to merely existing, has to involve risks if you're to reap its rewards. Only you can decide when and whether your desire to get involved with a co-worker is worth the risk that there could be some consequences to deal with down the road. Consider whether it is a mild attraction or something that feels very special. Perhaps the best advice is to go ahead if your feelings are strong, but try to be mature, circumspect, and insistent that your privacy be respected. Your personal life is not the business of your co-workers unless you decide to share it.

Should you try to keep the relationship a secret? Again, the answer is, "It depends." Use your head. Do you work in a veritable den of hot gossip? Some places make keeping a secret nearly impossible, although I've heard from friends in these circumstances that having to be clandestine can give the romance an extra dash of intrigue. What is the company's attitude toward relationships in the workplace? Most companies, especially larger ones where men and women work together, are accustomed to the development of relationships between co-workers—after all, it's only natural. On the other hand, an alliance can be seen as a threat in a small, highly competitive workplace.

Consider the overall level of harmony among the workers. How does the other person feel? Are you both comfortable with others knowing, or is one of you worried that it will make things difficult? One key question is: What is the work relationship between you and the other person? Dating your boss or anyone on another level in the hierarchy can be especially difficult and lead to charges of favoritism or other nasty insinuations. But if you truly care about the person who happens to be a boss or subordinate, this should not have to affect your personal choice. It can work. I know at least two women who have been involved in relationships with a direct supervisor. In both cases they chose to keep the relationship secret and managed to do so—for several years in one case. Again, only you can make this decision, but think it over carefully.

In short, common sense, reasonably dignified behavior, and a healthy dose of business savvy go a long way in shortcircuiting many problems at work. But sometimes, no matter what you do to protect yourself, discrimination still happens. In the next chapter I will give you some methods to use in assessing your situation and figuring out what to do when a problem comes up.

⚖

# CHAPTER 7

# How to Assess and Approach a Potential Problem

When you begin to suspect you're not being compensated fairly, you're probably not sure what is going on, what or who is involved, or even if the way you're being treated amounts to discrimination. You're likely to feel frustrated and angry, and wonder what you should do first.

## Making Sure You Have a Claim

You need to step back and view your predicament with a critical, objective eye. Take a careful look at whether your suspicions are justified. Are you sure you actually have a claim for pay inequity or other discrimination? In all but the most obvious situations, there could be something you're not aware of, a factor that would change your perception of what is going on. Bear in mind that the law goes only so far. You are protected from discrimination based on sex, race, age, national origin, or disability. But these laws do not cover every action that may have an unjust result, nor do they prevent an employer from discharging or refusing to promote or hire a person who is not able, willing, or qualified to fulfill the requirements of the job.

An employer is almost always entitled to fire an employee for "good cause."

## IS IT DISCRIMINATION OR SOMETHING ELSE?

Many of the problems and challenges in the workplace are not caused by sex discrimination. We all have to make hard choices in our careers, and when things don't go well, we may be tempted to look for a place to put the blame. Trying to heap that responsibility on the wrong individual, company, or policy can be both unfair and potentially disastrous for you, your co-workers, your company, and your family.

If you believe you have been the victim of an act of sex discrimination, the first thing to do is to separate the facts from the emotions. If you didn't get a raise but the two other managers in your department did; or if you were passed over for a promotion, find out why. Ask the person who made the decision to explain. Schedule a meeting with your boss in which you can discuss the decision in a congenial manner. Don't go on the attack by saying, "I was counting on that raise, how come I didn't get it?" Begin by explaining that you want to understand how you can grow with the company and have a better chance the next time an opportunity comes up. The answer you get may not be satisfying, but at least you will get an idea of what's up and whether it's a case of discrimination or something else.

Most of us have experienced plainly unfair treatment that may be mean, rotten, and lousy, but it's not discrimination. If your boss simply does not like you—and personality conflicts are common on the job—this could explain the decision to promote someone else. It is also something you need to know about so you can make your choices about whether to stay on that job, move to another department, or consider leaving.

Here's an example of a situation that was unfortunate and perhaps unfair but not sex discrimination. My friend Janelle Wilde works for a large business equipment manufacturer. The very life of the business depends on a strong outside sales force, both to get new accounts and to service existing customers. Outside sales reps are well compensated and earn generous commissions, and these are considered by many to be the plum jobs in the company. However, the reps earn every dime they make, because the work requires long, flexible hours and often includes evening and weekend work as well as frequent travel.

Susan Green, one of the women in the company, was a bright, ambitious inside sales assistant. She was a single parent with sole custody of two preschoolers, yet she believed she could handle an outside sales position despite the demands of the job and the potential for conflict between her work and parenting obligations. The company was worried but wanted to be fair, so it gave Green a territory.

Not surprisingly, she had great difficulty once she started her new job. She refused to attend evening meetings, because her children came first and she had no support from relatives, friends, or the children's father that allowed her flexibility in her schedule. Her day-care center required that the children be picked up by 5:15 P.M., and she couldn't find another source of care. She complained loudly when asked to travel or to meet a customer after business hours, although she was well aware when she took the job that these were essential requirements.

The company tried to be flexible and accommodating but could push the parameters of the job only so far. In the end she failed and had to return to an inside position. Now she is bitter and angry and feels she was treated unfairly.

Was she? Who is responsible for her failure? As Janelle says, "If this were a perfect world, every company would have in-house day care or everyone could afford a live-in nanny. But we all have to make choices. I have only one child, plus a husband who does his fair share and others nearby who could help. But there is no way I would take that job."

Janelle also pointed out that one of the male sales reps had encountered similar problems when his divorce left him with custody of his two children. He tried to keep his territory for awhile but simply could not do the job. He voluntarily chose a transfer to an inside position after only a few weeks.

The outcome of Susan Green's dilemma has been unfortunate for everyone. Janelle tells me that now there has been a backlash effect—the company seems to be hiring and promoting only young, single sales reps. The company has both male and female reps and would never openly admit that parents are being discouraged or excluded from the job. But that seems to be the obvious policy today. About Susan, she says, "In a way I have to admire her ambition and her commitment to her children. But her decision was really selfish and unreasonable. Now, I can't really blame management for thinking that putting a single parent into that type of job is a bad risk."

Could your dilemma be similar? Give it some thought before you proceed with a charge of discrimination.

## INVESTIGATING ON YOUR OWN

If you have taken a hard look and decided that discrimination is the reason for your unjust treatment, start gathering all the information you can about your company, its policies and practices. If your company has a personnel manual, get it and read it (if you haven't already). Sometimes wage and salary information, as well as an explanation of job classifications, is not included in a manual but is available from your boss or the personnel director. Don't be shy about asking for this information. You're entitled to have it, and there is nothing wrong or suspicious about wanting to be informed. Remember, too, that this information may amount to an implied contract. Read it carefully to see if the way you're being treated violates any stated procedures.

The next step is to begin gathering your facts. As any good detective knows, you can't prove a case without ample evidence. By accumulating both the subjective materials—rumors, hearsay, gut feelings, your general sense that something isn't right—as well as the hard facts that prove what is or is not happening, you will be able to accomplish two essential tasks: first, determining whether you have a claim; second, preparing a well-organized, factual presentation for your co-workers, employer, and anyone else who may become involved, such as an attorney or EEOC officer.

Buy a notebook and divide it into two sections. In the first section begin with a short summary of your own perspective about what's going on. Write down your version of the perfect job—either an ideal version of the job you have, a different job, or both. Then ask yourself what changes you would have to make to get there. Continue by writing down everything you see and hear that might support your feeling that there is discrimination in your workplace. This is the place to put your hunches, your sixth-sense reactions, everything other than the hard facts. Those will be kept separate.

While gossip and rumor often turn out to be exaggerated or simply wrong, we all know that the office grapevine can be a good source of information. You can investigate what you hear through more reliable channels later. Just be sure you make a note of the source of each bit of information. If Mary Jane, who is known to spread any rumor, tells you she just heard that Tom got a huge raise even though he has been with the company only six months, take it with a grain of salt, but write it down and label it accordingly as gossip from Mary Jane.

Take special care to record anything blatantly discriminatory, such as an off-the-cuff comment someone overheard from the boss, like "No damn broad will ever be a line manager as long as I have the say-so." Keep your ears perked for paternalistic remarks, too, such as "Dock foreman is no job for a lady." Note the climate of your workplace, how people act, and how other women on the job are treated. Pay special attention to who else may be aware of the discrimination or harassment, especially managers or supervisors. State when and how you know or believe they became aware of the incidents. Also note any money you have lost or had to spend because of what happened. Keep receipts and copies of any bills.

In this section of your notebook, you should also put down your feelings about the work you're required to do, your hours, your benefits, what you do and don't like about the job, your boss, the department head, or the personnel manager. Note the co-workers you like, those you don't trust, and those who may want to join or support you in your claim. Leave some pages blank so you can add more later. This is your "stream of consciousness" section, so feel free to include your general thoughts and feelings, observations on office atmosphere, and perceptions on morale. Think of it as a diary where anything goes.

These records should always be kept separate from any personal journal or diary. You may have to produce them if you get into a litigation process. If you mingle your accounts of what goes on at work with what goes on in your personal life, all these materials could end up in front of prying eyes.

The second part of the notebook will be more of a checklist to help you look for specific things and pull together the hard facts. This section should include:

1. Your title, job description and requirements, work hours, and pay scale. Include the schedule for reviews and raises, starting salary, and any promises or assurances that were made when you were hired or during your last review. If there are written manuals or policy statements, note this and keep them with the notebook.

2. The title, job description and requirements, work hours, and pay scale (if you know it) for all the workers, male and female, that you believe are doing the same work you are. Also describe recent openings and promotions, who got the job, who applied, and what criteria were required for the position.

3. Your education, work background, and the skills you use on the job. Include any special training that you received for this job, either on the job or prior to starting. Be sure to think carefully about any special qualifications or abilities that help you perform the job. What makes you special or, even better, what makes you indispensable? Think about things besides your education or training. For example, in my display manager position at a department store chain in Illinois, the main store and most of the branches were

in the Chicago area, but a few were downstate in small rural cities. None of the Chicago people wanted to be transferred to "the sticks," but I wanted to remain downstate where my family lived and my husband had a good job. When a display management position opened up in another rural store, I was in a good bargaining position because of my geographic location and preference. The company needed someone in the store immediately, and as the only qualified and willing employee ready to move into the position, I was able to negotiate a substantial raise.

4. Your responsibilities. Record what you are responsible for getting done, what specific tasks you have been assigned, and everything you actually do over the course of several days. Do you create a product? How much or how many did you work on or complete? Do you perform a service? What is it and how did you do it? Did you meet quotas, quantities, or deadlines? What duties did you perform, what activities went into completing these duties, and how much time did you spend on each activity? What does your work contribute to the company? Why is this work essential to what the company does or makes?

5. The effort you put into your work. Does your job require intense mental concentration? Do you have to deal with the public? Do you perform physical labor? Perhaps a combination? Think about the type of energy and amount of effort that goes into completing your work.

6. Your total compensation package. Start with your base wage or salary and add all fringe benefits and other extras. Do you know if others have the same benefits? Try to place a dollar amount on your benefits. For some, such as insurance, this will be fairly simple; for others, you may need to make an estimate or ask your personnel director. Also consider the value of the benefits to you personally. On one hand,

if the company has a health club membership you never use, this does not add to your personal compensation. On the other hand, a company day-care center may be saving you several hundred dollars a month. Do you regularly work overtime? Is this optional or mandatory? Are others given the same orders or opportunity?

7. All events that indicate discrimination. These should be recorded in detail. Limit them to things you actually experienced, saw, or know for certain, as opposed to secondhand information, which goes in the first section. Has a male co-worker with the same title, seniority, and training told you his salary, which is higher than yours? Did you train a male worker who has since advanced to a higher position than you? Have you or other qualified females been passed over for a promotion in favor of a male from outside the company? Are there different job classifications with suspect titles, as in secretary-clerk, host-hostess, stewardess-purser? Do you know for a fact that the workers in a male-dominated division of the company get paid at a higher scale than workers in a female-dominated division where the work is comparable in terms of skills, qualifications, effort, and duties? Have you or other female workers been singled out for mistreatment or made to feel unwelcome on the job?

It will take time to amass this information, and not all will be easy to acquire. But it is essential that you have as many facts as possible in order to evaluate and present your case. You may discover that you were overlooking legitimate differences in job responsibilities—that the worker you thought was expending equal effort for more pay actually has a harder job with more requirements and responsibilities. Or, you may learn that things are even worse than you thought. But how do you get this information? Personnel files are confidential (at least until an agency investigation begins or a lawsuit is filed), and most people consider direct questions about their earnings to be rude and in poor taste. Also, it's best not to broadcast your suspicions until you are sure they are justified and you have had a chance to consider your next move carefully. So how do you get your facts?

The best way to learn about your co-workers' salaries is usually to broach the subject in a friendly, nonthreatening way during the course of normal conversation. Ask indirect questions rather than demanding information in touchy areas. People love to talk about themselves and their background. Most people can be led into areas such as their education, former jobs, and opinions about the company and its pay policies through casual, everyday talk.

Is this sneaky? Manipulative? Perhaps some would consider it so. But your colleagues are free to tell you as much or as little as they like, and there is no harm that can come to your co-workers by your having this information. It is absolutely illegal to lower the males' pay to match the females', as some employers have learned the hard way in court. Furthermore, your goal is not to take anything from them, only to equalize the playing field and make sure you are getting treated in a fair and legal manner. Also, developing a good rapport with your co-workers can only make the workplace more pleasant and efficient. So don't be afraid to get to know your colleagues, and avoid the trap of viewing them as rivals or enemies. Many of them, both male and female, may turn out to be your supporters in working for equal pay.

At this early stage, it is also a good idea to get a copy of your written employment records before you speak up or file any type of complaint or grievance. Seal these records in an envelope and mail them to yourself. Leave the envelope sealed. This can provide valuable evidence of the true state of your records on the date they were mailed, and prevent any bogus claims of performance problems or other false information from being added later.

A word to the wise: When you're gathering information for your case, don't let your enthusiasm go too far. Midnight raids on the personnel office might turn up all sorts of juicy documents, but none of them could be used. And if you get caught, your case could fly right out the window. In several cases, employees with good, solid discrimination claims have tried these tactics and have been thrown out of court on their ears, often when they were caught halfway through the pretrial procedure and had invested considerable time, emotion, and expense in the case. Nearly everything will be available through legitimate discovery channels once your case is into the EEOC investigation or your lawsuit is filed, so resist the temptation to snoop.

Also, if there are skeletons in your personal employment closet, be prepared to tell your lawyer at the start of your work together. Did you lie on your résumé? Did you do something that violated company policy? Your lawyer will know how to minimize the damage that this type of information could cause if it comes out. Remember, discovery works both ways, and your opponent will be able to take a very close look at all your records and ask you just about any relevant question. Keep in mind that anything you tell your lawyer in helping to prepare your case is absolutely confidential and will never be revealed. Also, behavior such as lying on your application will not necessarily prevent you from winning your case; it certainly does not give your employer an excuse for discriminating. But your lawyer needs to know to figure out the best way to deal with what could become a serious problem.

Once you have accumulated enough information to feel confident that you have an accurate picture of what is truly taking place in the company, step back and look at it objectively again. Imagine that a friend has come to you and asked whether you think there is a problem. Or have a friend who works elsewhere evaluate what you've learned. Play devil's advocate. Put yourself in the position of an employer trying to explain the discrepancies. Could there be something you missed?

## Steps to Take Once Discrimination Is Determined

When you have concluded that sex discrimination is indeed the problem, what should you do next? Consider your personal goals. Think about what you would like to see happen if you could write your own best-case scenario. Do you want to quietly enforce your rights and get your equal pay without making waves? Do your want to be another Norma Rae and lead all the women in your company in a revolt? Do you want to expose the injustice, be compensated for your losses, and move on? Your personal goals will determine the ultimate strategy you choose. But whatever you eventually decide, there are a few steps you will be wise to take regardless of the outcome you seek.

First, line up all your ducks in a row so you will be prepared for whatever may happen. Update your résumé, using what you wrote about your job duties and responsibilities. Be sure your résumé accurately and completely reflects your duties, responsibilities, and experience. Don't exaggerate, but don't be modest either. Whatever path you may take, a solid, timely résumé will be an essential tool.

Second, think your options through. Learn about what your field does and should offer. What salary ranges can you realistically expect? Do these differ by size of the organization, geographic location, or other variables? Do you need additional training to advance in your field? Do you want to change careers and enter an entirely different type of employment?

In looking at your industry, take care that you don't fall prey to any preconceived notions. For example, retail store management is a notoriously low-paying field. Both male and female managers are poorly paid just because of the nature of the industry. But in 1979 the female managers of one of the nation's largest department store chains discovered that they were being paid a flat 20% less than the male managers. The women got together, fought in court, and won a judgment that required the company to pay them equally, as well as awarding them the back pay they should have received. The final outcome was a victory for the women, but had they realized sooner that they were underpaid, the problem might have been resolved before it became so entrenched, without a long court battle.

Third, look at available employment in your field and consider whether you want to change jobs. Talk to your boss or your company's personnel director about available openings, anticipated opportunities, and what qualifications are required for you to advance. Get a frank, honest picture of what your own company has to offer or says it has to offer. Then check with other local employers to find out about comparable jobs in your area.

Fourth, throughout this process, make a record of every significant conversation or event that occurs. If your boss promises a promotion or raise by a certain date, write a letter or memo confirming exactly what was said in that conversation, and send it to your boss. Send copies of the memo to the department head and personnel manager. If you have an interview with another potential employer, write a thank-you letter summarizing the essential information you discussed, including title, salary, and job requirements. No matter how casual or trivial the subject may seem, keep a written record by at least noting the date, subject, and people involved in the conversation in your notebook. If any potentially significant information is exchanged, send a letter or memo to the other person.

Fifth, see where your employer really stands. Your next step, whatever you believe your ultimate course of action will be, should be to meet with your current employer or a company representative. This will usually be your own supervisor or a personnel officer. Many problems can be solved quickly and informally, especially those that have occurred due to a misunderstanding, lack of communication, or ignorance of something going on in the workplace. Also, many companies have a structure set up for informal conciliation through collective bargaining agreements, personnel policies, or formal equal employment opportunity programs.

Even if you are angry, disillusioned, and certain you don't want to stay with the company, you need to know your employer's attitude toward both you and the issue of compensation. Plan to state your case and ask for a raise, promotion, or other solution to the problem in the workplace and see what happens. This is an important part of any game plan.

Schedule a meeting with your employer. Set it up in a quiet, businesslike atmosphere where you will not be distracted or disturbed, such as an office not shared by others. In some companies you may be put off or told you will have to wait until evaluation time rolls around. If something intolerable or dangerous is going on, such as intimidation or threats from a co-worker, insist on a meeting. Your employer has a duty to listen and put a stop to this kind of behavior.

When you do meet with your boss to request a raise, this usually is not the time to bring up pay inequities. The topic should be limited to your compensation. In this context it will be easier to learn just where you and the company stand. With the information you have gathered and organized, you will be well prepared to make your presentation in a confident, professional manner. Attitude is everything. Don't go in with a chip on your shoulder or allow yourself to appear emotional or defensive. The key is to be assertive, not aggressive—neither on the defensive nor on the attack. Being assertive means stating what you want and what you expect in a calm, straightforward, and nonconfrontational manner. It means maintaining a cool, pleasant, and above all professional demeanor.

This can be achieved even if your stomach is full of butterflies. Write out your objectives before your meeting. State your case on paper, in detail, before you do it in person. This will help you organize your thoughts, prepare the right questions, and build your confidence. As soon as the meeting is over, write down everything that was said. Again, prepare a follow-up letter or memo outlining what was discussed in the meeting.

If you did not get the raise, consider the merits of the reasons you were given. Were they legitimate reasons? Or were you given the brush-off? Try to be objective. If you know that others equally qualified are making more, reasons such as "It's not in the budget" or "You haven't been with the company long enough to reach that pay level" are clearly brush-offs. On the other hand, statements such as "Your sales performance does not warrant the increase you request at this time" may or may not be legitimate. Review your performance record. If any company policies, quotas, or other objective standards are mentioned, request a copy in writing.

Take a few days to mull over the results of the meeting. What do they tell you? Do they change your initial assessment of your claim, or your feelings about whether you want to stay with the company? Do you need more information?

If you still have doubts about either the merits of your claim or your desire to take action, it might be best to schedule a second meeting with your employer to discuss what you were told at the first. This will be the one where the topic of pay discrimination should come up. Review your legal rights, prepare carefully, and go in with a plan. Again, attitude is everything. Whether or not you want to keep your job, you will be better off if you keep an assertive, professional attitude. You may be furious at your employer, but burning bridges usually is a bad idea, even if you are ready to go the distance through litigation.

Prepare just as you did for the first meeting by writing down your all the information you want to present. Draw heavily on the factual section of your notebook and prepare a clear, concise picture of what is wrong in your workplace. Again, you need not approach your employer in a confrontational manner. A cooperative approach—"There is a problem here we need to discuss, and I would like to try and work it out"—is still the best way to start.

Begin by giving the company the benefit of the doubt, even if there is no real doubt in your mind. Lay out your facts. Don't stray from the point or allow yourself to become too emotional. Let your employer respond. In doing so you are not only being fair but saving face on the outside chance that you may still be mistaken. Perhaps the higher-paid male employee whose qualifications and seniority you presumed to be identical to yours actually worked five years for the company in another state before relocating to this office. If you get such a surprise, you can end the discussion, thank your employer, and leave with your dignity intact. If you launch into a full-scale attack and then your employer drops this kind of bomb, you will look and feel like a fool. Proceed cautiously and professionally.

When the facts have been discussed, presuming there is no adequate explanation for the discriminatory acts you have outlined, you must carefully consider your next move. With some employers it can be very effective to show your smarts. Do you believe your employer may be genuinely concerned and open to change? Do you trust this person, or could you picture him or her engaging in unethical, devious behavior? Do you think the company cares about being fair? If so, you may want to let your employer know that you know your rights and have done your homework. A simple statement such as "I believe this kind of pay structure might violate the federal Equal Pay Act as well as Title VII" can make a strong impression.

However, think it through carefully before you make any statement that could suggest you're going to file a complaint. Some employers may view any reference to your legal rights as a threat to take action, and will immediately fall into a defensive posture, which can be disastrous. An employer who fears reprisal by a disgruntled employee can quickly begin to manufacture all sorts of information about you that will justify not only paying you less but possibly providing a reason to fire you as well, and even tainting your personnel record in ways that could be cleared only through a long, ugly, and expensive legal battle. Although retaliation against an employee who files a complaint is strictly illegal and can be severely punished by the court, it can be harder to prove if there has been time to manufacture reasons to fire, demote, or otherwise punish you that could, if true, be considered legitimate. Remember, one of the key things required to win on a claim of retaliation is evidence that retaliation was the cause, the motivating factor, in the firing or other action. As appalling as this sounds, manufacturing bogus personnel reports is not uncommon.

## INFORMAL SOLUTIONS

Creative solutions are often the best. A group of women I know worked in a law office in which the "secretaries" (all female) were paid one rate, while the "legal assistants" (all male at that time) were paid at a higher rate. Although the job descriptions were different, the work was essentially the same. Two paralegals, one male, one female, were above both groups in the office hierarchy and had college degrees and jobs with substantially more responsibility. They were paid more than either the secretaries or legal assistants, with no discrepancy between the man and the woman.

The attorney in charge of the office was a good-hearted, absent-minded tax and estate lawyer who was brilliant in his particular niche but knew almost nothing about employment law. The secretaries had all worked for the attorney for several years, knew he had no real intention of discriminating, and would never be prone to retaliate against them for trying to gain their equal rights. The only problem was getting him to listen to their claims. First, they tried the direct approach. He heard them out but insisted that the legal assistants had different duties. In fact, the secretaries knew far more about the actual workings of the office than their boss, and they knew that the everyday work of the two groups was virtually the same. To complicate matters, all were essentially happy in their jobs, fond of their boss, and liked their male co-workers.

Finally, one of the women enlisted the help of the male paralegal, who agreed with the secretaries but had also been unable to convince the lawyer that the pay scheme was unfair. The paralegal went to another attorney in the same building who routinely did legal research for the tax and estate lawyer when a question outside the scope of the usual practice came up. He had this lawyer prepare a memo outlining the requirements of the FLSA, the EPA, and Title VII, with an explanation of why these laws prohibit the pay difference, and what penalties were available for violation. The paralegal then gave the memo to his boss, who laughed and proclaimed that the secretaries had made their case. The women received a raise that brought them in line with the legal assistants.

In many cases, a sincere threat may be enough. Tread carefully if you go this route, but it can work. Dr. Jennifer Mayfield was employed in a research facility with other physicians, both male and female. Mayfield and everyone else in the department found their immediate supervisor, a woman, impossible to work with. Eventually the situation became intolerable. The supervisor had become so hostile and unpleasant that it interfered with Mayfield's work. When she received an unfair performance review, she scheduled a meeting with the man who had authority over her immediate supervisor, in order to challenge the review and request a transfer to another office location. His first comment was, "You women just can't get along."

Mayfield's response was to point out that her supervisor had also alienated the men in her department. She named several who weren't even on speaking terms with their boss. Then she told him point-blank that his remark was sexist and if he refused to take responsibility to correct the situation and persisted in his attitude, she would file a complaint with the EEOC. He whined that Mayfield was putting him between a rock and a hard place, but he eventually took action to correct the review and moved Mayfield to a new office. She is glad she stood up to him. "This time, a threat worked," she says.

There are many different ways to approach the problem of unequal compensation and related discrimination, depending on each unique situation, and resolving the problem often will be easier than you think.

## GETTING READY TO GO THE DISTANCE

If informal strategies haven't worked or don't seem right for your situation, it's time to approach either an agency, an attorney, or both. The agencies have strict time limits, so it's important to contact the EEOC, your local FEPA, or another agency as soon as possible.

First of all, don't be hesitant to call the EEOC or another source of information such as your state FEPA office. The people at these agencies can help you make the decision as to whether you have a good claim and whether you should go ahead and file. And remember, it is against the law to discriminate against anyone for starting proceedings under Title VII, opposing an illegal practice, or participating in an investigation.

Once you're ready to take the next step, the formal complaint process is certainly not the only option available, and the best course of action can be determined only by those who know the human beings involved. Before making your decision, try to consult with an attorney, employment counselor, agency representative, or community-based organizations that offer referral, counseling, and legal assistance. While you're still deciding whether to file, you may also want to call the agency that handles your type of complaint just for information, including deadlines. Most of these agencies, as well as many federal offices such as the Women's Bureau of the U.S. Department of Labor and the U.S. EEOC Office of Communications and Legislative Affairs, print pamphlets filled with useful information that are free for the asking. These agencies are listed in the Appendix.

It is always wise to contact a lawyer as soon as you have your facts gathered and decide you have a claim for discrimination. A good employment lawyer can answer questions, advise you on all of your various choices, and provide insight into what strategies are likely to work best in your particular situation. A legal memo or opinion letter may be enough to convince your employer that equal pay is a serious issue that must be addressed. Albuquerque employment attorney and legal counselor Eric Sirotkin always begins with a letter to the employer or the employer's attorney stating the facts, describing what laws appear to have been violated and what claims the employee may have. He stresses settlement negotiations and mediation over litigation. More and more employers are responding to these efforts and settling suits before they reach the courthouse, in a way that minimizes the financial and emotional costs of litigation. Even if you feel certain that you never want to go so far as the courtroom, you may want to contact a lawyer to act as an adviser to you and your fellow employees, and to present the problem and suggested solutions to the employer.

Whether you go directly to an agency or meet with a lawyer first, you need to get your notebook out again and add still more information. Get your data organized before you talk to a lawyer or contact an agency. They will be grateful, and the chances of your case being processed efficiently will be greatly increased. Be sure to include answers to these questions:

- Were other employees affected by the same or similar actions or forms of discrimination?
- What are any weaknesses of your case?
- What reasons did your employer give for the decision or conduct?
- What explanation is the employer likely to use to justify the conduct or decision?
- Is there someone at work who knows or saw what happened but has no personal interest in the outcome? (For instance, a male co-worker who is not a potential target of sex discrimination, someone you don't know very well, or someone from another department.)
- What damages and losses have you suffered because of the discrimination? Did you lose wages, lose your job, lose benefits, commissions, bonuses? Did you suffer physical or emotional illness?
- What other damages could there be that you hadn't thought about? Did you have to pay service charges because you couldn't pay loans or mortgages? Did you have to move to get another job and pay relocation expenses? Was your credit rating damaged? Was anything repossessed?

Be prepared to give information on when you started the job; how long you worked there; when you got promotions; the name of each position you held, how long you held each position, and what you were paid for each; all your raises and bonuses; names and titles of all supervisors; company policies, rules, and regulations; all contracts or other documents you were given when hired and later; performance evaluations (both oral and written); training, classes, meetings, and conventions you attended; and problems, warnings, or reprimands you received.

You also need to have all the facts about what happened lined up: When did the problems start? What happened? What was said? Did anyone complain, and if so, to whom? Have others had problems? What do you think really caused your problems? Were there other contributing factors? Have you had other problems with this employer? With others? Were you ever fired, and if so, by whom and why?

In preparing your case, be sure to focus on everything that shows how your current problems, including your employment situation (or lack thereof), your loss of income, and any anxiety or other physical, emotional, or financial problems, were caused by your employer's discrimination. This is important whether the case goes to court or not, because you need to be able to demonstrate just how your employer caused your damages and exactly what these damages are.

If you're case is based on a pattern and practice of discrimination, such as having to work in a hostile and offensive work environment, you need to focus on the environment as well as its effect on you. When this kind of case goes to trial, it's as though the work environment is being put on trial. The best support in this kind of a case is the testimony of three or four other workers, especially female employees who had to endure the same atmosphere. In short, try to gather everything you can that proves (1) that there is a discrimination problem; (2) that your employer is the cause of the problem; and (3) that this discrimination has hurt you.

The importance of proving causation can't be emphasized enough. This can be one of the most difficult things to prove, because it's often easy to see that someone has a problem, but it's hard to see what is causing her distress. Also, the employer will be anxious to find any reason besides discrimination to blame for your problems.

Eric Sirotkin draws upon a fishing analogy to explain how this works in a trial setting. "The discrimination or harassment is like a fishhook. The fish, or the employee, is swimming along, minding her own business, when suddenly she sees the bait, takes it, and gets hooked. She starts struggling and suffering, which will often impact her work. The surface observer or co-employees will see that there is a struggle going on, but they won't know what caused it—as they can't see the hook. It will often appear as if the employee is causing the disruption to the waters of the workplace. The trick at trial, or for a skilled internal investigator, is to discover and explain how the discrimination is the hook, the struggle is caused by the hook—the original harassment or discrimination against the employee." He explains, "This is the approach we take with a jury at trial. The defense will focus on the struggle and try to explain it away by blaming the employee. We need to focus on the hook and explain that the blame for the struggle lies with the abusive employer who set the struggle in motion by its harassment of the employee."

Sirotkin recommends looking for a list of key factors that can be used to build a case of discrimination. Any of these things can provide a valuable tool in building your case and preparing to take on the struggle against discrimination. Thirteen things to watch for are listed below.

1. If you were fired, what reason were you given? Some states' department of labor laws and regulations require employers to keep written records on the reasons employees are terminated. Often, if an employee files a complaint, the employer will give the investigator a different explanation as to why the person was fired. Sometimes, if the case stretches on to trial, the employer will give three or four different reasons through the course of the proceedings. This can be devastating evidence to attack the credibility of an employer. Write a letter or memo to your boss stating the reason you were given for termination. Ask others your boss may have talked to what they were told about why you were being fired. According to Sirotkin, in the majority of employment discrimination cases, the first reason an employer gives for terminating someone will change at some point later in the process. The same principles may apply if you were demoted, transferred to a less desirable position, or passed over for a promotion.

2. If you're fired or you quit, keep abreast of what goes on after you leave. Who was hired to take your place?

Has anyone else been fired? How are other employees being treated, especially similarly situated employees, both men and women? Employers sometimes try to mask discrimination by hiring another woman. Did you apply for unemployment compensation? Were you awarded unemployment insurance? On what basis was there a finding of wrongful termination?

3. What kind of numbers, counts, and statistics might help show discrimination? Obviously, you will want to think about the number of women in different jobs and at different levels in the company. But don't stop there. Are there patterns in the way people are treated, assigned, or given assistance? Are women given more work and less help than men? Did the others have to work overtime occasionally, while you had to work overtime constantly? Consider the big picture.

4. How is discipline meted out at your job? Are women disciplined in a different way than the men? Are some individuals always disciplined, while others get by with reprimands or nothing at all? Are inappropriate or demeaning disciplinary methods ever used?

5. Have there been any sudden changes in the qualifications for a job? Were certain requirements added or dropped from job descriptions just before or after someone was hired or promoted? Have job titles changed for no apparent reason? For instance, did two people apply for an opening with listed requirements, one male and one female, then the job description was changed after the man—who did not meet the original criteria—was hired?

6. Take another look at any company policies and manuals. Are they being applied equally to all workers? Are there rules that certain favored employees are not expected to follow? Are there guidelines on promotion requirements that are relaxed to let men progress faster than women? This can be tremendously impor-

tant, because if your employer is acting contrary to the requirements of the job manual, you may have a breach of contract claim as well.

7. Get your notebook out again and do a couple of homework assignments. First, write out a narrative of what happened, start to finish, and how it affected your work and personal life. This should be like a letter to a close friend—pour your heart out and just write whatever comes to mind. Then prepare a chronology of what happened, with the most accurate dates you can get, including not only factual events but also how your work, the environment, and your co-workers were affected. Pay special attention to changes. Did your own work performance decline? When? Why? Did you get negative reviews? When? What did they say? This can be essential in showing how the discrimination damaged you. Were you harassed into leaving? List each and every action you can remember. This may also give you another claim for constructive discharge. If you suffered stress, loss of self-esteem, difficulty keeping your work performance up, or other emotional problems, these are real damages that entitle you to compensation, not only for any costs you incurred for therapy, counseling, or physical distress, but also for your pain and suffering.

8. Who else may have seen the discrimination taking place and noticed what was happening to you? Could anyone with supervisory authority have been aware of what was going on?

9. Consider whether you might have been set up to fail. Insidious as it is, this goes on. Were you given impossible assignments, then held accountable? Did you do what you were told, only to hear later that you misunderstood, goofed, or did it wrong when you know you did exactly as you were instructed? Were you given faulty equipment or the wrong equipment?

10. Have you seen any indication that your employer may have secret logs or files on employees, information that doesn't go into the personnel files? This is the sort of juicy tidbit juries love.

11. How are evaluations and reviews conducted? Is your performance judged on objective criteria or is it subjective? Some subjective comments are usually expected, but if decisions on your pay and progress on the job are almost entirely subjective, this is a red flag.

12. If you have been the target of overt discrimination, abuse, or harassment by a co-worker or supervisor, was that person disciplined, terminated, or at least reprimanded? Did anyone sit you both down and try to deal with the problem? When higher-ups do nothing, this implies that they approve of what is going on.

13. Is there any evidence you might be able to get that would help prove your case? Do a little detective work on your own (just be sure you don't get carried away and violate any legitimate company policies or laws). For example, in one case an employee was fired in part for not having a mandatory bumper sticker on her car. She took pictures of the other employees' cars in the parking lot and showed that only a few of the others had the stickers. Take pictures, copy memos, make notes of demeaning jokes or comments, including who made the comment, to whom it was directed, and who overheard it. Think about why people do these things—what's their motive?

## GOING IT ALONE OR GATHERING THE TROOPS

Should you enlist the support of your co-workers or go it alone? Again, this will depend on each situation. There is certainly strength in numbers, and if you share a good relationship with your co-workers, along with a definite, mutual desire to correct your equal pay problem, this may be a very effective approach. A group can present a united front, share legal expenses, and provide mutual support.

But don't reveal too much, too early, to too many people. Keep your suspicions to yourself until you've completed your analysis. There could be company loyalists who would fly to the boss at the first hint of dissent and tell all. Your employer may then begin to put together a strategy to oppose you, or even to manufacture justifications to fire the rabble-rousers before you can take any action. Wait until you have a clear picture of what's happening, then try to get the support of your co-workers, especially if they are also the victims of the discrimination. In gathering your allies, think about who else might be hurt by the policy or practice you're challenging. For instance, in one case, a minimum height requirement was found to discriminate against both women and Hispanic males.

You will probably want to test the waters by initiating informal discussions about the work situation to gauge how your co-workers feel before trying to organize a group. One thing to keep in mind if you believe your co-workers would be reluctant to take formal action is that much can be accomplished by working informally as a group. Your colleagues can provide mutual support, encouragement, and a broader range of backgrounds and personalities. Approaching your employer with a united front lessens the chance of retaliation or firing. If you do put a coalition together, plan to share memos, employee manuals and policy statements, recruiting materials, and pay records, as well as any evidence of discriminatory actions.

Some believe that a group meeting with higher-level management is the best place to start. Make the managers aware that you know your legal rights and available recourses. Have a written agenda, with organized, detailed grievances and concerns. Think through what you want and be prepared to state your goals with precision. Think about how the changes you seek will benefit not just you but the company. Emphasize that you are not making unreasonable demands; rather, you are seeking what you are entitled to receive under the law. A coalition of workers with an organized plan and clear goals is more powerful and more intimidating to management than an individual.

Before scheduling the group meeting with your employer, get everyone together to meet with a lawyer to discuss your questions and the goals you have set. Going into the meeting represented by legal counsel can also be a very strong advantage. You can count on your employer to rally the forces at the first sign of trouble. Think about how you can even the odds by recruiting your band of soldiers as well.

Another important reason you may need to involve others is to get the support of witnesses to your employer's acts of discrimination. Witnesses can be essential in proving your claim, and you should do everything possible to convince any witnesses to help you if the complaint goes that far. Emphasize the need to keep your activities confidential, and also stress that most cases will not require courtroom testimony. Also remind them that your employer cannot retaliate against either you or your witnesses, and any attempt to do so will mean serious trouble.

If you decide not to involve your co-workers, you still don't necessarily have to proceed entirely on your own. A good source of support can be found through women's business and equal rights organizations, some of which are listed in the Appendix of this book. The members have often been through similar ordeals and can provide objective advice and encouragement. Enlist the support of anyone who can help, not necessarily through direct involvement, but by providing moral support and general assistance. Your supporters may include family members, friends, other workers who have dealt with discrimination, local politicians, women's groups, civil rights groups, or anyone who can offer advice, evidence, testimony, financial assistance, or emotional support.

Fighting discrimination has its personal costs. Some workers report being ostracized after filing a complaint, excluded from social events, and shut out at work. Others experience criticism as rabble-rousers or whiners. The "blame the victim" mentality is all too common, and it can be difficult to carry on at a job where you're made to feel like a pariah. But most of the women I know who have stood up for their rights are glad, even if the consequences can be harsh. One woman explained that if she had left her job without filing a complaint, she would be sending her employer a message it is okay to discriminate. She felt that if you don't take a stand for your rights and beliefs, you can't blame anyone else for your problems, nor can you hope that your daughters will have anything better.

## ENTERING THE COURT SYSTEM

First, you will work with your lawyer to decide which legal theories apply to your case and to draft your complaint. This is the document that gets the ball rolling. It is often fairly long and detailed, and it tells the court what happened, what laws entitle you to relief, and what kind of remedies you want. It is filed with the court and served on the defendants.

The defendants then have a set period of time, usually 30 days, to file an answer. This is where they tell their side of the story and offer any legal defenses to your charges. At this point they may also file a motion to dismiss, which says you don't have a case even if the facts you stated in your complaint are true. You will get a chance to answer this motion and argue why it should not be granted. If you have a good lawyer and have planned your complaint carefully, a motion to dismiss usually will not be granted, though sometimes the case will get pared down—for example, if some of your claims were "iffy." This is one reason why it's usually best to include as many strong claims as you can.

Then discovery begins. Both sides will have a chance to serve each other with written questions, called interrogatories, which have to be answered, and requests for production of documents, which request copies of all the documents you think your employer might have that would help your case. The other side also has the right to make discovery, so be prepared to answer questions and produce documents of your own, too.

Discovery also involves taking depositions. Each lawyer gets to ask questions of the opposing parties and their witnesses. This is usually done in a lawyer's office. The questions must be answered under oath and recorded by a court reporter. The transcribed depositions can then be used in trial preparation, in motions, and in court.

More pretrial motions usually follow discovery. Such motions include a variety of requests that the judge orders the other side to do or refrain from doing, or to eliminate portions of the case. One common pretrial motion is a motion for summary judgment. A motion for summary judgment argues that there is "no genuine issue of material fact" to be decided at trial; that the undisputed facts of what happened, when applied to the law, are enough to decide the case. These motions are often granted, in whole or in part, where the facts and law are clear and the proof strong.

At some point in this process the judge will usually call a pretrial conference to see where everyone is going, what motions are going to be filed, and to set deadlines for finishing discovery, exchanging witness lists, and taking care of the other business of preparing for trial. The court may also order a settlement conference, a type of court-ordered mediation, or make other orders.

Then the waiting game starts. Motions fly back and forth, and discovery proceeds. This will usually take at least a few months or sometimes longer, depending on how complex the case is. If a "dispositive" motion is granted—one that throws out all or part of either side's case—it can be appealed, and this can take years to resolve.

It is rare to get everything ready for trial in less than a year, although many cases are settled fairly early in the process. In one I worked on, we settled in about six weeks.

Once trial is set, don't be surprised if there are delays or continuances. After trial, there may be appeals. But remember, it is common to settle at any stage of the game, and as time drags on the settlement talks tend to get more serious. But this, in a basic nutshell, is how the process works.

So if you have to take your case to court, you will need to be patient and resilient, but the rewards for your perseverance can be handsome. One civil rights employment case I worked on last year produced a jury verdict of more than $450,000 for the employee.

Usually, though, the complaint will never get this far. Smart employers, when presented with solid proof of their pay discrimination, will correct the problem, give you a fair salary adjustment, and work out a compromise, often at the conciliation conference. Approximately 85 to 90% of all legal cases never get to court. Unless your case is weak or you have a very stubborn or foolish employer, this is what is likely to happen. Going to court is expensive and time consuming and generates bad publicity for a company accused of discrimination.

However, if you do go to court, the rewards, both monetary and emotional, can be great. While most people face the thought of getting on the witness stand with some trepidation, a full-fought courtroom victory can be among life's most exhilarating and rewarding experiences.

## One Woman's Story

One of the most uplifting success stories, both from a legal and a human point of view, is that of Muriel Kraszewski, who fought the system and won big time. Muriel describes herself as "never one to make waves," but when she came up against blatant sex discrimination that prevented her from getting the job she wanted only because she was a woman, she was furious enough to take action. As a result of her battle—which took 17 years—State Farm Insurance Company was ordered to pay her more than $400,000 and a total of nearly $250 million to other women who had been unfairly denied the chance to work in high-paying positions. It was the largest settlement ever awarded in a civil rights case. As Muriel said in an article she wrote for *Ladies' Home Journal,* despite the long, hard fight, "It was worth every minute." The trial showed her how strong she was, and where she once would never have dreamed of fighting the system, today she is eager to keep doing just that. Looking back now, she warns other women, "Among men who think that way, if they think they can buffalo you, they will!"

Muriel was hired as a secretary for two State Farm sales agents in 1963 and was eventually promoted to office manager. Over the 12 years she held the position, she learned about the duties of a sales agent and began selling policies under the agents' supervision. Once, when an agent was on vacation, she sold so many policies for him that *he* was named the top-selling agent in his region! Yet when she approached management about becoming a sales agent herself, she was unsuccessful. Although no one came right out and said women were not hired as agents, she wasn't given the job. Instead, she was led on for two years until she finally met with the division agency manager, who told her that she was not qualified to be appointed as an agent. When she pressed the issue, he started offering excuses. He said she didn't have a college degree. She replied that she had never worked for an agent who graduated from college. He said they preferred agents with experience running their own businesses. She pointed out that most never had. It dawned on her then that she had wasted two years pursuing an appointment they never intended to offer her because she was a woman. She decided that she would be one of the people who was doing something about discrimination. She gave notice and got a job as a sales agent with another insurance company and went on to become one of the top-selling agents within a matter of months. This company, Farmers Insurance, had offered her an agent's job before, but she declined, out of hope that State Farm would also appoint her as an agent.

Though she had a new and fulfilling job, Muriel was determined to make State Farm accountable for its sexist policies. She began to research what was going on and gathered her proof. Then she filed a complaint with the EEOC. They were too overloaded to prosecute, but they issued her a right-to-sue letter, and she phoned a civil rights attorney who informed her that he had been deluged with complaints from other women at State Farm and was already considering filing a class-action suit. Since Muriel's track record with her new employer proved that she could handle the job, she was asked to be one of the main plaintiffs. Her attorney was willing to advance the costs of the suit and wait for his fees to be awarded by the court, on a contingency basis, to be paid by State Farm. He felt that the case would be stronger with other named plaintiffs, including a woman who had taken college courses to meet the "requirements" State Farm had told her were needed for an agent job, only to learn that she still would not get the position.

The case was filed in federal court in 1979 but was delayed by unsuccessful settlement attempts and took nearly three years to go to trial. It was brought for Title VII violations under the theories of disparate impact and a pattern and practice of disparate treatment. Muriel was nervous about testifying but found she was calm on the witness stand, because she knew there was no question she could not answer. Several of the male agents she had sold policies for as office manager backed up her testimony. Her attorney showed that male applicants for the agent position did not have to meet the requirements Muriel was told were mandatory for the job.

What was actually a four-month trial dragged on for almost a year due to delays. Then the judge took another two years to hand down the decision. Meanwhile, Muriel continued to enjoy her success with Farmers Insurance, eventually earning a six-figure salary. Finally, the judge ruled that State Farm had committed sex discrimination. Judge Thelton Henderson wrote in his opinion that women were "lied to and/or given false and misleading information when they inquired about the possibility of being agents . . . told about educational requirements that did not exist, financial requirements not founded in fact, and false information about the availability of positions."

Appeals followed, and the case was finally settled in 1988. Sadly, one of the other named plaintiffs had died by that time, but her estate, Muriel, and the other plaintiff would each receive $420,822, based on what they proved they could have been expected to earn if they had been hired as agents when the discrimination took place in 1975. Muriel claims she would have "been happy with $5.95, but for me, the important thing was ensuring that no other woman would ever have to go through the indignity I suffered."

Muriel's case also revealed that thousands of women in California alone had applied for the almost 1,100 sales agent jobs that had gone only to men from 1974 through 1987. Any woman who could prove discrimination would receive compensation for lost earnings. State Farm also agreed to hire at least 50% women as new California agents, and to reform its policies nationwide. By April 1992, 814 women had been awarded an average of $193,000 each. As Muriel's attorney, Guy Saperstein, said, "This sends a pretty powerful message—that women can stand up [against discrimination], and that they can prevail."

Nor surprisingly, Muriel's case has received a great deal of attention. Attorney Merrick T. Rossein wrote about the case in his book *Employment Discrimination: Law and Litigation,* a guide for employment lawyers, as an excellent example of a case done right. He notes that the plaintiffs "discovered and presenting detailed, varied and voluminous examples of the employer discouraging women from applying for highly lucrative 'career sales agent' and 'sales trainee' positions."

The plaintiffs in Muriel's case worked hard to discover all the evidence they could to support their claim. They contacted as many members of the plaintiff class as they could and put together a complete picture of the way State Farm discouraged female applicants for the better jobs, including:

1. An all-male management staff that recruited only other men through word of mouth.
2. Employer documents encouraging agents to use personal contacts to seek recruits through friends, community and social groups, business associates, and community "centers of influence," as well as testimony to show the all-male orientation in recruiting.
3. Recruitment brochures and advertising materials, showing pictures of entirely male agents and referring to agents as "he," "guy," as well as print and broadcast samples showing only male agents.
4. The testimony of women who were deterred by these projections of agents as only men, in addition to the

testimony of employees and job seekers who knew
State Farm had a reputation for not hiring women.
Some of these people had actually been told by man-
agers that women were not hired.

5. Real stories from the women who were victims of the
discrimination, including their accounts of how this
discrimination had impacted their lives.

No doubt the case was long and tough, but it gives a clear picture not only of how to fight and win—but also why. Today,
Muriel advises any woman faced with this type of discrimination to "Be tough and go for it!"

## Other Alternatives besides Agencies or Court

You may also want to consider one of the methods of resolving
a case that comes under the heading of "alternative dispute resolution," or ADR. These include mediation and arbitration, as
well as minitrials and other methods of working out a solution
to a problem without going through the administrative process
or court proceeding. Arbitration involves putting your case to
one to three people, generally lawyers, who decide what should
be done. Their decision is usually binding and can be enforced
in court. Some employment contracts have an arbitration
clause, which says that this method will be used if any disputes
arise between you and your employer. It may specify certain
rules or procedures to be followed, such as those of the
American Arbitration Association. The main advantages to
arbitration are that it is quicker, less expensive, and not as formal as a courtroom proceeding.

Arbitration is still an adversarial process, so mediation is
the method many prefer to resolve disputes. Mediation involves
getting everyone together in a fairly informal setting and basically just trying to hash things out. It is similar to the conciliation procedures used by the agencies. Both sides have the
opportunity to tell the mediators their story, then the mediators

have several discussions with those involved, both together and alone. The goal of mediation is to get the parties to agree to a mutually acceptable solution, and while the mediators will offer advice, including an explanation of what is required by law, they will not make a decision for you.

While there are no strict requirements in most states about who can be a mediator, most have training and certification programs. Sometimes only one mediator is used, sometimes a team of two, often a lawyer and a psychologist.

Make sure you get a good mediator or mediation team. The mediator should be familiar with your type of case and what it's reasonably worth. "A good mediator does two things," says Jean Bannon, an employment lawyer who frequently uses mediation to resolve her cases. "First, he or she has to understand the value of the case. This will generally lead to convincing the plaintiff that she has overvalued the case, and convincing the defendant that he or she has undervalued the case, or sometimes dropping hints that one or the other isn't expecting enough. Second, the mediator should be able to point out the weaknesses of the case on each side. It is through this process that the mediator usually 'convinces' a party that they may have unrealistically valued the case."

One of the advantages of mediation is that it is a peacemaking process rather than a battle, and if the parties can't agree to resolve the problem, there is no effect on your right to continue with a lawsuit. The mediator, as a neutral party not involved in the outcome or emotions of the case, can give a fresh perspective. An impartial viewpoint can be extremely valuable, even when it seems the parties are so far apart that the case has no hope of settlement.

I've been surprised more than once. One of my cases that started out with the parties literally millions of dollars apart was resolved shortly after the second settlement mediation. The attorneys on both sides thought the second conference would be futile and tried to cancel, but the judge ordered us to go. The mediator, himself an experienced judge, wasn't shy about stating exactly what he thought of our clients' positions on both sides in colorful and emphatic language! He made us feel like kids caught fighting on the playground and hauled into the principal's office to be read the riot act. But his technique worked—everyone took a more realistic look at the case, and we worked it out to a fair settlement.

Mediation or arbitration can be set up at any time. There are private groups that provide these services, as well as court-affiliated groups. To prevent having to go the full route to trial, a judge will sometimes order people to use some form of ADR after a lawsuit is filed.

All forms of ADR are becoming more common in employment law cases, especially mediation. If you want to keep your job, an amicable solution is always preferable to a long battle that is bound to result in anger and resentment and can make returning to your job uncomfortable, even if you win.

## Choosing the Right Lawyer

It is essential in an employment discrimination case to find a lawyer who understands the applicable laws thoroughly. The family lawyer who drew up Uncle Harry's will and helped you beat that speeding ticket may or may not be this person. How do you decide which lawyer is right, and how do you find a lawyer in the first place?

Lawyers, unlike doctors, don't widely identify their expertise by specialty. Most states do recognize some legal specialties, such as tax attorneys. But both the requirements for certification and the specialties that are endorsed vary widely from state to state.

The traditional way lawyers make their abilities known and promote their services is through word of mouth. If you know someone who has had an employment problem, ask who represented her or him. Ask any lawyer you happen to know to recommend someone well versed in employment law. Many states have lawyer referral services, often through the state bar association. Or find out whether there is a local or state chapter of NELA, the National Employment Lawyers Association, in your area. The national headquarters of NELA, as well as other groups that provide referrals to attorneys, is listed in the Appendix.

Bear in mind that you may have to talk to a number of lawyers before you find someone who is both qualified and willing to take your case. This does not mean that you do not have a good case or that you should give up. Sometimes lawyers are simply too busy to take a case or choose only a very few cases that involve a certain amount of money. Keep trying. If a lawyer declines your case, ask if she or he might be available to counsel you in an advisory position as you go through the agency process, or if she or he could give you a few pointers before you begin. Or ask if she or he may be able to refer you to another attorney.

The importance of choosing not only a good lawyer but the right lawyer can't be emphasized enough. If you get the feeling that the lawyer is too busy to really listen to you, or if you are uncomfortable for another reason, be wary about hiring that person. Listen to your instincts. Employment lawyer Jean Bannon believes the most important part of the relationship is trust: "You have to have a lawyer you can trust, who you can feel comfortable asking any question. You have to feel that your lawyer has your best interests at heart and will be candid with you. A lot of this is gut feeling, intuition. But it's so important because you have to be intimately involved with this person for what will sometimes amount to years."

Bannon believes the most important question a lawyer should ask a client is simply, "What do you want?" It is vital that the lawyer and client understand and accept their common goals. The client should also understand that she is the final decision maker in the case—the lawyer is employed by the client and cannot ethically make any decisions on her behalf. The final approval for any significant step in the case must come from the client after the lawyer has explained the effect of the decision and alternative choices.

Beware the gladiator personality. The lawyer who approaches each case with an adversarial "defeat the enemy" attitude may seem like a worthy advocate but usually does the client more harm than good. Too often, trial attorneys who carry a heavy load of litigation cases are too busy to fulfill the lawyer's other traditional role—that of counselor. A few, like Eric Sirotkin, have given up litigation almost completely in order to focus on this aspect of the practice and to help their clients avoid litigation whenever possible. The counselor function is especially vital in employment law cases, so much so that the NELA has begun to conduct frequent seminars to emphasize the importance of counseling clients and to help employment lawyers learn how to do so effectively.

Most good lawyers, even those with large litigation practices, agree that going to court should be the last resort. Jean Bannon, who represents both plaintiffs and defendants in employment disputes, says, "Litigation is always horrible. It exhausts you emotionally and financially and frequently drags on for years. If there is a way to avoid it, find it and use it." She also emphasizes the importance of finding a lawyer who understands and explains the rigors of litigation. "The lawyer should be right up front about what it takes to go through a trial—the time, cost, and trauma. Many clients come in thinking they want a fight, want to expose the employer's wrongdoing and drag them through court. But there are better ways to vindicate your rights, and a lawyer should always take the time to explain all the alternatives and why they are probably better than a full-scale court battle."

Eric Sirotkin feels that even if the parties do go into litigation, the goal should be finding a solution to a problem, not trying to win a war: "Litigation should have a rehabilitative effect as opposed to a destructive effect upon the client, and for that matter, the lawyers." He explains that the goal should be reconciliation and healing, not battle. "Shedding the image of the other party as 'the enemy' and interjecting more humanity into the process will go a long way toward achieving this goal and bring back a true sense of justice."

In his practice Sirotkin usually begins by preparing a detailed letter to the employer outlining the client's claims. The letter can be signed by either the attorney or the client, if it appears that the stigma of "bringing in the lawyers" would put the employer on the defensive and damage the worker's chances of settling. Unfortunately, he estimates that only about 10% of the initial letters he sends out result in a true give-and-take settlement discussion. He feels that mediation is still not used enough in employment cases, and the concept is unfamiliar to many employers. Yet they, too, benefit when litigation is avoided. "Employers haven't begun to value these cases, either monetarily or in terms of the psychological and emotional costs to the entire workplace. Until employers come to understand the victimization process, this will be difficult. So much of the damage is not tangible in terms of dollars. How do you place a money value on divorce, insomnia, constant physical and emotional discomfort?"

This is one reason cases often take months or years to reach a resolution. Sirotkin stresses that a good lawyer should be willing to negotiate continually to try to resolve the dispute, and be prepared to stand by the client throughout the process, however long it may take.

## How You Can Help Your Lawyer

I'm not going to preach about how to be a "good client" at any length; for the most part it's a matter of common sense, cooperation, and basic human consideration. But there are some things you can do and refrain from doing that not only can make your lawyer like you and be more excited about your case, but will help you a great deal in building a winner.

First, use your head. You don't have to be a rocket scientist, but try to understand your case and the basics of the legal process so you will know what to expect and be able to help your lawyer put together the best possible presentation. Trust does not mean abdicating all interest and responsibility. If there is something you don't understand, don't hesitate to ask for an explanation. There may be something vital at stake that you didn't bring up because you thought it was unimportant.

Second, be willing to help by gathering materials and documents, assisting in investigation, cooperating in discovery, and getting ready for trial. You can often save yourself a good deal of money on costs this way as well. On the other hand, you may need to spend money to make money. It is often essential that you involve experts, such as psychologists or vocational analysts, to prepare a winning case. Be prepared to pay their fees. If you win your case, these costs will usually be reimbursed.

Third, be realistic about what you expect, and try not to let your emotions override reason. The legal system can't always give you exactly what you want—things like revenge, absolution, or wealth. Talk to your lawyer about what you really want to accomplish, what you can and can't expect, and accept the reality of the system. If you're willing to take less money if a formal apology is made, say so—this type of settlement can be made. Again, be sure your lawyer knows what is most important to you. This seems simple, but it is amazing how often clients and their attorneys get all the way to trial with fundamentally different assumptions about what goals they are trying to achieve.

Finally, show your lawyer confidence and appreciation. This person is working hard for you, often without compensation, for a period that may amount to years. Show some give and take. Schedule your calls and meetings during business hours whenever possible. Don't call at unreasonable hours like 7 A.M. on a Sunday unless you have a true emergency. Ask all the legitimate questions you need to, but don't demand an explanation of every paper clip in your file. Be patient, too. Justice does happen, but it takes time. Your lawyer can keep things moving along, but he or she can't force an immediate resolution.

If you are going to trial, you have to trust your lawyer and follow his or her directives absolutely. This is not to say that you should stop thinking for yourself, stop asking questions, or fail to speak up if something does not seem right. Accept constructive criticism and don't be offended. Remember, you have to make a jury like you and convince them that you're worthy of their consideration and deserve to be compensated.

Unfair as it may be, small things can affect this. If your lawyer tells you you have to dress a certain way, or attend to such things as bad teeth, speech patterns, your temper, gestures, or distracting habits, do it without argument. You can assert your individuality later, but for now you have to appeal to mainstream sensibilities. "Jury appeal" can make or break a case, and even outstanding cases have been lost because the jury simply did not like the plaintiff. The importance of this can't be stressed enough, and your willingness to cooperate is absolutely essential.

Above all, if your attorney suggests settling, don't assume he or she is selling you out. In most situations, if a fair offer is made, early settlement is preferable for many financial, strategic, political, and legal reasons. If your lawyer recommends that you take an offer, have a frank discussion about why, and listen carefully. The decision is ultimately yours. But always consider any serious settlement offer, not only in terms of money but also in human terms, taking into account your emotional state, the time you've put in, and how much more will be required to continue. What will be the costs, both monetarily and personally?

If you agree to accept a settlement offer, be absolutely certain that you understand what you are signing. Don't let yourself be dazzled by all those lovely dollar signs and zeros. Step back and take a good look at what you're getting. Are there tax consequences you may not understand? For example, damages you receive to compensate you for personal injury—including damages in a Section 1983 case—are not taxable. But both back wages and punitive damages are, and this can reduce the number you see by a quick one-third. Be certain to sit down with your lawyer and review the proposed offer, line by line.

What if there has been no fair settlement offer, and your trial date is looming ahead in the uncomfortably near future? The best thing you can do is begin to prepare early, in every way that you can. Your lawyer will probably schedule several meetings devoted entirely to trial preparation. Good trial preparation is vital for you as well as for your lawyer, because it gives you a realistic idea of both the process and the outcome you can expect at trial. You must also be well prepared as a witness. Your lawyer may want to actually rehearse your testimony or put you through a mock cross-examination to get you ready to face the defense attorney. This can be excellent preparation and training to keep your cool under fire—something that will be vital in court. If your lawyer doesn't suggest this kind of practice, but you think it would be beneficial, bring it up yourself.

The trial process can be confusing and intimidating, and you may even want to spend a few days in court watching other, trials to get a feel for it. Be sure you have a clear and realistic picture of what you should expect to win. Clients are often disappointed when they get what is actually a very good award, simply because their expectations were too high. Ask your lawyer about what others in similar cases have received.

Bear in mind that before a court can award you any money damages, you have to prove these damages with reliable, competent evidence. Discuss the range you can realistically expect with your lawyer. The jury's award must bear a reasonable relationship to the losses suffered. If the jury gets overly generous and makes an award that "indicates passion or prejudice" or is "flagrantly outrageous and extravagant," the judge can take action to reduce it, or it can be reduced on appeal.

For example, in *Hill v. GTE Directories Corp.*, a sales representative proved that she suffered blatant sex discrimination and was constructively discharged. At trial, a jury awarded her $40,000 in lost income and $410,000 in noneconomic damages for emotional distress. The court reduced both awards. First, the judge pointed out that the economic expert who calculated her lost income testified that she was deprived of a little over $16,000 in direct income, and that a co-worker testified that she would have been eligible for some small bonus payments as well. So the judge reduced the $40,000 in lost income to $19,000. What is fair compensation as noneconomic damages is always more difficult to determine, because this type of damage doesn't involve numbers. But the award must be in proportion to the injury suffered and must be supported by competent evidence. Hill had suffered stress and frustration and had seen a doctor who prescribed antianxiety medication. She also saw a psychiatrist twice. But the judge thought $410,000 in noneconomic damages was out of proportion to her injury and reduced the award to $125,000.

In another case, *Robinson v. Jacksonville Shipyards, Inc.*, a female welder working in a shipyard endured a constant barrage of verbal harassment, pornography, exclusion, and intimidation. Yet she did not show the court that she suffered any economic losses. So although the court found that the "hostile work environment" form of sexual harassment indeed took place, and issued an injunction ordering the employer to adopt and enforce policies that would stop the harassment, Robinson was not awarded any money damages. The court commented that since she offered no proof of lost money, any such award would be speculative, a common problem that reduces or prevents people from getting money awards.

These cases did not involve punitive damages, but where these damages are allowed, they, too, have to be in proportion to the injury and the conduct they are designed to punish. The defendant's financial state is also considered sometimes, so a big corporation will pay more than a small company. Punitive damages are also reduced by the court when they are considered to reflect passion and prejudice or be out of proportion to the actual damages.

## GOING TO COURT WITHOUT A LAWYER

What if you absolutely can't find an attorney who is qualified or one you can afford? Should you ever represent yourself? Of course you should, if this is absolutely your only alternative. If you find yourself in a position where you will lose your rights if you don't act soon, then by all means go for it! You can file a complaint and begin some preliminary discovery. This will show the other side that you're serious, and you can keep looking for an attorney after you file your complaint to stop the clock from running out. Your complaint doesn't have to be a masterpiece of legal literature; it can be a plain, simple statement of facts, telling what happened to you and what laws you believe were violated. It can be amended later if necessary. Sample complaints can be found in form books in any law school library, as well as in legal self-help books at both public and college libraries.

While you should be wary of taking legal advice from anyone other than a lawyer, others with some knowledge of law or experience in their own suits may be able to help you analyze what claims you have available and put them into the right form. As I mentioned, NELA is beginning to establish legal clinics, staffed by paralegals who work under the supervision of an attorney. Other groups and private lawyers run such clinics in some places as well. Law students, paralegals, legal secretaries, people who have worked for government agencies, people who own small businesses, court reporters, government clerks—all may be able to help. Most public libraries and college libraries have copies of your state's statutes, local laws, and legal self-help books that can help you put together a complaint. You may also want to look at some case files from the court where you will be filing your complaint to get an idea of the form and language used.

If you decide to start on your discovery, the same books and sources can help you draft interrogatories and requests for production of documents. In the meantime, keep looking for a lawyer. Attorneys are impressed by clients who have the gumption to get things going on their own and share the burden of work on their case. The same person who was "too busy" may see that you're too valuable a client to pass up.

# CHAPTER 8

# COMMON PROBLEMS AND PRACTICAL SOLUTIONS

## The Pink-Collar Ghetto

The "pink-collar ghetto" refers to the type of jobs that have traditionally been held by women and tend to pay low wages. Commonly included in this classification are nurse's aides, food service workers, clerical workers, and retail salespersons. Many such jobs are not low skilled, but all are low paying.

Like other problems of equal treatment and compensation, the reasons for this disparity are many. First, when women were denied entry into other professions, these jobs became overcrowded, so the supply of workers exceeded the demand and wages were driven down. Second, such jobs have not been organized by labor unions, as have many of the male-dominated unskilled or semiskilled occupations. Third, the persistent view of women as secondary wage earners who do not need to make as much as male heads of households resulted in lower wages for female workers. Fourth, many women in such jobs have interrupted their work to spend periods at home with young children, and either changed jobs within the occupation or did not keep their seniority on their return. Fifth, these jobs tend to have a high rate of turnover and employ a large number of part-time workers and students.

How did this distinction between "women's work" and "men's work" get started? It probably dates back to the Industrial Revolution in England, which began in the mid-1700s. Sex roles had been established for centuries among farm families, based mostly on physical strength and the expectation that mothers would nurse babies, then continue as primary care-givers. When people left the farms to pursue factory work, these traditions continued. Men did the heavier labor while women took jobs such as textile mill work that required manual dexterity and mirrored work formerly done by women in the home.

On the other hand, several of the occupations in this category were once among the better-paying jobs when they were held entirely by men. Clerical workers and bank tellers earned more than blue-collar workers at the turn of the century. Now that these jobs are held mainly by females, they earn much less.

What can be done about this? It's a difficult dilemma, since these are often the jobs that come up in discussions of "comparable worth." As you will recall from chapter 2, challenges to unfair pay based on a theory of comparable worth are difficult to win. However, some of the pink-collar pay problems fit precisely into the "similar work" pay gap that is strictly prohibited by both Title VII and the Equal Pay Act. For instance, if you are a nurse's aide and do the same work as the male orderlies in the same hospital but are paid less, this is blatant pay inequality. Remember, the factors to look at in comparing the two jobs are whether they require essentially the same skill, effort, and responsibility and are performed in the same workplace. Other pink-collar jobs that may fall into this category are female beauticians and male hairdressers, or female secretaries and male clerks. Others may be less obvious, such as factory jobs in which women are assigned to tasks that require special dexterity assembling small parts, while men work with heavier components that require more brawn but little finesse.

One way to fight the pink-collar syndrome is to organize with other workers to gain more respect for your contributions.

For example, child-care workers are beginning to earn more recognition for the value and the importance of their work through professional organizations and publications. A lot of ideas are beginning to emerge. Add your voice. And remember, the most effective way to bring about change is usually little by little, one company at a time.

## Double or Triple Discrimination

Women of color have a double disadvantage in employment opportunities. There has been a dramatic narrowing of the wage gap between white and nonwhite women since World War II, but unemployment rates are still much higher for minority women, and there is further segregation within the job market along racial and ethnic lines.

This and related forms of discrimination, such as the obstacles faced by women with a disability, are sometimes called sex-plus discrimination. This refers to a policy or practice based on sex, *plus* an additional characteristic, such as refusal to hire or give certain jobs to women of certain races, women with preschool children, women of a certain age, or women who are married. This kind of discrimination may also involve demeaning stereotypes (such as a case in which women, but not men, were required to wear uniforms because the employer assumed women could not exercise good judgment in choosing business attire). One interesting case established that employers may not base decisions on sexual stereotypes relating to notions of "proper" role and behavior for women. An accounting firm refused to offer a qualified female employee a partnership because she was described by others as "macho," accused of "overcompensating for being a woman," "a lady using foul language," and advised to "walk more femininely, dress more femininely, wear makeup, have her hair styled, and wear jewelry," in order to improve her chances to be promoted to partner. The Supreme Court found that her employer had discriminated.

Sex-plus discrimination may also occur when a woman has a medical or psychological problem that may be contributing to the unfair treatment. Employment attorney Jean Bannon once represented an administrative assistant who suffered severe psychological problems after her husband died suddenly. Her employers insisted she return to work soon after her loss, before she had recovered from her shock and grief. Then they refused to let her have time off to see her psychiatrist, even though temporary workers could have covered her job. The administrative assistant tried her best but ended up suffering a nervous breakdown and was hospitalized.

The case settled soon after Jean contacted the employer. However, she was prepared to seek remedies under the state anti-discrimination law which is similar to the Americans with Disabilities Act (ADA). "The employer knew how serious the problem was, yet refused to take the relatively easy step of using temporary or part-time help one day a week so my client could get the treatment she needed," Bannon explains. "Under the state counterpart to the ADA, an employer is required to make reasonable accommodations to enable an 'otherwise qualified' employee with a disability to do her job. That is, if the employee is able to do the job after the employer provides an accommodation, the employer is required to do so. This type of disability (psychological or emotional) is included in the act, and I believe the employer's refusal to accommodate her needs violated the law."

Keep in mind that if you are a member of another group protected by anti-discrimination laws, you may want to consider whether the discrimination is due to your being female, your other characteristic, or both. For example, if you are female, black, and over the age of 50, this suggests there may be issues of sex, race, and age discrimination to consider. Both federal and state laws may protect your rights, and the laws vary. For example, federal laws only prohibit age discrimination against people over the age of 50. But in some states, there is no such limitation. If you skipped grades and took summer school classes so that you're out of college at 18, but an employer tells you, "Sorry, kid, I only hire people at least 22," this may be another kind of age discrimination.

## Passed Over for a Promotion

Promotional decisions are one of the most common areas in which discrimination occurs. Aside from the broad problem of the glass ceiling, discussed later in this chapter, individual workers who thought they were working in a fair environment often receive a rude awakening when they are passed over for a promotion.

First, how is a fair decision made? Understandably, employers are entitled to look at a broad range of criteria in deciding who is the most qualified person for a job. Objective factors such as seniority, test scores, education, licenses, job performance evaluations, productivity, and special training are usually legitimate considerations as long as they relate to the requirements of the job. As in hiring, subjective criteria can be considered, too. Personality, interest in the work, ambition, and communication skills may all be taken into account, provided they are relevant to the job and don't have the effect of excluding women or other protected groups. If a case goes to court, this will be scrutinized carefully.

Openings for higher positions are supposed to be publicized so that everyone who is interested can apply. If an employer fails to do this and instead hand-picks someone for the position, another qualified employee may have a case for discrimination if she can show that if she had known about the opening, she would have applied. Evidence that one or more women were discouraged from trying for the job, or statistics showing gross disparities between the percentages of women in the upper- and lower-level positions can be very convincing.

A lateral move can also mean a step ahead in your career when a promotion does not seem likely. Changing to a different job at the same level can give you a new perspective on the company, an opportunity to learn about another aspect of the business, and a broader set of experiences in the company. This is especially true if you can move from a staff position to a line position, one that sets you on the track for advancement. Many executives emphasize this kind of structuring as one of the key considerations in charting your way up the ranks.

Look before you leap. Get all the details of the job, including the specific job description and requirements, to whom you will be accountable, budget figures, training, and the structure of the department. Find out as much as you can about the people you will be working with. Get to know them in advance if you can. And always go for a raise with the transfer, even if it's only a modest increase or your standard yearly adjustment.

# The Glass Ceiling

One of the most frustrating positions a career woman can find herself in is that of having done everything right and still not be advancing to the level where she is receiving the rewards she has earned. She may find herself stalled below her male colleagues who have far less impressive résumés.

The latest studies on the glass ceiling show that it is very real, very persistent, and very broad. Women have made far more progress against the wage gap in some fields than others, according to statistics compiled by the U.S. Department of Labor in conducting the study dubbed the Glass Ceiling Initiative, as ordered by the Civil Rights Act of 1991. The study showed women earning well above the average 70% of male salaries in several fields: 83% of men's wages in computer programming, 99% among registered nurses, 88% among secretaries, stenographers, and typists, 89% in the elementary teaching field, and 87% among nurse's aides and orderlies. The trouble is, most of these professions have traditionally been female dominated to begin with, so wages tend to be lower for all workers when compared to other jobs.

In the many of the more lucrative professions, the gap persists at or below the average: Female lawyers and judges make 70% of the salaries of their male colleagues, financial managers 67%, personnel and labor managers 69%, production workers 59%, and salespeople 58%. The report concluded that women workers are indeed blocked by a glass ceiling of subtle discrimination that limits employment opportunities. *TV Guide* magazine reported in 1993 that median annual salaries in broadcasting are $49,400 for men and $33,400 for women.

According to a study conducted early in 1993 by the National Association of Female Executives (NAFE), although women have made progress in the business world, overall they still make less money, are less powerful, and find fewer opportunities for advancement than men. One of the biggest problems seems to be the inability of executive women to move from lower-level management into the highest levels of professional decision making. This discrimination persists in corporations, in the nonprofit sector, and in government. Also, in professions such as law and medicine, more and more women are entering the field but are being channeled into certain specialties and barred from other positions with greater earnings and influence. Although women now account for 21% of the attorneys in the United States, as opposed to only 3% 20 years ago, statistics from 1991 show that men still hold 89% of the partnerships in the nation's largest law firms.

The NAFE study looked at statistics on the positions of businesswomen compiled over the last 25 years. The numbers show that corporate America is one of the worst architects of a thick glass ceiling. Women in corporate positions continue to trail men in both earnings and promotions. As of 1990, only 4.3% of corporate officers were women. NAFE also learned that while women now hold 40% of all executive, managerial, and administrative positions, these jobs are mostly lower and middle management and staff positions. Front-line jobs that directly involve business operations, as well as the upper echelon decision-making positions, are still male dominated. "Women are just not breaking through," said NAFE director

Wendy Reid Crisp in a June 1993 interview. "Discrimination exists at every step of the way."

Some of the most shameful stories I heard in researching this book came out of my own profession. A lawyer formerly with a big Wall Street firm said women are weeded out by reviews that suddenly turn bad in their sixth or seventh year, just when they are coming up for partnership. The firm is a mammoth, with 115 partners, 7 of whom are female.

In 1987 the New Mexico Bar Association appointed a Task Force on Women and the Legal Profession to conduct a two-year study on the needs of women lawyers in New Mexico. It found, among other things, that although progress toward eliminating gender bias has been made, the bias still exists in the administration of the law and in the treatment of women as professionals. Among the problems identified were lower salaries, more dissatisfaction, more problems achieving partnership, and closer scrutiny of hours and work. And as explained below, female lawyers face some of the worst problems of any working women when it comes to getting derailed on the "mommy track."

Another area in which women are still not advancing at the rate they should be is academics. The number of women in high-ranking faculty positions in our nation's universities has not kept pace with the number of women earning doctoral degrees.

One of the professions with the thickest glass ceilings is medicine. According to a 1992 article in the *Journal of the American Medical Association,* even pediatrics, a specialty that has long attracted female physicians, shows widespread disparity. The journal reported that only 6 of the 126 pediatric departments in the United States is chaired by a woman, and that a survey of those teaching pediatrics showed American women in academic pediatrics earning an average $11,000 a year less than men. Even in a profession with children at its center, child rearing was cited most frequently by the female pediatricians as to why their careers had slowed. Perhaps most disturbing was the fact that 55.8% of the women polled felt their career progress had been delayed due to sex discrimination. At a meeting of physicians and scientists to discuss how to overcome obstacles to full participation by women in the biomedical sciences, several reforms were recommended. The ideas included programs to facilitate the retraining of female scientists to help them get back into research after taking time off or slowing down to raise children; the need to reform the tenure system in medical schools; and more and better mentoring of women scientists.

Though many of the findings were grim and the ideas slow in coming, the conference showed optimism as well. Bernadine P. Healy, M.D., director of the National Institutes of Health, said that "despite the barriers we face, I believe we are on the verge of a revolution that will end the outrages and accord women their rightful place in society's most important endeavors . . . [I am] more than ever convinced that gender disparities in medical treatment and research will be reduced by increasing the number of women in leadership positions in the teaching, research, and practice of medicine."

Likewise, former Surgeon General Antonia C. Novello, M.D., said, "There will be a day when the descriptors of what I am will no longer be used, because there will be so many minorities and women being surgeon general that it will be obsolete to mention that I am the first, and I want to be around when that day comes."

Also, though the statistics may be disheartening, some of the individual success stories are remarkable and inspiring. NAFE studied 50 of the top career women in America and reported its findings in the September/October 1992 issue of *Executive Female* magazine. Though most of these women reported having been passed over for a promotion at least once in their careers, and most believe that gender is still a barrier to the executive suite, each now makes over $225,000 a year (some over $1 million) and have reached the highest pinnacles of success.

When asked about the glass ceiling and its causes, many of these women mentioned both the time required for anyone to move into top-level positions, as well as the comfort factor—the tendency of top executives, who are mostly male, to promote the people who are most like themselves. They believed that getting the attention and support of the CEO and other top executives is the single most important thing women can do individually to eliminate the glass ceiling. NAFE has established an annual program of Golden Hammer awards to honor companies that are doing the most to shatter the glass ceiling and promote women into senior management positions.

NAFE also reported some encouraging news in a study released in mid-1993. Women have been especially successful in entrepreneurial ventures. There are currently at least 6.5 million female business owners in the country, and the variety of women-owned businesses is expanding into fields traditionally dominated by males. Women are starting construction firms, manufacturing operations, and auto repair shops. Margie Seals, an Atlanta mechanic, runs her own garage, and business is booming. It's a far cry from when she graduated from automotive school in 1974 at the top of her class but couldn't find a job. One garage owner let her fill out an application, then told her to drop it in the wastebasket on the way out. When she finally got a job in a tune-up shop, the manager explained that the only reason he was hiring her was that he couldn't find a man with her credentials who would work for what he was about to pay her.

But things changed when Margie became her own boss. Like many successful entrepreneurs, she started out by finding a niche—a need in her profession that wasn't being met by the existing market. Before she opened her own shop, she ran a garage on wheels and made house calls, mostly to professional women. Today, 70% of her customers are female, and she employs four other mechanics, two women and two men. Experienced female mechanics remain rare, and though she is committed to giving other qualified women in her field a chance, Seals says she has had difficulty. According to government statistics, only 7,000 of the 864,000 auto mechanics in the country are female.

Each of these stories represents another victory, another important indication of progress. The glass ceiling may not be shattering all at once, but little by little women are chipping away and breaking through.

## The Mommy Track

One of the toughest decisions faced by women in the workplace is how to reconcile the conflicting demands of work and family. Mothers of young children who work outside the home find themselves torn between their dedication to their job and their dedication to their children. Some workplaces perpetuate the belief that motherhood and career are incompatible, and this hurts women, children, and men.

Why does this happen? Perhaps the main reasons are history and tradition. Earlier in the century, when the big companies were in their formative years, the norm was an executive male who could give the company his all because he had a wife who was a full-time homemaker. This ideal became entrenched, and although times have changed, many corporations are still mired in this outmoded ideal. Also, many employers believe that women will be less loyal to a job, less ambitious, and more likely to miss work or be less productive than male workers. Child care is viewed as a woman's private problem. Employers also tend to be resistant to new ideas such as company-supported day care, flexible working hours, job sharing, paid child-care leave, and other innovations that encourage both male and female workers to achieve a more harmonious blend of work and family life.

By the age of 40, 90% of all women have had a child. Yet among the women occupying the top executive levels, less than 50% are mothers. Most other western democracies have made much more progress in helping women and men balance their work and child-care responsibilities, despite the view of most that America is a more liberated country. There remains a serious gap between the ambitions of modern women and the realities of our lives.

Surprisingly, some of the greatest problems are faced by women who have made the greatest gains in their careers.

Professional women often report appalling hostility in the workplace when they choose to become mothers. Dubbed "the maternal wall" by Deborah Swiss and Judith Walker, authors of *Women and the Work/Family Dilemma,* women at the executive level often face direct punishment or more subtle roadblocks in their career advancement, even when they take only modest maternity leaves.

Swiss and Walker polled Harvard graduates and reported shocking stories among women most would assume to be among the most empowered in the nation. Several female lawyers with large law firms reported having babies on Friday and returning to work on Monday for fear that any leave would jeopardize their careers. An obstetrician reported that a plum promotion was withdrawn when she announced she was pregnant. Others reported direct insults from supervisors, and some said they felt obligated to lie, go to work sick to save sick days for times their children were ill, or work at home during their maternity leaves.

These studies point to a deplorable lack of value for the family and a sickening greed in the professional world. They suggest that American commerce places much less importance on babies than on the bottom line. The prime years for establishing a career tend to be the same prime years for starting a family, and the women who want to move up the corporate ladder often feel that they have to choose between motherhood and professional success.

It would be easy to place at least a part of the blame on the women who allow these practices to continue, but this would ignore the recurrent theme running through these stories: fear. Women who have worked hard and fought to gain high-level positions are terrified that if they don't play the game, they will lose even more than they are losing now. There seems to be no room for babies on the fast track. Some economists believe that career interruptions due to childbearing explain up to half the wage gap between men and women. In addition, most women still carry the larger burden of domestic chores in the home, even in two-career families. And many homes are run by women alone.

But the news isn't entirely grim. The Family and Medical Leave Act of 1993, enacted to help working families, reflects a changing focus in American values. Many companies are starting to wise up to the value of keeping trained, loyal workers happy.

The best setting for working mothers seems to be in large companies, such as those in the insurance and financial industries. *Working Mother* magazine recently compiled its eighth annual list of the 100 top companies that are supportive of working families. *Working Mother* evaluated the companies on four criteria: pay, advancement opportunities, child care, and family-related benefits such as job-protected maternity leave, flexible scheduling, job-sharing, and allowances for the care of elderly parents. Editor Judith Culbreth reported that even in a troubled economy, companies were still anxious to make the list. She characterized this attitude as a good sign of the nation's economic strength and an indication that companies are looking down the road.

The magazine found that time is the biggest issue working women face. As a result, more companies are beginning to realize the value of varying the traditional 40-hour work week and allowing flexible alternatives. For example, Aetna Life & Casualty has more than 2,000 people who do their jobs from home, which can also cut company overhead.

What can be done to fight this form of discrimination if you don't work for one of the progressive companies? Some of the responsibility must be taken by women, and many are standing up for this very personal right. With their efforts things seem to be changing, slowly but surely. In many workplaces, practices such as part-time work, flex time, and job sharing are no longer considered odd.

Fine, you may say. But your boss is still stuck in the old workaholic mentality and equates loyalty with slavery. What can you do? Aburdene and Naisbitt, authors of *Megatrends for Women,* advise that you needn't wait for your company to take the first step. You can negotiate the life and work style that works for you. Come up with a proposal, and show your employer how it will work. With laptop computers, modems, cellular telephones, and other technical advances, it's becoming easier to work at home, and this can save an employer money, as well as increase your productivity. Find some examples in your field through associates, trade journals, professional groups, or any other source available, and show your boss how your idea has worked for someone else. If you would be willing to take a cut in pay or make adjustments to lower overhead, say so. Remember the old saying: Those who ask don't always get what they want, but those who don't ask never do.

Beth Ozmun, an attorney in Austin, Texas, described what worked for her in an article in *Barrister* magazine. When her daughter was born, she decided to propose a part-time arrangement to her law firm. She has compiled a list of potential negotiating points for others, particularly lawyers, who approach employers to request a part-time schedule. Her guidelines include the following eight tips:

1. Do your homework first. Know your firm's track record for allowing scheduling concessions.
2. Be up front. When you realize you won't be returning to work on a full-time basis, let the firm know.
3. Be discreet. Approach someone you know, trust, and/or work with often for support before making an official announcement.
4. Know your options. Set your own priorities for reduction in hours, loss of benefits, salary, client contact, responsibility. Rank these things and separate those you must have from others where there may be room for compromise.
5. Have one or more proposals. Think through a number of options you can offer the company. Propose a pay scale that reflects your reduced hours. Consider working as an independent contractor. Think about alternatives such as staff classification or other changes in your job description.
6. Know your selling points. Stress your positive attitude: Say that the change will be temporary, that you're willing to slow down your progress up the

corporate ladder, and that you won't cost the firm as much overhead. You are already trained and skilled and won't have to be replaced by a fresh recruit. If you have special talents, training, or an established clientele you will still service, emphasize this.

7. Know your limitations. If your job demands a kind of flexibility that you can't mesh with a part-time schedule, think seriously about switching to another area within your field.

8. Keep your eyes and ears open for other opportunities. That way, if your plan doesn't work, you're not left high and dry.

Many women are moving successfully in similar new directions, both in their present jobs and by starting business ventures of their own. Part-time, flex time, and job sharing—in which two workers generally share what was previously one full-time (or more than full-time) position—are becoming accepted alternatives in many companies and firms. The number of female entrepreneurs is at an all-time high, with a 50% increase since 1980. Plus, there are indications that corporate America is beginning to realize the value of the human talent that is lost when women are driven from the workplace. Fertility rates are on the rise, with the 1990 birthrate reported as the highest since 1963. Smart employers can see that unless they rethink old ideas about the work environment, they will lose essential human resources.

Even old professions dominated by males for centuries, in the decrepit traditions based on the workaholic father and stay-at-home mother, are showing signs of moving into the twentieth century. The tide seems to be turning, and those companies and firms willing to change with the times are seeing rewards of the kind the business world understands the best—those in the bottom line. Reports indicate that flexibility in employee scheduling, especially allowing part-time work arrangements, increases productivity and profits and gives the firm a competitive edge in the marketplace. Employers willing to allow their employees more flexible scheduling arrangements are rewarded with greater effort and loyalty among their workers. According to employers, the most common advantages to flex time are better employee morale; increased productivity; reduced absenteeism, tardiness, and overtime; better service to customers; lower turnover; and increased recruitment.

Businesses around the country are learning that when such accommodations are offered, talented people (and not just parents) at other firms are drawn to change over. This is becoming especially common in the world of law, known for brutal scheduling demands. One law firm that reduced its annual billable hour requirements to a figure that represented a more reasonable nine-to-five approach, far below most firms of a similar size, was inundated with truckloads of résumés, many from the country's best and brightest students and lawyers. Others have found that arrangements including part-time, job sharing, work at home, and flex time can reduce expenses, increase morale, lower turnover, and keep valuable employees who might otherwise leave to seek a more humane employer.

Child-care options seem to be improving for working parents, too. Some unions, especially those with a large female membership, have been leaders in making changes especially desirable to female workers. For example, the Amalgamated Clothing Workers of America was the first to establish its own child-care center, operated by the union and parent-workers.

Overall, today's society is placing less emphasis on money and more on meaning in life. The birthrate is on the rise, and at the same time companies are learning that they can't afford to lose good, trained workers. More fathers are taking parental leave. The number of companies offering child-care assistance for their workers is steadily rising as studies show the tremendous impact of this type of benefit. Working parents who are free of the distraction of worrying about their children have much higher morale, lower attrition, and greatly reduced absence and tardiness. Productivity and profits soar.

Of course, not every company has the ability to offer on-site day care, but those who can't are discovering many creative options. Some help subsidize the cost of day care or set up a relatively small child-care area with on-call staff to provide emergency day care for parents when their regular caregivers are unavailable or can't accommodate special needs, such as occasional evening care.

The same three choices available in any situation exist when a woman is pressured to sacrifice the needs of her family or lose hard-earned gains in her career. First, she can put up with it—as always, balancing the rewards with the costs. Do you really want to leave your two-month-old baby in day care 12 hours a day? Dedication should not have to mean selling your soul. If you feel that you must remain in a situation you dislike, is there something you can do to make this choice more tolerable or temporary? Only you and the other members of your family can make these tough choices.

Second, can you change the situation? Sometimes it's tough to separate unfounded fears from real threats. Most people have more choices than they think they do. You may not realize that alternatives are available simply because no one has ever tried anything different from the usual practice. At one law firm, a six-week maternity leave was the norm, with some women taking as little as four weeks. Everyone assumed that a short leave or quitting was the only choice. Then a woman decided she wanted to take a year's leave of absence and return to work part-time. There was the predictable grumbling, and the question of how this affects her accumulated seniority toward partnership remains unsettled. But she has the schedule she wanted, because she asked for it.

Your third choice, again, is to leave. This may be the step you need to take. Search your own soul. If you decide to leave, don't feel as though you have caved in or done something wrong. Eric Sirotkin says that the people who leave are often the happiest. For them, there is a sense of closure, of putting something unpleasant behind and moving on. Remember, if you have suffered discrimination you can still bring your case.

If this is the choice you make, don't let anyone make you feel guilty. Child care is one of the most important and least valued jobs in our society, whether it's performed by mothers or child-care workers. Some women who have chosen to be full-time mothers until their children are older have learned that this can enhance their careers. Dr. Patricia Murphy has found that the majority of women do not hit their career stride until they are around 40, whether they have children or not. Many men are following similar patterns as career changes are becoming more common among both sexes.

A sabbatical or job change can be a smart career move. One of my friends, a music teacher, took time off when his son was born. During this period, he developed his own private instruction business, which he is much happier pursuing.

Whatever your situation, if you are miserable, something has to give. The mommy track is the same as any other employment problem in that nothing will happen if people don't assert their power. The family rights of both men and women are gradually gaining importance, but obviously we have a long way to go. Don't let yourself be bullied into doing what's not right for you, whether it's being denied a reasonable maternity leave, being forced to take a longer leave than you want, or having your seniority threatened because of your choices. If you do, you're being unfair to yourself, your family, and others who need leaders willing to push for change. You may not be 100% successful in getting everything you ask for, but so what? At least you tried. And you never know—sometimes you will get what you ask for, or even something better.

In short, the bulk of the problem rests with attitudes and values—things that are slow and difficult to change. But many employers and the law are finally beginning to show some real progress.

## The Law and Other Family Choices

A pregnant woman often will lose her job because, the employer claims, she had poor job performance not related to her pregnancy, or she could not perform the functions required for the job. Timing is important. If the employee's reviews had found her job performance adequate, then suddenly plummeted when she announced her pregnancy, this is highly suspicious. Also, the job requirement must be a real requirement, not a preference. Some of the justifications offered by employers in court cases are incredible. A waitress was fired because her boss thought having a pregnant waitress "looked tacky."

An employer may wait until the worker has her baby or returns after maternity leave, then discharge or demote her. This is especially common when the mother is single. In most cases, discharging a pregnant employee or single mother because of her marital status violates Title VII.

Echoes of the old protective laws are still heard in the troubling area of fetal vulnerability policies. These policies limit pregnant women or, in some cases, all women who might become pregnant, from jobs that involve exposure to chemicals, toxins, or other substances that might cause reproductive injury.

This is a highly controversial topic. Although most would agree that an employer may be legitimately concerned when pregnant workers are exposed to harmful substances in the workplace (for both humanitarian and liability reasons), many of these policies are overbroad or unfairly applied. For example, women have been excluded from jobs where there is little proof that the materials they use are truly hazardous. The harmful impact of continued wage gaps, unemployment, and fewer job opportunities on both the woman and her offspring cannot be ignored. In an especially shocking situation reported in 1978, five women working at a chemical company underwent unwanted sterilizations because they feared they would lose their jobs.

Several court cases have looked at these policies. In one case, the court reminded the employer that it had a duty to find a less discriminatory alternative than forcing a female X-ray technician to resign after she became pregnant. In addition, the employer is required to consider whether devices such as protective filter masks could allow the worker to continue safely on the job.

In others, fetal protection policies have been allowed, but only if the employer shows strong scientific evidence that there is a substantial risk of harm to the offspring of the worker, that the harm is confined to only one sex, and the policy effectively eliminates the risk. Where such policies have been allowed to stand, they have often been narrowed. For example, one employer's policy presumed that all women between the ages of 5 and 63 were fertile!

One positive side effect of these cases is that the effects of such toxins on all workers, male and female, have been explored. In some cases, even where existing OSHA standards were implemented, courts have found that chemicals had harmful effects on the reproductive capacities of both sexes—but true to the protective tradition, only women had been restricted from exposure.

## Sexual Harassment

Sexual harassment has been much in the news since the Senate confirmation hearings of Supreme Court Justice Clarence Thomas in 1991. But the problem has been around for centuries, though it has only received official recognition in the law as a form of discrimination for a period of less than 20 years.

Sexual harassment impacts on your right to equal compensation in several ways. First, men who treat women as objects prove their disrespect for women as equals in the workplace. They will almost certainly outright oppose or at least fail to support policies giving women equal opportunity to advance into positions of authority. Psychologists agree that forced sexual attention—whether it be rape or harassment on the job—is about power more than it is about sex. The perpetrators want to keep you in what they believe is "your place." Sexual harassment causes loss of self-confidence and self-esteem, and prevents both the victim and others from seeing her as an able, competent, and equal worker.

In addition to the costs to the individual, there are serious costs to society and industry when sexual harassment is allowed to continue. A federal government study in the early 1980s estimated that the government alone lost $189 million over a two-year period due to job turnover, absenteeism, medical insurance claims, and reduced productivity, all because of sexual harassment.

As prevalent as harassment is, a great deal of confusion still surrounds this uncomfortable topic. The easiest type of sexual harassment to identify as sex discrimination—and the first kind to be recognized as clearly illegal—is called quid pro quo sexual harassment. This occurs when an employer conditions a raise, promotion, continued employment, or other employment benefits on the employee's submission to sexual demands. Obviously, this amounts to sex discrimination in its most insidious form, and workers who have taken their employers to court for such behavior have been handsomely compensated, and the employers severely punished.

The second type of sexual harassment is called hostile work environment. This generally occurs where an employer allows employees to engage in a pattern of behavior that interferes with female employees' ability to work by creating an offensive, demeaning, hostile, or intimidating work environment.

In determining whether a particular behavior is sexual harassment, the standard is what is offensive to a reasonable person (or, some say, to a reasonable woman). If you are especially sensitive to certain things that would not offend most others, such as common swear words, that does not make the action sexual harassment.

It is essential to assess any situation carefully because of the immense damage done when a woman cries sexual harassment where none exists. Not only is there damage to the man accused, the woman herself, and the workplace, but "cry wolf" cases of false or mistaken charges make it harder for the woman who is truly harassed to get others to believe her. This kind of backlash is becoming a serious problem in some companies. And while no one with any scruples would ever intentionally make a false claim of harassment, some sensitive women misperceive a gesture or comment as having sexual overtones where none are intended.

This is not to say that you should ever put up with behavior that makes you uncomfortable, no matter what the other person's intentions may be. But tread lightly until you are sure. Some people are simply more "touchy-feely" than others. If you have a boss who is a hugger, and you would prefer he not hug you, find a way to tell him in a friendly, nonaccusatory way that you're just not used to physical affection on the job. If he persists, then you know there is a problem. But good people often do not realize their behavior offends, and it's both unfair and unprofessional to jump to conclusions before you try a more gentle approach.

This also relates to the requirement that the conduct be unwelcome. You are expected to let the offender know if his conduct makes you uncomfortable. This often will be enough. Many women find dirty jokes funny; many do not. If the joke-ster hasn't been told, he won't know if his humor is unwelcome. Likewise, if creepy Rick from the packing department asks you out on a date once, this is certainly not sexual harassment. On the other hand, if creepy Rick is your supervisor, asks you out every day even after you've made it clear you don't want to date him, and subtly suggests that going out with him could enhance your promotion opportunities, this is sexual harassment.

It's an especially tricky area because of all the subtle dynamics of the workplace. Behavior that may be perfectly legal and considered by most to be normal in a nonwork environment—such as telling raunchy jokes, decorating the walls with *Playboy* centerfolds, commenting on a woman's physical attributes—is usually inappropriate in the workplace, and if extreme or constant, it is enough to constitute a hostile work environment and sexual harassment.

What kind of behavior can create this type of hostile environment? Courts agree that it has to be severe enough or pervasive enough to alter the working conditions and create a work environment that is abusive. This is decided by looking at the situation as a whole, or what the law calls the "totality of the circumstances." This means that no one, single factor is required, and a series of events can add up to harassment, even if any one event would not be that serious by itself. In *Sanchez v. Miami Beach,* a female police officer sued the city of Miami Beach. The court found that being forced to work around "a plethora of sexually offensive posters, pictures, graffiti and pinups" and listen to "innumerable childish, yet offensive sexual and obscene innuendos and incidents aimed at her on the basis of sex" created a hostile, abusive, and offensive working environment. The Miami Police Department did have a policy banning sexual harassment, giving responsibility to supervisors to prevent such behavior and providing discipline for violators. But the fact that the city had a policy but failed to enforce it was probably more damaging than having no policy at all.

However, sexual harassment does not necessarily involve prurient or overtly sexual conduct. A hostile environment is often created when a person is treated differently from other employees only on the basis of her sex. It is only necessary to show that gender is a substantial motivating factor in the treatment, and that if the worker had been a man, she would not have been treated that way. For example, when co-workers spread rumors that a person has poor work skills, complain about her work without reason, steal her equipment, mimic and make fun of her, or threaten her safety, this can create a hostile work environment. Another example is when a supervisor gives a woman heavier work assignments than the male workers, allows her less help, sends her to less desirable locations, allows derogatory or condescending remarks to be made about her, and does nothing to stop the mistreatment. In one 1988 case, male members of a construction crew decided to show a woman on the site that she was unwelcome by urinating into the gas tank of her car. The court found this was indeed sexual harassment. This was obviously a hostile and offensive thing to do, and the message was clear: The woman was not welcome on the job because of her gender.

In a hostile work environment type of sexual harassment case, it is important to gather support from co-workers if possible. The more evidence of incidents directed toward women besides yourself in the workplace, the better. Even if your co-workers do not want to join in your claim, having them as potential witnesses can be very powerful whether your case goes to trial or not.

Make sure to keep careful records of what goes on, how often, and how severe it is. One nude pinup does not a hostile environment make, but a hundred of them strategically located so they are visible to all employees just might. Erotic but not obscene photos change the picture, so to speak. It depends on the seriousness, frequency, and pervasiveness of the acts or exhibitions, and the courts will look at the total setting.

As with other types of discrimination, the worker faced with sexual harassment has a number of choices in how to deal with the problem. Three of your choices are definitely to be avoided. First, never give in to a harasser's demands. Remember, sexual harassment is defined as unwanted sexual attention from a supervisor, co-worker, customer, or client. If you give in to unwanted demands for any sexual behavior, you are degrading yourself and sending a message to the perpetrator that he can get away with this. Don't let him, no matter what.

The second common mistake is to ignore the person and simply try to avoid the issue. It's easy to see why this route is tempting. If you ignore the creep, he may eventually give up and leave you alone, but he may still get away with his vile behavior, by harassing someone else. If the person is your supervisor or in a position to affect your opportunity to advance in this company or others, avoidance is not practical or desirable. A 1993 decision of the U.S. Supreme Court made it clear that a woman does not have to prove that she suffered psychological harm to win her case. You do not need to endure the harassment until you are on the verge of a nervous breakdown. Insist it stop immediately.

Third, you can quit the job. Sometimes this may be the best choice. But you still can still see to it that the perpetrator is punished and the behavior stopped. Otherwise, you will be selling yourself short and allowing the harasser to get away with it. You shouldn't be driven from a job you want to keep, and you don't have to be.

This leaves the alternative of doing something to stop the behavior. As with all problems in the workplace, there are many ways this can be done. Very often, an unmistakable order to cut it out will do the trick. When I was tending bar in college, I worked in a small saloon with limited space behind the bar. On a busy night, there was little room for three bartenders to move around, so bumping into one another was inevitable. However, one of the guys always managed to run his hand across my posterior as he passed behind me. It was a minor annoyance in my mind, and I was too busy to give it much thought. But one night when we were especially swamped he did it again. I simply lost my temper and yelled, "Get your hand off my butt!" A number of his friends were sitting right in front of me. They laughed at him, and he turned red in the face and slunk away. He never bothered me again. It never occurred to me that I was being harassed; the term *sexual harassment* hadn't yet been coined. In my mind it was just a matter of setting a jerk straight. This is usually the best place to start.

If this doesn't work, the next step to take is to complain to someone above the harasser. Employers who are made aware of sexual harassment are required by Title VII and other laws to take all necessary steps to stop the harassment and prevent it from happening again. This may include disciplining the harasser, implementing a policy prohibiting harassing practices, or conducting programs to educate the employees about sexual harassment.

The rules of what your company must do to protect you are slightly different depending on whether the harasser is your supervisor or a co-worker. The EEOC guidelines, which are often used by the courts, include two important rules on employer responsibility. First, the employer is absolutely responsible for the acts of his *supervisory employees,* regardless of whether the employer knew or should have known that the acts occurred.

Second, your employer is responsible for the acts of your fellow employees (at the same level or below) where the employer (or his supervisory employees) knew or should have known about the conduct, unless he can show that he took immediate corrective action. A hostile environment can't be allowed to continue. This standard also applies to harassment by customers or clients.

As mentioned in chapter 2, if you are a government employee, you may also be able to bring a claim under Section 1983 that sexual harassment violated your constitutional right to equal protection under the law. In order to prove this type of case, you will have to show that the harassment is part of a custom or practice condoned by your employer. In one case, a female firefighter won by showing that sexual harassment was business as usual at the fire department where she worked. She proved that it was ongoing and accepted, and that the supervisory and management officials—the people responsible for the working conditions at the department—not only knew about it but also participated in the behavior.

Sexual harassment can cause devastating damage to a career and terrible emotional pain. Under Title VII, Section 1983, and state common law claims, damages can be recovered for emotional distress. It is not necessary to show that you were demoted, lost an opportunity to advance, or were fired or otherwise forced out of your job.

If the harassment involved unwelcome physical touching, confinement to an area against your will, coerced sex acts, or other behavior intended to intimidate or frighten you, you may have claims for assault, battery, or other acts prohibited by both civil and criminal law in your states. In one case, a woman recovered on a state common law claim of tortious interference with contractual relations when sexual harassment interfered with her ability to do her job and earn a living.

Many of the torts described previously are also crimes. Most states have laws against fraud, blackballing, assault, and battery. You may want to contact a local law enforcement agency. This is especially important if the harassment caused you physical injury or if you were sexually assaulted. Don't hesitate to call the police immediately, and never let the perpetrator intimidate you with threats. Get witnesses, if there are any, even if they didn't witness the actual incident. They may be able to help place the criminal at the scene or provide other information. Don't wait until you have calmed down, showered, or seen a doctor to report the incident to the police (though you should see a doctor right away if you are hurt or have been sexually assaulted, of course). Much of the essential evidence in this type of case disappears quickly. Also, reporting the incident to the police right away helps show your credibility later if the perpetrator tries to deny what happened. It also helps in a civil suit as well.

Under Title VII, you can't directly sue your co-workers for sexual harassment (although as mentioned above, you may have common law or other claims against them for battery, assault, or other torts). But you can sue your employer under Title VII, as well as many state antidiscrimination laws, for allowing your co-workers to harass you continually and/or turn the place where you work into a hostile environment.

Don't ever tolerate sexual harassment. You are entitled to work in an environment where you are treated with respect. Also, from a practical standpoint, if you allow the harassment to continue, then decide it eventually becomes intolerable, the fact that you did not speak up earlier can hurt your legal claims. Tell both the harasser and your supervisor what is happening and that you expect it to stop. You can get help from many private organizations such as rape crisis centers, campus women's centers, or groups listed in the Appendix.

The NOW Legal Defense Fund produces a free information packet on sexual harassment. The packet includes a sample letter to be sent to someone who is sexually harassing you. The letter can be tailored to suit your particular set of facts and is designed to let the harasser know in no uncertain terms what the sexual harassment is and what will happen if it does not stop.

## Other Types of Abuse and Intimidation

Your employer has a legal duty to provide a work environment for you that is safe and reasonably comfortable. This includes a duty to protect you from other employees. When Becky Ralston worked in print sales, she was required to oversee the jobs she contracted with her clients from start to finish. She had to communicate the essential requirements of each individual order to the press room workers, then follow through until the job was finished, including overnight press checks during the course of the final printing. While she generally got along well with the plant workers, one of the press room supervisors deeply resented what he perceived to be a woman telling him or his pressmen how their job was to be done. He made threatening remarks to her on three occasions, telling her she had better stay away from his presses and his workers or she'd "get it." The first two times time this occurred, Ralston ignored him and went on about her business. But when he threatened her at 3 A.M. in a dark area of the plant, she was genuinely frightened. "I went straight to my desk put everything that had happened in writing, in a formal, detailed letter to the general manager," she recalls. "After that, I never had any problems with this man. I wish now that I had done it after the first time he threatened me."

This is what is supposed to happen when an employee is threatened, harassed, or intimidated. Your boss is required to put a stop to such behavior. Don't be hesitant to speak out if a co-worker is behaving unprofessionally, and don't wait until you're truly terrified. Violence in the workplace is one of the most rapidly increasing areas of violent crime. We read about disgruntled and deeply disturbed employees going on shooting sprees. Usually, after the tragedy, the individual's co-workers will recall threats, odd behavior, or loss of temper beyond what could be considered normal that could have tipped them off that this person had serious problems. No one likes to get a fellow worker in trouble, but by speaking out you may be saving yourself and your co-workers from injury or even death. The law guarantees you a safe workplace. Don't hesitate to insist on it.

## One Woman's Story

In 1981 Barbara Bovee began working for the New Mexico State Highway Department, an agency with a very strong male tradition. She progressed to the rank of supervising construction engineer in her third year, managing the largest project in the state. She consistently received positive performance evaluations and praise for doing exceptional work.

But the workplace was never welcoming toward female employees. Rude comments were common, and the women were forced to work in areas festooned with pornographic pin-ups. When one woman complained about the pinups, Barbara noticed a campaign of subtle retaliation against the woman. Her supervisors denied her access to information she needed to complete her work, and then criticized her for not meeting deadlines. In short, Barbara says, they set her up.

From the start, Barbara also noted that she was given a heavier workload and less help than her male counterparts. Women who complained inevitably faced retaliation. "These tactics were commonly used by the department to force people out," she explained. "The state personnel procedures are so rough when someone is fired that actual discharges were rare. So if they wanted someone to leave, they made it impossible for them to stay. Men never faced this treatment unless they did something truly bad, like stealing or risking the safety of others. All a woman had to do was complain and the pattern would start."

Barbara was disturbed by this. She knew it was wrong, but she didn't want to rock the boat or risk her job. Plus, with her background, she had a hard time believing the problem was real. Barbara had never faced sex discrimination before, although she had attended a predominantly male high school and studied engineering in college with a majority of male students. She had always enjoyed a good rapport with men. So she decided to work hard and expected she would be recognized and rewarded for her abilities.

Six years later, Barbara was still working hard—far harder than men in the same position—with three times the workload, yet only 40% of the help the males who supervised construction crews were given. Her only promotions had been those required by the state based on time spent in a particular job classification. Her reviews were still excellent. Yet she was consistently passed over for merit promotions, all of which went to men. She was consistently understaffed and forced to work overtime without compensation.

Barbara was then asked to serve on the STRIDE committee—a loose acronym for Striving for Departmental Equality. The committee was formed in response to an inquiry by a state legislator about why there were not more women in management in the Highway Department. Its purpose was to ascertain why there were few women in management, and to determine whether pay inequity and other forms of discrimination existed.

Due to her isolation from other professional women Barbara was of the opinion she was the only woman experiencing inequitable treatment compared to male employees in similar jobs. Through her association with the other men and women appointed to the committee she soon realized the problem was systemic. At the end of three years she was the fourth woman to chair the committee—the three women who had previously held that position had left the department under questionable circumstances. But the committee completed its study and found that women were not given the same opportunities as men. Their recommendations to the department included correcting inequities in pay as well as in training and recruitment procedures. They also recommended eliminating pinups and exercising more control over inappropriate comments and other sexist behavior in the workplace.

The report was whitewashed, however. Upper management blamed the problems on an inadequate applicant pool and said that this should have been the finding of the committee. A high ranking official at the department stated that the finding wasn't anything new and he had hoped for a more novel solution. A short time later, Barbara was again passed over for a promotion in favor of a man. Her supervisor justified the decision by saying the man had a family to support.

These problems were minor compared with what happened in 1988 when she began to assist another woman who had been sexually harassed. Until this time, she had maintained a good working relationship with her direct supervisor, who always praised her work and referred to her as one of his favorite project managers. When she agreed to be the woman's department representative, retaliation against her began in earnest.

"Things went downhill fast," she says. "The supervisors tried to do everything they could to keep me from helping this woman. My boss gave me an extra workload, then asked me point-blank if I thought I would still have time to help her. I just took the work and told him sure, I would have time."

Barbara did her best to fulfill even the extra burden and continue to represent her colleague, as the retaliation got steadily worse. In fall of 1988, she was in charge of the largest highway construction project in the state, a multimillion-dollar endeavor. Yet she was transferred to an office with no computer and no telephone. She was also threatened, insulted, harassed, and intimidated. Her performance evaluations suddenly dropped. She was denied vacation time, comp time, sick and educational leave. When she made complaints, they were ignored, and management did nothing to protect her from abusive conditions.

Finally, she filed a complaint about the retaliation with the department according to federally-mandated internal grievance procedures. An internal investigation was conducted. The "official" finding Barbara received stated that there was "insufficient evidence" of retaliation. But Barbara later learned that the report had been altered. The original found that retaliation had occurred, and she had cause to litigate.

In the meantime, however, Barbara continued working hard. She was often required to put in a 60- or 70-hour week while continuing to serve on the STRIDE committee and representing her co-worker. Predictably, the retaliation got worse. She was still responsible for difficult, important work, but denied the opportunity to enjoy her accomplishments. For example, she was excluded from a final inspection of the largest highway construction project in the state—a project she had supervised. Then she was assigned one job 90 miles south of her office location and another job 40 miles to the east, in addition to office work not pertaining to either project. She was expected to travel to both sites as well as complete her office duties every day.

Barbara still had hope that she might be able to resolve her problems, so she filed a complaint with the local EEOC office in early 1989. It took 18 months before the agency made an on-site investigation, which was hurried and relied a good deal on the department's whitewashed report. The investigation was still pending when Barbara decided to sue. Since the employer received federal funds, a right-to-sue letter had to be issued by the Department of Justice.

Meanwhile, Barbara continued to do her best under increasingly difficult conditions. The same abuses continued, and she felt increasingly isolated from her co-workers. Her staff reported to a different office than the one where she worked. Her performance evaluations took a radical dive, even though she was managing to complete her work and do a good job despite the obstructions. Her faults were outlined as "failure to communicate," "failure to act for the good of the departmernt," and "not a team player."

Then, in 1989, Barbara was again asked to act as a departmental representative for another woman. She agreed and found herself in a very upsetting situation. The woman was a maintenance laborer who had worked for the Highway Department in this capacity for 14 years. She had been raped by her supervisor. Even though she filed a complaint, she was left under his supervision, and he retaliated by making her do work she was prohibited from doing by her doctor due to an on-the-job injury. By the time an internal hearing was scheduled, the woman was on medical leave because the work had aggravated her condition.

Barbara attended an internal hearing in which the woman was forced to tell her story to a room full of men who showed no compassion and instead asked accusatory questions such as "Couldn't you have fought him off?" The woman was nervous, inarticulate, and embarrassed, and by this time did not want to pursue the complaint further. The final result? The woman was fired.

"After this, I was truly disgusted," Barbara said. "But it wasn't over yet." Barbara was asked to represent yet another employee who had also been raped by her supervisor under very similar circumstances. Because this woman worked at a distant location, Barbara did not feel she could represent her. But she did file an anonymous complaint with the union, and the woman filed her own internal complaint. In this case, the woman was again forced to work with the rapist for some time, then was transferred to a job site miles from her home, with no transportation. The supervisor was transferred too, but he was given a company vehicle and per diem, daily expenses.

By this time Barbara was so incensed that her determination to proceed with her own complaint was reinforced. She began to give serious thought to filing a lawsuit.

"I had several advantages in preparing to go to court," she says. "First, I am a strong person to begin with. I was single and independent, and didn't have other problems like commitments at home to deal with during the process. I had a lot of time to devote to the issue. Second, I had worked on many court cases in my job involving contract disputes, accidents, and others. I knew something about the law, so I could do some research on my own. Most important, I knew the game plan. Management would try to make you hysterical so they could bring it up in hearings and in court to make you look bad. I knew the strategy they would use and the strategy I had to use. So throughout the whole process, I made myself stay objective. I could have easily been lost in cynicism and sympathy for the other women, but instead I looked at how I could use any details to win my case and help others. I detached myself from the emotion and made rational, calculated decisions."

Not surprisingly, this proved to be difficult. "I had to work every day with the people who were involved in all the retaliation and other discrimination. I had to sit down with them and discuss work matters. It wasn't easy to maintain that control. But you have to know what you're up against and have power over it to be successful."

By 1990 Barbara was getting frustrated with the EEOC delays. She was ready to file suit, but she was hesitant. She still had hope that the problems might be resolved by the EEOC and the work of the STRIDE committee, and she had worked on enough construction lawsuits to understand what an ordeal a trial could be. But then her direct supervisor, who had engineered the retaliation that had been making her life miserable and her job impossible, was appointed to the STRIDE committee. She realized that there would be virtually no chance of an internal solution. That was the last straw.

At this point Barbara began looking for an attorney. Several lawyers she knew recommended Eric Sirotkin, so she retained him. The ACLU also offered to represent Barbara free of charge, but Barbara decided to stay with Sirotkin. In October of 1990 Barbara filed suit against the State Highway Department, her direct supervisor, and six others. The suit charged retaliation for exercise of her First Amendment rights and sex discrimination in violation of her right to equal protection under the law (both under 42 U.S.C. 1983).

By this time Barbara didn't think things could get any worse, but she was unpleasantly surprised. She began to get threats, and the retaliation took an ugly turn. On one occasion, she got a call in the middle of the night reporting an accident at one of her project sites. According to her duty as a supervisor, she got up and traveled to the site, only to learn that no accident had happened. At the end of the workday, she would go to her car and discover that the lights, wipers, and radio were on. Her car was always locked and showed no signs of a break-in, so someone had apparently copied her keys.

Barbara knew there was a campaign being waged to force her out, but she was determined not to give in. The pretrial work progressed, and Barbara learned then that the first report on her internal complaint had been altered. She got a copy of the original report, which found that retaliation had indeed occurred.

A settlement conference was scheduled in the summer of 1992. One month before the conference, she received a performance evaluation, which rated her work as "average." About two weeks later, she received a six-page letter of reprimand, containing a litany of contrived complaints—such things as defective paint on structures, even though Barbara had no responsibility for the paint or painting operations, which had taken place at the fabricator's plant in Colorado. Also, the reprimand appeared to be part of a weak strategy to confuse a jury if the case went to trial. It was written in complex, highly technical language, so Barbara wrote her reply in simple, straightforward terms.

At the settlement conference, the department made an offer, but both Barbara and her attorney felt it was far too low. Trial was eminent. Then, at work, her supervisor went berserk. "I was lucky I wasn't there," she says. "I was told that he was holding a sledgehammer and began shouting that it was all my fault. He threatened me and the women I'd helped, and he knocked holes in the walls. He said, "The next time someone around here pisses me off I'm gonna fire their ass." He was off work for a couple of weeks after that. So what happened when he came back? He got promoted!"

Barbara's working conditions were becoming unbearable. "Before, I was losing sleep because I was mad," she says. "Now I was losing sleep because of fear." The worst part was the effect on her co-workers. "My crew was afraid. They knew this man and thought he might come after me at some remote job site or even in the office. Some of them started bringing guns to work." Barbara finished the projects she was working on and then resigned in December 1992, shortly before the trial was scheduled to begin. "I felt I was in a lose-lose situation. The outcome of the trial wasn't relevant. The retaliation would intensify after court."

The trial itself was difficult, even though Barbara was fully aware of what she was getting into. Barbara knew what to expect. She knew her employer would say she hadn't done her job. But she had objective proof—documents and records—to overcome this. The hardest part was the subjective assessment and the psychological evaluation. "In this type of case, your opponent can make you see a psychologist of their choosing," she explains. "The worst part of the trial was hearing someone get up and say things that were not true—that I was crazy."

Barbara had been seeing a psychologist of her own, initially to understand why these men were acting unfairly, and then to help her cope with the stress, anxiety, and loss of sleep she had suffered since things deteriorated on the job. This doctor, as well as another who worked with Barbara after the litigation started, testified that she was very healthy until the continued abuse at work directly caused anxiety, depression, and stress disorder. But even this was hard for Barbara to have aired in public. "I didn't want the defendants to know how much they had injured me," she explains. "And even though the press was fair and reported what both psychologists said in court, it's very hard to read in the paper that someone says you're crazy and says other things about you that just aren't true. It's even worse to think that all of your friends, co-workers, and everyone you know will read this, too."

But Barbara had been fortunate in an important way. She had always been well liked on the job. Most of her co-workers supported her once her suit was filed, though they didn't know the details of her internal complaint or her representation of the other women, because of internal policy requiring confidentiality. Also, some had backed away from her earlier, out of fear. "When people are in an environment like this, they sometimes shun the person going through it out of fear for their own jobs. Some of my friends quit talking to me at work, but when the suit got going, they spoke up. They didn't let me down in the end."

Several of the men she had worked with testified on her behalf at the trial. Barbara actually received more support from the men at her job than from the women. "Women have to stick by other women when something like this is going on," she says. "I got more support from the men, especially when the retaliation became obvious. I couldn't have made it without their support."

Despite the unpleasant nature of the case, relations between the attorneys on the case remained businesslike and professional throughout the lawsuit and trial. "It's much better to avoid getting into an adversarial situation," she emphasizes. "When you're in court, you have to listen to people making accusations and saying terrible things about you, then get up on the witness stand and smile and act professional. You can't get emotional. You have to show the jury that what the others are saying is not true."

Barbara also knew the importance of a making a good visual impression on the jury. "Appearances are essential. You have to be very conscious of your demeanor, gestures, and manner of dress. For instance, when the defense psychologist was going to testify that I was this pathetic, crazy woman, I made sure I wore a suit that gave me a very powerful look."

During the pretrial motion process, the judge in Barbara's case ruled that much of the evidence, including evidence of the rapes, could not come in because of a rule that allows a judge to exclude evidence that is deemed more prejudicial than important to the case. "It's really hard to have to testify and leave certain things out—important things that you can't refer to or you will risk a mistrial," Barbara admits.

The trial was long and difficult, and the jury deliberated for more than two days. But the ordeal was well worth it. The jury awarded Barbara over $1.8 million—$900,000 in compensatory damages and $900,000 in punitive damages against three managers at the Highway Department. When the verdict was challenged by posttrial motions and the defendants filed an appeal, she settled the case for $725,000—still a handsome sum, received without delay and structured under the terms of the agreement so it would be nontaxable.

"I still have to wonder why they didn't try to correct the problems, why they didn't make any real effort to settle my case instead of pushing to trial," Barbara says. "By 1988, when I filed my complaint, these people knew me well enough to know that once I made up my mind, I would not back down. My supervisor saw me take control of meetings with tough contractors and back them into a corner to get my point across. They knew my abilities. This was one reason I had received good performance reviews. I was not easily intimidated."

Looking back, Barbara says she wouldn't change anything about the way she handled her situation. "I didn't make any snap decisions. I researched it, thought it out first, then came to an educated conclusion. I would tell other women in similar circumstances to try everything within reason to get your employer to change the behavior, but if they don't act like responsible individuals, then *you* have to make the change." She adds, "It's unfortunate that an individual has to go to this extreme in order to provide a dignified workplace for women."

Her attorney, Eric Sirotkin, said he hoped that employers would take notice and take charges seriously. "We often put a stigma on those who complain, rather than praise them," he says.

Barbara is also pleased that other women at the Highway Department have filed a complaint with the Department of Justice claiming a pattern and practice of discrimination. The investigation is under way.

As for Barbara, she is now pursuing a new career. Her final thoughts? "The courtroom process isn't about justice, it's about compensation. The settlement process isn't about compensation, it's about compromise. When it's over, get over it and get on with your life. Living well is the best revenge. I now drive over New Mexico's roads in my Mercedes-Benz."

## The Road Ahead

As we enter the mid-1990s, what can women on the job expect for the future? I believe there is every reason to be optimistic. The law continues to grow and develop so that nearly every woman working is now protected from sex discrimination.

True, the laws are increasingly complex, the agencies are overloaded, and fighting for your rights can be an exhausting, seemingly endless battle. But these very problems bring about more solutions. Increasing numbers of women are standing up for their rights and refusing to accept unfair treatment. The tools for winning equality are in place, they are being used, and they work. The wheels of justice do turn slowly, with a lot of squeaks and groans, but they do turn, as Barbara Bovee and countless others have learned.

Moreover, attitudes and values are changing. Overall, the wage gap has narrowed sharply in the past 10 years. Employers are learning the importance of treating their workers with dignity and respect. They are seeing the rewards of keeping good workers satisfied and encouraging each and every person to reach his or her potential. More and more companies are progressing toward greater diversity and tolerance through such innovations as flex-time work, new styles of management, and better access to advancement opportunities.

Individually and collectively, through public support and in the private sector, we are moving toward a time when true equality in the workplace will be the norm. In the meantime, we must continue to do whatever is necessary to insist on our rights and reap the rewards we have earned. We're *all* worth it!

# RESOURCES AND
# SUGGESTED READINGS

Abramson, Joan. *Old Boys, New Women: The Politics of Sex Discrimination.* New York: Praeger Publishers, 1979.

Abramsky, Michael F. "Work Traumas and Psychological Damage." *Trial,* July 1992, 48–52.

Aburdene, Patricia and John Naisbitt. *Megatrends for Women.* New York: Villard Books, 1992.

"After 30 Years of 'Equal Pay,' Women's Pay 70% of Men's." (AP) *Daily Pantagraph,* June 7, 1993, Section D.

Anderson, Howard J. and Michael D. Levin-Epstein. *Primer of Equal Employment Opportunity.* Washington, D.C.: Bureau of National Affairs, 2d Ed. 1982.

Austin, Nancy K. "Create a Pocket of Excellence." *Executive Female,* January/February 1992, 42–45.

Austin, Nancy K. "Now About This Female Management Style . . ." *Executive Female.* September/October 1992, 48–51.

Baer, Judith A. *The Chains of Protection.* Westport, CT: Greenwood Press, 1978.

Bergman, Barbara R. *The Economic Emergence of Women.* New York: Basic Books, Inc., 1986.

Cahalan, Diane. *Americans With Disabilities Act* Chicago: American Labelmark Corp., 1993.

Cook, Alice H. *Comparable Worth: The Problem and States' Approaches to Wage Equity.* Honolulu: University of Hawaii at Manoa, 1983.

Cotton, Paul. "Women Scientists Explore More Ways to Smash Through the 'Glass Ceiling'." *Journal of the American Medical Association,* 268:2, July 8, 1992, 173.

Dusky, Lorraine. "The New Old Boy." *Glamour,* February, 1992, 162.

Fisher, Anne B. "When Will Women Get to the Top?" *Fortune,* September 21, 1992, 44–48.

Foner, Phillip S., Editor. *Frederick Douglass On Women's Rights.* Westport, CT: Greenwood Press, 1971.

Frug, Mary Joe. *Postmodern Legal Feminism.* New York: Routlege, 1992.

Graham, Gerald. "Term 'Facilitation' Signals Shift in Leadership Style." Knight-Ridder Newspapers, (AP) *Albuquerque Journal,* August 23, 1993. Business Outlook Section, Page 22.

Heim, Pat, with Susan K. Golant. *Hardball for Women.* Los Angeles: Lowell House, 1992.

Hellwig, Basia. "Executive Female's Breakthrough 50." *Executive Female,* September/ October 1992, 43–46.

Hewlett, Sylvia Ann. *A Lesser Life: The Myth of Women's Liberation in America.* New York: William Morrow & Co., Inc., 1986.

Husband, John M. "Legal Overview of Equal Pay and Comparable Worth." *The Colorado Lawyer,* July, 1986, 1201–1203.

Institute for Research on Women's Health: *Sexual Harassment and Employment Discrimination Against Women: A Consumer Handbook for Women Who Are Harmed and For Those Who Care.* Bethesda, MD: The Feminist Institute Clearinghouse, 1988.

Jennings, Ken and Robert L. Willits. "A Neglected Consideration in Sex-Based Wage Discrimination Cases." *Labor Law Journal,* July, 1986, 412–422.

Kagan, Julia. "Woman's Work: See How Our World Has Grown." *Executive Female,* September/October 1992, 52–57.

Kirby, Emily B. *Yes You Can: The Working Woman's Guide to Her Legal Rights, Fair Employment, and Equal Pay.* Englewood Cliffs, New Jersey: Spectrum/ Prentice Hall, Inc. 1984.

Kraszewski, Muriel. "I Fought the System—And Won." *Ladies' Home Journal,* November, 1992, 24.

Larson, E. Richard. *Sue Your Boss: Rights and Remedies for Employment Discrimination.* New York: Farrar, Straus & Giroux (1981).

Lusk, Alice. "The Jobs That Lead to Better Jobs." *Executive Female,* January/February 1992, 38–41.

"Magazine Credits Top Family Firms." *The Pantagraph,* September 16, 1993, D3.

Maupin, Joyce. *Talking Union.* San Francisco: Union W.A.G.E., 1979.

Moore, Lynda L. *Not as Far as You Think: The Realities of Working Women.* Lexington, Mass: D.C. Heath & Co., 1986.

Moskowitz, Milton and Carol Townsend. "Working Mother 100 Best: 8th Annual Survey." *Working Mother,* October, 1993, 28–69.

Murphy, Patricia. *Making the Connections: Women, Work and Abuse.* Winter Park, FL: PMD Publisher's Group, Inc. 1993.

Continuing Legal Education of New Mexico, Inc. *1993 Sex, Race, Employment and You.* Albuquerque: 1993.

Nelan, Bruce W. "Annie Get Your Gun." *Time,* May 10, 1993, 42–43.

Oehmke, Thomas H. *Sex Discrimination in Employment.* Detroit: Trends Publishing Co., 1974.

Omilian, Susan. *Sexual Harassment in Employment.* Wilmette, IL: Callaghan & Co., 1987.

O'Neill, June. "Women and Wages: Gender Pay Ratios." *Current,* March/April 1991, 10–16.

Painton, Priscilla. "The Maternal Wall." *Time,* May 10, 1993, 44–45.

Perry, Nancy J. "If You Can't Join 'Em, Beat 'Em." *Fortune,* September 21, 1992, 58–59.

Player, Mack A. *Federal Law of Employment Discrimination in a Nutshell.* St. Paul, MN: West Publishing, 3rd. Ed., 1992.

Reardon, Kathleen. "The Memo Every Woman Keeps in Her Desk." *Executive Female,* July/August 1993, 29.

Reich, Robert B. "The Day I Became a Feminist." *Executive Female,* March/April 1993, 48–51.

Reich, Robert B. *The Resurgent Liberal and Other Unfashionable Prophesies.* New York: Times Books, 1989.

Reynis, Lee A. *A Woman's Guide to the Workplace: A Self-Help Manual for New Mexico Women.* Albuquerque, NM: University of New Mexico, 1984.

Roberts, Cindy. "A Woman With Differential Ideas." *Associated Press,* 1993.

Rossein, Merrick T. *Employment Discrimination: Law and Litigation.* New York: Clark Boardman Co., Ltd., 1990.

Sachs, Andrea. "Desperately Seeking Daycare: The Secret Lives of Women Lawyers." *ABA Journal,* June 1993, 58–62.

Saltzman, Amy. "Trouble at the Top." *U.S. News and World Report,* June 17, 1991, 40–48.

Sirotkin, Eric. *Employment Law in New Mexico.* Clearwater, FL: Butterworth Legal Publishers, 1994.

Sirotkin, Eric and Advocates for Equal Rights. *How to Handle Employee Rights Litigation: A Nuts and Bolts Primer.* Albuquerque: CLE of New Mexico, 1993.

Smith, Anne Mollegen. "Clinton's Top Women." *Executive Female,* March/April 1993, 38–43.

Steinem, Gloria. *Outrageous Acts and Everyday Rebellions.* New York: Plume Books, 1984.

Swiss, Deborah and Judith Walker. *Women and the Work/Family Dilemma: How Today's Professional Women are Finding Solutions.* New York: John Wiley & Sons, 1993.

Task Force on Women and the Legal Profession. *Summary Report.* Albuquerque, NM: State Bar of New Mexico, 1991.

United States Commission on Civil Rights. *Comparable Worth: An Analysis and Recommendations.* Washington, D.C., United States Government Printing Office, 1985.

United States Department of Labor, Women's Bureau. *A Working Woman's Guide to Her Job Rights.* Washington, D.C.: United States Government Printing Office, 1992.

Wahl, Melissa. "Diversity Training—The Fun Way." *Executive Female,* March/April 1993, 20.

Watts, Patti. "Hey, That's My Idea!" *Executive Female,* November/December 1992, 61–62.

Webb, Marilyn. "Why We Don't Get Paid What We're Worth." *Ladies' Home Journal,* June, 1993, 110.

Whitehead, Geraldine Chelius. *Women in America.* Fort Worth: Sperry & Hutchinson Co., 1971.

"Women Trail Men in Business World." *Associated Press: The Pantagraph,* June 15, 1993.

Women's Labor Project of the National Lawyer's Guild. *Bargaining for Equality.* San Francisco: National Labor Law Center, 1981.

"Women's Rights Convention Site Added To Historical Park." *The Pantagraph,* September 16, 1993, C2.

Wyer, E. Bingo. "No Promotion in Sight? How to Move Ahead Anyway." *Executive Female,* November/December 1992, 29.

Zetlin, Minda. "I've Been Passed Over for a Promotion—Now What?" *Executive Female,* May/June 1993, 55–56.

# ACKNOWLEDGMENTS

Grateful acknowledgment is made for use of portions of the following:

"Making it Work" by Beth Ozmun, *Barrister* magazine, Vol. 20 No. 3, Fall, 1993. Copyright 1993, American Bar Association. Reprinted by permission. All rights reserved.

*Megatrends for Women* by Patricia Aburdene and John Naisbitt. Copyright 1992 by Megatrends, Ltd., Published by Villiard Books, a division of Random House, Inc. Reprinted by permission. All rights reserved.

"The Jobs That Lead to Better Jobs" by Alice Lusk. Reprinted from *Executive Female*, the official publication of the National Association for Female Executives (800-927-NAFE), copyright 1992 by the National Association for Female Executives, Inc. Used by permission. All rights reserved.

"I Fought the System—And Won" by Muriel Kraszewski, *Ladies' Home Journal*, © copyright 1992 Meredith Corporation. All rights reserved. Reprinted from Ladies' Home Journal Magazine with permission from the author, Andrea Gross.

"Women Scientists Explore More Ways to Smash Through the 'Glass Ceiling'" by Paul Cotton. *Journal of the American Medical Association*, 268:2, July 8, 1992, p. 173. Copyright 1992, American Medical Association. Used by permission. All rights reserved.

# APPENDIX

The following information is as accurate as I could possibly make it, but bear in mind that telephone numbers change, offices move, and organizations restructure frequently. If you have trouble reaching one of these offices, check with directory assistance in the appropriate city, or check the State or Federal "Yellow Book" in the reference section of your local library, or call the national headquarters of the organization or government office. Your reference librarian can give you additional ideas. TDD telephone numbers refer to Telecommunications Device for the Deaf. This list is by no means complete. I have tried to include all of the national groups and agencies I am familiar with that assist in achieving equal rights for working women. There are many fine organizations that operate on the local or regional level as well. Check your local telephone directory, newspapers, bulletin boards, the *Encyclopedia of Associations* and other books at your public library for other sources of information and help.

## FEDERAL AGENCIES: NATIONAL HEADQUARTERS

U.S. Equal Employment
Opportunity Commission
1801 L St. NW,
Washington, D.C. 20507
(202) 663-4900
(202) 663-4494 (TDD)
Or toll free:
(800) 669-EEOC
(800) 800-3302 (TDD)

The EEOC publishes several helpful brochures, including "EEOC Information for the Private Sector" and "Laws Enforced by the EEOC," which may be ordered free of charge by calling the numbers above.

U.S. Department of Labor
200 Constitution Avenue NW
Washington, D.C. 20210
General Information:
(202) 219-7316
Publication Information:
(202) 219-1221

The Department of Labor is divided into different offices which

serve different functions, including:
Job Training Partnership Act (JPTA) Programs
(202) 219-6236
Occupational Safety and Health Administration
(202) 219-8151

Office of Federal Contract Compliance Programs
Employment Standards Administration
(202) 219-9475

This office handles complaints for violations of Executive Order 11246. It has local offices listed in the US Government section of your telephone directory, or contact the national or closest regional office for a referral.

Office of Labor Management Standards
(202) 219-6065
Office of Workers' Compensation Programs
(202) 219-7503
Pension and Welfare Benefits Administration
(202) 219-8233
U.S. Employment Service
Employment and Training Administration
(202) 219-5257

This office, through more than 1700 offices nationwide, provides various employment information and services to job seekers.

Services include employability assessments, job counseling, training, referral, job placement, and information on job openings and opportunities, training programs, and the demand for particular types of work in various regions.

Veteran's Employment and Training Service
(202) 442-2VET
Wage and Hour Division
(202) 219-8305
Women's Bureau
(202) 219-6611

Federal Trade Commission
Sixth Street and Pennsylvania Avenue, NW
Washington, D.C. 20580
(202) 326-2222

Internal Revenue Service
U.S. Department of the Treasury
1111 Constitution Avenue, NW
Washington, D.C. 20224
(800) 829-1040
(800) 829-4059 (TDD)

National Labor Relations Board
1099 14th Street NW
Washington, D.C. 20570
(202) 273-1991
(800) 736-2983 (Toll-free hotline)

Pension Benefit Guaranty Corp.
1200 K Street NW
Washington, DC 20005-4026
(202) 326-4000

U.S. Department of Health and
Human Services
Office for Civil Rights
200 Independence Avenue SW
Washington, D.C. 20201
(202) 619-0403
(202) 863-0101 (TDD)
Social Security Administration
Baltimore, MD 21235
(800) 772-1213

U.S. Department of Justice
Civil Rights Division
P.O. Box 66118
Washington, D.C. 20035-6118
(202) 514-2151

Office of Special Counsel for
Immigration-Related
Unfair Employment Practices
(202) 616-5528

U.S. Small Business
Administration
Office of Equal Employment
Opportunity and Compliance
409 Third Street SW
Washington, DC 20416
(202) 205-6750
(800) 827-5722 (SBA hotline)

Office of Financial Assistance
(202) 205-6490

Office of Women's Business
Ownership
(202) 205-6673

# Department of Labor
# Regional Offices

Following is a list of the 10
regional offices of the U.S.
Department of Labor and the
states served by each. The telephone number of each of the agencies within each office, such as the
Women's Bureau and the Wage
and Hour division, should be
listed in the U.S. Government section of your telephone directory.

U.S. Department of Labor
1 Congress St.
Boston, MA 02114
(Connecticut, Maine,
Massachusetts, New Hampshire,
Rhode Island, Vermont)

U.S. Department of Labor
201 Varick St.
New York, NY 10014
(New York, New Jersey, Puerto
Rico, U.S. Virgin Islands)

U.S. Department of Labor
Gateway Building
3535 Market St.
Philadelphia, PA 19104
(Delaware, District of Columbia,
Maryland, Pennsylvania, Virginia,
West Virginia)

U.S. Department of Labor
1371 Peachtree St., NE
Atlanta, GA 30367
(Alabama, Florida, Georgia,
Kentucky, Mississippi, North
Carolina, South Carolina,
Tennessee)

U.S. Department of Labor
New Federal Building
230 S. Dearborn St.
Chicago, IL 60604
(Illinois, Indiana, Michigan,
Minnesota, Ohio, Wisconsin)

U.S. Department of Labor
Federal Building
525 Griffin St.
Dallas, Texas 75202
(Arkansas, Louisiana, New
Mexico, Oklahoma, Texas)

U.S. Department of Labor
Federal Office Building
911 Walnut St.
Kansas City, MO 64106
(Iowa, Kansas, Missouri,
Nebraska)

U.S. Department of Labor
Federal Office Building
1801 California St.
Denver, CO 80202-2614
(Colorado, Montana, North
Dakota, South Dakota, Utah,
Wyoming)

U.S. Department of Labor
71 Stevenson St.
San Francisco, CA 94105
(Arizona, California, Hawaii,
Nevada)
U.S. Department of Labor
1111 Third Ave.
Seattle, WA 98101-3211
(Alaska, Idaho, Oregon,
Washington)

# EEOC District Offices

The EEOC has 23 district offices,
one field office, and 26 area and
local offices that process charges
of discrimination. Information on
area and local offices that serve
your region can be obtained by
calling 1-800-669-4000. A list of
these offices and the locations they
serve follows.

Atlanta District Office
75 Piedmont Ave., NE, Suite 1100
Atlanta, GA 30335
(404) 331-6093
(404) 841-6091  (TDD)
(Georgia)

Baltimore District Office
111 Market Pl., Suite 4000
Baltimore, MD 21202
(301) 962-3932
(301) 922-6065  (TDD)
(Maryland, southwestern Virginia)

Birmingham District Office
1900 3rd Ave. N., Suite 101
Birmingham, AL 35203-2397
(205) 731-0082
(205) 229-0095  (TDD)
(Alabama, Mississippi)

Charlotte District Office
5500 Central Ave.
Charlotte, NC 28212
(704) 567-7100
(704) 628-7173  (TDD)
(North Carolina, South Carolina)

Chicago District Office
536 S. Clark St., Room 930-A
Chicago, IL 60605
(312) 353-2713
(312) 353-7173 (TDD)
(northern Illinois)

Cleveland District Office
1375 Euclid Ave., Room 600
Cleveland, OH 44115-1808
(216) 522-2001
(216) 942-7296 (TDD)
(Ohio)

Dallas District Office
8303 Elmbrook Dr.
Dallas, TX 75274
(214) 767-7015
(214) 729-7523 (TDD)
(Oklahoma, northern Texas)

Denver District Office
1845 Sherman St., 2nd Floor
Denver, CO 80203
(303) 866-1300
(303) 564-1950 (TDD)
(Colorado, Montana, Nebraska,
North Dakota, South Dakota,
Wyoming)

Detroit District Office
477 Michigan Ave., Room 1540
Detroit, MI 48226-9704
(313) 226-7636
(303) 226-7599 (TDD)
(Michigan)

Houston District Office
1919 Smith St., 7th Floor
Houston, TX 77002
(713) 653-3377
(713) 522-3367
(southeastern Texas)

Indianapolis District Office
46 E. Ohio St., Room 456
Indianapolis, IN 46204-1903
(317) 226-7212
(317) 331-5162 (TDD)
(Indiana, Kentucky)

Los Angeles District Office
3660 Wilshire Blvd., 5th Floor
Los Angeles, CA 90010
(213) 251-7278
(213) 251-7384 (TDD)
(southern California, Nevada)

Memphis District Office
1407 Union Ave., Suite 621
Memphis, TN 38104
(901) 722-2617
(901) 222-2604 (TDD)
(Arkansas, Tennessee)

Miami District Office
1 Northeast First St., 6th Floor
Miami, FL 33132-2491
(305) 536-4491
(305) 350-5721 (TDD)
(Florida, Canal Zone)

Milwaukee District Office
310 W. Wisconsin Ave., Suite 800
Milwaukee, WI 53203-2292
(414) 297-1111
(414) 362-1115 (TDD)
(Iowa, Minnesota, Wisconsin)

New Orleans District Office
701 Loyola Ave., Suite 600
New Orleans, LA 70114
(504) 589-2329
(504) 682-2958 (TDD)
(Louisiana)

New York District Office
90 Church St., Room 1501
New York, NY 10007
(212) 264-7161
(212) 264-7697 (TDD)
(Connecticut, Maine,
Massachusetts, New Hampshire,
New York, Rhode Island,
Vermont, Puerto Rico, Virgin
Islands)

Philadelphia District Office
1421 Cherry St., 10th Floor
Philadelphia, PA 19102
(215) 597-9350
(215) 597-5314 (TDD)
(Delaware, New Jersey,
Pennsylvania, West Virginia)

Phoenix District Office
4520 N. Central Ave., Suite 300
Phoenix, AZ 85012-1848
(602) 640-5000
(602) 261-2692 (TDD)
(Arizona, New Mexico, Utah)

San Antonio District Office
5410 Fredricksburg Rd., Suite 200
San Antonio, TX 78229-3555
(512) 229-4810
(512) 730-4858 (TDD)
(southwestern Texas)

San Francisco District Office
901 Market St., Suite 500
San Francisco, CA 94103
(415) 744-6500
(415) 484-7329 (TDD)
(Northern California, Hawaii,
American Samoa, Guam, northern
Mariana Islands, Wake Island)

Seattle District Office
2815 Second Ave., Suite 500
Seattle, WA 98121
(206) 553-0968
(206) 399-1362 (TDD)
(Alaska, Idaho, Oregon,
Washington)

St. Louis District Office
625 N. Euclid St., 5th Floor
St. Louis, MO 63108
(314) 425-6585
(314) 279-6547 (TDD)
(southwestern Illinois, Kansas,
Missouri)

Washington Field Office
1400 L St., Suite 200
Washington, DC 20005
(202) 275-7377
(202) 275-7518 (TDD)
(District of Columbia)

## Regional Offices of Other Federal Agencies

These agencies also provide
information and/or enforce various laws prohibiting sex discrimination:

REGION 1: CONNECTICUT,
MAINE, MASSACHUSETTS,
NEW HAMPSHIRE, RHODE
ISLAND, VERMONT

U.S. Department of Education
Office for Civil Rights
Post Office and Courthouse,
Room 222
Boston, MA 02109-4557
(617) 223-9662
(617) 223-9695 (TDD)

U.S. Department of Labor
Office of Federal Contract
Compliance Programs
One Congress St., 11th Floor
Boston, MA 02114
(617) 565-2055
(617) 223-4067 (TDD)

U.S. Department of Health and
Human Services
Office for Civil Rights
JFK Federal Building, Room 203A
Boston, MA 02203
(617) 565-1340
(617) 565-1343 (TDD)

U.S. Small Business
Administration
155 Federal St., 9th Floor
Boston, MA 02110
(617) 451-2023

REGION 2: NEW JERSEY, NEW
YORK, PUERTO RICO, VIRGIN
ISLANDS

U.S. Department of Education
Office for Civil Rights
26 Federal Plaza, 33rd Floor
New York, NY 10278-0082
(212) 264-4633
(212) 264-8797 (TDD)

U.S. Department of Labor
Office of Federal Contract
Compliance Programs
201 Varick St., Room 750
New York, NY 10014
(212) 337-2007

U.S. Department of Health and
Human Services
Office for Civil Rights
Jacob Javits Federal Building
26 Federal Plaza, Suite 3312
New York, NY 10278
(212) 264-3313
(212) 264-3656 (TDD)

U.S. Small Business
Administration
26 Federal Plaza, Room 31-08
New York, NY 10278
(212) 264-7772

REGION 3: DELAWARE,
DISTRICT OF COLUMBIA,
MARYLAND, PENNSYLVANIA,
VIRGINIA, WEST VIRGINIA

U.S. Department of Education
Office for Civil Rights
3535 Market St., Room 6300
Philadelphia, PA 19104-3326
(215) 596-6791
(215) 596-6794 (TDD)

U.S. Department of Labor
Office of Federal Contract
Compliance Programs
Gateway Building
3535 Market St., Room 15240
Philadelphia, PA 19104
(215) 596-6168
(215) 596-6186 (TDD)

U.S. Department of Health and
Human Services
Office for Civil Rights
3535 Market St., Room 6350
Philadelphia, PA 19101
(215) 596-5831
(215) 596-5195  (TDD)

U.S. Small Business
Administration
475 Allendale Rd., Suite 201
King of Prussia, PA 19406
(215) 962-3700
(215) 962-3806  (TDD)

REGION 4: ALABAMA,
FLORIDA, GEORGIA,
KENTUCKY, MISSISSIPPI,
NORTH CAROLINA, SOUTH
CAROLINA, TENNESSEE

U.S. Department of Education
Office for Civil Rights
101 Marietta Tower, 27th Floor
P.O. Box 2048
Atlanta, GA 30301
(404) 331-2806
(404) 331-7236  (TDD)

U.S. Department of Labor
Office of Federal Contract
Compliance Programs
1375 Peachtree St., NE, Suite 678
Atlanta, GA 30367
(404) 347-3200

U.S. Department of Health and
Human Services
Office for Civil Rights
101 Marietta Tower, Room 1502
Atlanta, GA 30323
(404) 331-2779
(404) 331-2867  (TDD)

U.S. Small Business
Administration
1375 Peachtree St. NE, 5th Floor
Atlanta, GA 30367-8102
(404) 347-2797
(404) 347-5051  (TDD)

REGION 5: ILLINOIS,
INDIANA, MINNESOTA,
MICHIGAN, OHIO,
WISCONSIN

U.S. Department of Education
Office for Civil Rights
401 S. State St., Room 700-C
Chicago, IL 60605-1202
(312) 353-2520
(312) 353-2540  (TDD)

U.S. Department of Labor Office
of Federal Contract Compliance
Programs
230 S. Dearborn St., Room 570
Chicago, IL 60604
(312) 353-0335
(312) 353-2158  (TDD)

U.S. Department of Health and
Human Services
Office for Civil Rights
105 W. Adams, 16th Floor
Chicago, IL 60603
(312) 886-2359
(312) 353-5693  (TDD)

U.S. Small Business
Administration
300 S. Riverside Plaza,
Suite 1975 South
Chicago, IL 60606
(312) 353-0359

REGION 6: ARKANSAS,
LOUISIANA, NEW MEXICO,
OKLAHOMA, TEXAS

U.S. Department of Education
Office for Civil Rights
1200 Main Tower Building,
Suite 2260
Dallas, TX 75202-9998
(214) 767-3936
(214) 767-3639  (TDD)

U.S. Department of Labor
Office of Federal Contract
Compliance Programs
525 S. Griffin St., Room 840
Dallas, TX 75202
(214) 767-4771

U.S. Department of Health and
Human Services
Office for Civil Rights
1200 Main Tower Building,
Room 1360
Dallas, TX 75202
(214) 767-4056
(214) 767-8940  (TDD)

U.S. Small Business
Administration
8625 King George Dr., Building C
Dallas, TX 75235-3391
(214) 767-7643

REGION 7: IOWA, KANSAS,
MISSOURI, NEBRASKA

U.S. Department of Education
Office for Civil Rights
10220 N. Executive Hills Blvd.,
8th Floor
Kansas City, MO 64153-1267
(816) 891-8026
(816) 374-6461  (TDD)

U.S. Department of Labor
Office of Federal Contract
Compliance Programs
911 Walnut St., Room 2011
Kansas City, MO 64106
(816) 426-5384

U.S. Department of Health and
Human Services
Office for Civil Rights
601 E. 12th St., Room 248
Kansas City, MO 64106
(816) 426-7277
(816) 426-7065  (TDD)

U.S. Small Business
Administration
911 Walnut St., 13th Floor
Kansas City, MO 64106
(816) 426-3608

REGION 8: COLORADO,
MONTANA, NORTH
DAKOTA, SOUTH DAKOTA,
UTAH, WYOMING

U.S. Department of Education
Office for Civil Rights
1244 Speer Blvd., Suite 310
Denver, CO 80204-3864
(303) 844-5695
(303) 884-3417  (TDD)

U.S. Department of Labor
Office of Federal Contract
Compliance
1961 Stout St., Room 1480
Denver, CO 80294
(303) 844-5011
(303) 844-4481  (TDD)

U.S. Department of Health and
Human Services
Office for Civil Rights
1961 Stout St., Room 1185
Denver, CO 80294-3538
(303) 844-4774
(303) 844-3439   (TDD)

U.S. Small Business
Administration
999 18th St., Suite 701
Denver, CO 80202
(303) 294-7001

REGION 9: ARIZONA,
CALIFORNIA, HAWAII,
NEVADA, GUAM, TRUST
TERRITORY OF THE PACIFIC
ISLANDS, AMERICAN SAMOA

U.S. Department of Education
Office for Civil Rights
50 United Nations Plaza
San Francisco, CA 94102
(415) 556-7000
(415) 556-6806  (TDD)

U.S. Department of Labor
Office of Federal Contract
Compliance
71 Stevenson St., Suite 1700
San Francisco, CA 94105
(415) 744-6986

U.S. Department of Health and
Human Services
Office for Civil Rights
Federal Office Building,
Room 322
50 United Nations Plaza
San Francisco, CA 94102
(415) 556-8586 (voice or TDD)

U.S. Small Business
Administration
71 Stevenson St., 20th Floor
San Francisco, CA 94105-2939
(415) 744-6402

REGION 10: ALASKA, IDAHO,
OREGON, WASHINGTON

U.S. Department of Education
Office for Civil Rights
915 2nd Ave., Room 3310
Seattle, WA 98174-1099
(206) 553-1636
(206) 442-4542  (TDD)

U.S. Department of Labor
Office of Federal Contract
Compliance Programs
1111 Third Ave., Suite 610
Seattle, WA 98101-3212
(206) 442-4508

U.S. Department of Health and
Human Services
Office for Civil Rights
2201 Sixth Ave.
M/S RX-11
Seattle, WA 98121-1233
(206) 553-7483
(206) 553-7486  (TDD)

U.S. Small Business
Administration
2615 4th Ave., Room 440
Seattle, WA 98121-1233
(206) 553-5676
(206) 553-2872 (TDD)

## STATE AGENCIES

The states have structured their agency programs in different ways. Some have three or four separate locations administering the various state and federal programs; others have one or two offices in which several functions are combined. Additionally, many states have other special service agencies, such as Commissions on the Status of Women. I have included as many of these as possible, but there may be others which are not listed here.

Also, many private organizations such as NOW have branch locations in numerous cities. Check your state and local telephone directory for other helpful organizations.

The list below provides the address and telephone number of each state's Fair Employment Practices Agency (FEPA), Employment Service office, Job Training Partnership Act liaison, and Department of Labor.

Bear in mind that in many states, there are several locations where these programs are administered, and that the address below is for the main office for each agency. Check your local telephone directory or state Yellow Book (found in public libraries and updated several times each year). You can also call the main office to find out where you need to go to find the location nearest you.

### ALABAMA

FEPA:
Human Resources Department
EEO Office
Gordon Persons Office Building
50 North Ripley St.
Montgomery, AL 36130-4000
(205) 242-1550
or contact the EEOC:
2121 Eighth Ave. N., Suite 824
Birmingham, AL 35203
(205) 731-0083

Employment Service:
Department of Industrial
Relations
Industrial Relations Building
649 Monroe St., Room 204
Montgomery, Alabama 36131
(205) 242-8618
(205) 242-8608 (TDD)

Job Training:
Alabama Department of
Economic and Community Affairs
P.O. Box 5690
Montgomery, AL 36103
(205) 242-5846

Alabama Labor Department
1789 Cong. W.L. Dickinson Dr.
Montgomery, AL 36130
(205) 242-3460

Alabama Women's Commission
701 Montgomery Hwy., Suite 204
Birmingham, AL 35216-1833
(205) 822-7292

## ALASKA

FEPA:
Alaska State Commission for
Human Rights
800 A St., Suite 202
Anchorage, AK 99501-3669
(907) 276-7474
(907) 276-3177 (TDD)

Employment Service:
Alaska Department of Labor
Employment Security Division
1111 W. Eighth St.,
P.O. Box 25509
Juneau, AK 99802-5509
(907) 465-2711

Job Training:
Community and Regional Affairs
Department
P.O. Box 112100
Juneau, AK 99811
(907) 465-2700

Labor Department
1111 W. Eighth St.
P.O. Box 21149
Juneau, AK 99802-1149
(907) 465-2700

## ARIZONA

FEPA:
Arizona Civil Rights Division
1275 West Washington
Phoenix, AZ 85007
(602) 542-5263

Employment Service:
Department of Economic Security
P.O. Box 6123-010A
1717 West Jefferson
Phoenix, AZ 85007
(602) 542-4791

Job Training:
Arizona Department of
Employment Security
Division of Employment and
Rehabilitation Services
1717 W. Jefferson
Phoenix, AZ 85007
(602) 542-4910

Arizona Department of Labor
800 West Washington Street, 3rd
Floor
P.O. Box 19070
Phoenix, AZ 85005

Arizona Governor's Office for
Women
1700 W. Washington Street
State Capitol, West Wing
Phoenix, AZ 85007
(602) 542-4644

ARKANSAS

FEPA:
None. Contact the EEOC:
320 West Capitol Avenue
Suite 621
Little Rock, AR 72201
(501) 378-5060

Employment Service and Job
Training:
Arkansas Employment Security
Department
P.O. Box 2981
Little Rock, AR 72203-2981
(501) 682-2121

Department of Labor
10421 West Markham
Little Rock, Arkansas 72202
(501) 682-4500
(800) 285-1131 (TDD)

CALIFORNIA

FEPA:
California Fair Employment and
Housing Commission
1390 Market St., Suite 410
San Francisco, CA 94102-5377
(415) 557-2325

Employment Service and Job
Training:
Employment Development
Department
800 Capitol Mall, Room 5000
P.O. Box 826880, MIC 83
Sacramento, CA 94280-0001
(916) 654-8210

Department of Industrial
Relations
455 Golden Gate Ave.
San Francisco, CA 94102
(415) 703-4590

Commission on the Status of
Women
1303 J Street, Suite 400
Sacramento, CA 95814-2900
(916) 445-3173

COLORADO

FEPA:
Colorado Civil Rights Division
1560 Broadway, Suite 1050
Denver, CO 80202
(303) 894-7805
(303) 894-7832 (TDD)

Employment Service:
Labor and Employment
Department
600 Grant St., Suite 900
Denver, CO 80203-3528
(303) 837-3800

Job Training:
Governor's Job Training Office
720 South Colorado Blvd.,
Suite 550
Denver, CO 80222
(303) 758-5020 (Voice or TDD)

Rural Job Training Office
1900 Grant St., Suite 800
Denver, CO 80203

CONNECTICUT

FEPA:
Connecticut Commission on
Human Rights and Opportunities
90 Washington St.
Hartford, CT        06106
(203) 566-4895
(203) 566-3350 (TDD)

Employment Service and job
Training:
Department of Labor
200 Folly Brook Boulevard
Wethersfield, CT 06109-1114
(203) 566-5160

Status of Women Commission
90 Washington Street
Hartford, CT   06106
(203) 566-5702

DELAWARE

FEPA:
Delaware Department of Labor
Anti-Discrimination Section
Carvel State Office Building
820 North French Street, 6th
Floor
Wilmington, DE   19801
(302) 577-2710

Employment Service and Job
Training:
State Department of Labor
Employment and Training
Division
University Plaza, Stockton Bldg.
Wilmington, DE   19714-9029
(302) 368-6810

Office for Commission of Women
Carvel State Office Building
829 N. French St.
Wilmington, DE   19801
(302) 577-2710

DISTRICT OF COLUMBIA

FEPA:
D.C. Office of Human Rights and
Minority Business Development
One Judiciary Square
441 Fourth St., NW
Washington, D.C.   20001
(202) 724-3786

Human Rights Commission
One Judiciary Square
441 Fourth St., NW, 5th Floor
Washington, D.C.   20001
(202) 727-0656

Employment Service and Job
Training:
D.C. Department of Employment
Services
500 C Street NW, Suite 600
Washington, D.C. 20001
(202) 724-7133

Wage and Hour Office
120 Upsher St. NW
Washington, D.C.   20011
(202) 576-6942

Commission for Women
2000 14th St., NW, Room 354
Washington, D.C.   20009
(202) 939-8083

FLORIDA

FEPA:
Florida Commission on Human
Relations
325 John Knox Road,
Suite 240, Building F
Tallahassee, FL 32399-1570
(904) 488-5291

Employment Service and Job
Training:
Florida Department of Labor and
Employment Security
Hartman Building, Suite 303
2012 Capitol Circle SE
Tallahassee, FL 32399-2152
(904) 488-4398

GEORGIA

FEPA:
Georgia Office of Fair Employment
Practices
156 Trinity Avenue SW, Suite 208
Atlanta, GA 30303
(404) 656-1736

Georgia Commission on Equal
Opportunity
710 Cain Tower, Peachtree Ctr.
229 Peachtree St., NE
Atlanta, GA 30303
(404) 656-1736

Employment Service and Job
Training:
Georgia Department of Labor
Sussex Place
148 International Building, NE,
Suite 600
Atlanta, GA 30303-1751
(404) 656-3017

HAWAII

FEPA:
Hawaii Civil Rights Commission
888 Mililani St., 2nd Floor
Honolulu, HI 96813
(808) 548-7625
(808) 586-8800 (TDD)

Employment Service and Job
Training:
Department of Labor and Industrial
Relations
830 Punchbowl Street, Room 320
Honolulu, HI 96813
(808) 586-8844 or
(808) 586-9060

Commission on the Status of
Women
335 Merchant St.,Room 253
Honolulu, HI 96813
(808) 586-5757

IDAHO

FEPA:
Commission on Human Rights
450 West State St., 1st Floor West
P.O. Box 83720
Boise, Idaho      83720
(208) 334-2873

Employment Service and Job
Training:
Department of Employment
317 Main St.
Boise, ID 83735-0001
(208) 334-6100

Department of Labor and Industrial
Services
Statehouse Mail
227 North 6th Street
Boise, Idaho 83720-6000
(208) 334-2327

## ILLINOIS

FEPA:
Illinois Department of Human
Rights
100 West Randolph Street,
10th Floor, Suite 100
Chicago, IL 60601
(312) 814-6200
(312) 263-1579 (TDD)

Employment Service:
Department of Employment
Security
401 South State St., 6th Floor
Chicago, IL 60605
(312) 793-5700
(312) 793-9350 (TDD)

Job Training:
Department of Commerce and
Community Affairs
JTPA Programs Division
620 E. Adams, 6th Floor
Menden Hall
Springfield, IL 62701
(217) 785-6006 (Voice or TDD)

Department of Labor
160 N. LaSalle St.
Suite 1300-C
Chicago, IL 60601
(312) 793-2800

## INDIANA

FEPA:
Indiana Civil Rights Commission
Indiana Government Center North
100 Senate AVe. Room N-103
Indianapolis, IN 46204
(317) 232-2600
(317) 232-2629

Employment Service and Job
Training:
Workforce Development Dept.
Indiana Government Center South
10 North Senate Avenue,
Indianapolis, IN 46204
(317) 232-7670
(317) 232-7560 (TDD)

Department of Labor
402 W. Washington St.
Room W195
Indianapolis, IN 46204
(317) 232-2655
(317) 743-3333(TDD)

## IOWA

FEPA:
Iowa Civil Rights Commission
211 East Maple Street, 2nd. Floor
Grimes State Office Building,
c/o State Mailroom
Des Moines, IA 50319
(515) 281-4121 or
(800) 457-4416

Division of Labor
Employment Services Department
1000 East Grand Avenue
Des Moines, IA 50319
(515) 281-5387
(800) 562-4692

Iowa Human Rights Department
Status of Women Division
Lucas Building
Des Moines, IA 50319
(515) 281-4467
(515) 281-3164 (TDD)

KANSAS

FEPA:
Kansas Human Rights
Commission
Landon State Office Building,
Suite 851-S
900 SW Jackson St.
Topeka, KS 66612-1252
(913) 296-3206
(913) 296-0245 (TDD)

Employment Service and Job
Training:
Kansas Department of Human
Resources
401 SW Topeka Boulevard
Topeka, KS 66603-3182
(913) 296-7474
(913) 296-5044 (TDD)

KENTUCKY

FEPA:
Kentucky Commission on Human
Rights
832 Capitol Plaza Tower
Frankfort, KY 40601

Human Rights Commission
The Heyburn Building
332 West Broadway
7th Floor
Louisville, KY 40202
(502) 595-4024
(502) 595-4084 (DD)

Employment Service and Job
Training:
Department for Employment
Services
Cabinet for Human Resources
275 East Main St. 2-West
Frankfort, KY 40621-0001
(502) 564-5331

Workforce Development Cabinet
Capital Plaza Tower, 2nd Floor
500 Mero St.
Frankfort, KY 40601
(502) 564-6606

Labor Cabinet
1047 U.S. Highway 127 South,
Suite 4
Frankfort, KY 40601
(502) 564-3070

Commission on Women
614-A Shelby
Frankfort, KY 40601
(502) 564-6643

LOUISIANA

FEPA:
None: Contact the EEOC
701 Loyola Ave., Suite 600
New Orleans, LA 70113
(504) 589-2329

Employment Service and Job Training:
Department of Employment and Training
Department of Labor
1045 State Land and Natural Resources Building
P.O. Box 94094
Baton Rouge, LA 70804-9094
(504) 342-3111 (General Information
(504) 342-3016 (Employment Training)
(504) 342-7620 (Job Service)

MAINE

FEPA:
Maine Human Rights Commission
State House Station 51
Augusta, ME 04333-0051
(207) 624-6050
(207) 624-6064 (TDD)

Employment Service:
Maine Department of Labor
Bureau of Employment Security
20 Union Street
P.O. Box 309
Augusta, Maine 04332-0309
(207) 287-3377
(800) 794-1110 (TDD)

Job Training:
Bureau of Employment and Training Programs
Statehouse Station 55
Augusta, ME 04333
(207) 289-3377

MARYLAND

Human Relations Commission
William Donald Schaefer Tower
Six St. Paul St., 9th Floor
Baltimore, MD 21202-2274
(410) 767-8600
(410) 333-1737 (TDD)

Employment Service and Job Training:
Department of Economic and Employment Development
Employment and Training Division
1100 North Eutaw St.
Baltimore, MD 21201-2199
(410) 333-5070
(410) 333-1737 (TDD)

Economic and Employment Development Department
217 E. Redwood St.
Baltimore, MD 21202-3316
(410) 333-6917
(410) 333-6926 (TDD)

Commission for Women
Human Resources Department
311 W. Saratoga St.
Baltimore, MD 21201
(410) 767-7556
(410) 767-7025

MASSACHUSETTS

FEPA:
Massachusetts Commission Against Discrimination
1 Ashburton Place, Sixth Floor
Boston, Massachusetts 02108
(617) 727-3990

Employment Service and Job Training:
Department of Employment and Training
Charles F. Hurley Building
Government Center, 19 Staniford Street, 3rd Floor
Boston, MA 02114
(617) 727-6560
(617) 727-8660 (TDD)

Department of Labor and Industries
100 Cambridge Street, Room 1100
Boston, Massachusetts 02202
(617) 727-3454

## MICHIGAN

FEPA:
Michigan Civil Rights Department
303 W. Kalamazoo, 4th Floor
Lansing, MI 48913
(517) 335-3165
(313) 961-1552 (TDD)

Detroit Office:
Michigan Plaza Building
1200 Sixth St.
Detroit, MI 48226
(313) 256-2663
(313) 961-1552 (TDD)

Employment Service:
Michigan Employment Security Commission
7310 Woodward Ave.
Detroit, MI 48202
(313) 876-5000
(313) 876-5540

Job Training:
Michigan Department of Labor
201 North Washington Square
P.O. Box 30015
Lansing, Michigan 48909
(517) 322-1287

Jobs Commission
Victor Office Center
201 N. Washinton St.
Lansing, MI 48913
(517) 393-8500
(800) 649-3777 (TDD)

## MINNESOTA

FEPA:
Minnesota Department of Human Rights
500 Bremer Tower, 5th Floor
7th Place and Minnesota Street
St. Paul, MN 55101
(612) 296-5663 or
(800) 652-9747
(612) 296-1283 (TDD)

Employment Service and Job Training:
Economic Security Department
390 North Robert St.
St. Paul, MN 55101
(612) 296-2919
(612) 282-5909

Department of Labor and Industry
Space Center, 5th Floor
443 Lafayette Rd.
St. Paul, MN 55155
(612) 296-6107
(612) 297-4198 (TDD)

Commission on the Economic
Status of Women
85 State Office Bldg.
St. Paul, MN 55155
(800) 657-3949

MISSISSIPPI

FEPA: None.  Contact the EEOC:
New Federal Building
100 West Capitol St., Suite 721
Jackson, MS 39269
(601) 965-4537

Human Services Department
P.O. Box 352
Jackson, MS 39205-0352
(601) 359-4900
(601) 359-4854 (Jobs Division)

Employment Service:
Mississippi Employment Security
Commission
1520 West Capitol St.
P.O. Box 1699
Jackson, MS 39215-1699
(601) 354-8711
Job Training:

Department of Economic and
Community Development
Employment Training Division
1200 Walter Sillers Building
P.O. Box 39205
Jackson, MS 39205
(601) 949-2003

MISSOURI

FEPA:
Missouri Commission on Human
Rights
3315 W. Truman Blvd.
P.O. Box 504
Jefferson City, MO 65102
(314) 751-3325 (Voice or TDD)

Employment Service:
Division of Employment Security
3315 W. Truman Blvd.
P.O. Box 504
Jefferson City, MO 65102
(314) 751-3976

Job Training:
Economic Development
Department
Division of Job Development and
Training
221 Metro Drive
Jefferson City, MO 65102
(314) 751-4750
(800) 877-8698

Department of Labor and
Industrial Relations
3315 W. Truman Blvd.
P.O. Box 504
Jefferson City, MO 65102
(314) 751-4091

Women's Council
Economic Development
Department
221 Metro Dr.
Jefferson City, MO 65102
(314) 751-0810

MONTANA

FEPA:
Department of Labor & Industry
Human Rights Division
1236 6th Avenue
P.O. Box 1728
Helena, Montana 59624-1728
(406) 444-3870
(800) 542-0807
Employment Service and Job
Training:
Department of Labor and Industry
P.O. Box 1728
Helena, Montana 59624
(406) 444-4100

NEBRASKA

FEPA:
Nebraska Equal Opportunity
Commission
301 Centennial Mall South
P.O. Box 94934, 5th Floor
Lincoln, Nebraska 68509-4934
(402) 471-2024
(800) 642-6112

Employment Service and Job
Training:
Department of Labor
550 South 16th Street
Box 94600
State House Station
Lincoln, Nebraska 68509-6400
(402) 471-2603 (Employment
Service)
(402) 471-9000 (Job Training)
(402) 471-9977 (EEO/Civil Rights
Division)

Women's Commission
301 Centennial Mall South
P.O. Box 94985
Lincoln, NE 68509-4985
(402) 471-2039

NEVADA

FEPA:
Nevada Equal Rights Commission
1515 E. Tropicana, Suite 590
Las Vegas, Nevada 89158
(702) 486-7161
(702) 486-7164 (TDD)

Employment Service:
Nevada Employment Security
Division
500 East 3rd St., Room 200
Carson City, NV 89713
(702) 687-4635 (Voice or TDD)

Job Training:
State Job Training Office
Capitol Complex,
400 West King St., Suite 108
Carson City, NV 89710
(702) 687-4310

Labor Commission
Capitol Complex
Carson City, Nevada 89710
(702) 687-4850

Occupational Information
Coordinating Committee
Frontier Plaza
1923 N. Carson St., Suite 211
Carson City, NV 89710
(702) 687-4577

NEW HAMPSHIRE

New Hampshire Commission for
Human Rights
163 Loudon Road
Concord, NH 03301
(603) 271-2767
(800) 735-2964 (TDD)

Employment Service:
Department of Employment
Security
32 South Main St.
Concord, NH 03301-4857
(603) 224-3311
(800) 735-2964 (TDD)

Job Training:
New Hampshire Job Training
Coordinating Council
64 Old Suncook Rd.
Concord, NH 03301
(603) 228-9500
(800) 772-7001

Department of Labor
State Office Park South
95 Pleasant St.
Concord, NH 03301
(603) 271-3171

Commission on the Status of
Women
State House Annex, Room 22
Concord, NH 03301
(603) 271-2660
(800) 735-2964 (TDD)

NEW JERSEY

FEPA:
Department of Law and Public
Safety
Civil Rights Division
CN 089
383 W. State St.
Trenton, NJ 08625
(609) 984-3100

Employment Service and Job
Training:
New Jersey Department of Labor
John Fitch Plaza
P.O. Box CN 110
Trenton, NJ 08625-0110
(609) 984-5666

NEW MEXICO

FEPA:
New Mexico Human Rights
Division
1596 Pacheco Street, Aspen Plaza
Santa Fe, NM 87502
(505) 827-6838

Employment Service:
New Mexico Department of
Labor
P.O. Box 1928
Albuquerque, NM 87103
(505) 841-8437

Job Training:
Job Training Division
P.O. Box 4218
Santa Fe, NM 87502
(505) 827-6827

Status of Women Commission
4001 Indian School Road NE,
Suite 220
Albuquerque, NM 87110
(505) 841-4662

NEW YORK

FEPA:
New York State Division of
Human Rights
55 West 125th Street
New York, NY 10027
(212) 870-8400

Employment Service and Job
Training:
New York State Department of
Labor
W.A. Harriman Campus,
Building 12, Room 592
Albany, NY 12240
(518) 457-9000

Job Development Authority
605 Third Avenue
New York, NY 10158
(212) 818-1700

NORTH CAROLINA

FEPA:
North Carolina Civil Rights
Division
P.O. Drawer 27447
Raleigh, NC 27661
(919) 733-0431 (Voice or TDD)

Employment Service:
Employment Security Commission
of North Carolina
P.O. Box 25903
Raleigh, NC 27611
(919) 733-3098

Job Service:
Department of Economic and
Community Development
Division of Employment and
Training
111 Seaboard Ave.
Raleigh, NC 27604
(919) 733-6383

Department of Labor
Labor Building
4 West Edenton St.
Raleigh, NC 27601
(919) 733-7166
(919) 733-7167 (Training
programs)

Human Relations Commission
217 W. Jones St., 4th Floor
Raleigh, NC 27603-1336
(919) 733-7996

Council for Women
Merrimon-Wynne House
526 N. Wilmaington St.
Raleigh, NC 27604-1199
(919) 733-2455

NORTH DAKOTA

FEPA:
North Dakota Department of
Labor
EEO Division
State Capitol Bldg., 6th Floor
600 East Boulevard Ave.
Bismarck, ND 58505
(701) 224-2665

Employment Service and Job
Training:
Job Service of North Dakota
P.O. Box 5507
Bismarck, ND 58502-5507
(701) 224-2825
(701) 224-3262 (TDD)

Labor Department
State Capitol, 6th Floor
600 E. Boulevard Ave.
Bismarck, ND 58505
(701) 224-2660

OHIO

FEPA:
Ohio Civil Rights Commission
220 Parsons Avenue
Columbus, OH 43215-5385
(614) 466-2785
(614) 466-9353 (TDD)

Employment Service:
Ohio Employment Services Bureau
145 S. Front St.
Columbus, OH 43215
(614) 466-4636
(614) 644-9186 (TDD)

Job Training:
Job Training Partnership Act—
Ohio Division
Bureau of Employment Services
145 S. Front St., 4th Floor
Columbus, OH 43215
(614) 466-3817
(614) 644-9186 (TDD)

Department of Industrial
Relations
2323 West 5th Avenue
P.O. Box 825
Columbus, OH 43266-0567
(614) 644-2223

OKLAHOMA

FEPA:
Oklahoma Human Rights
Commission
2101 North Lincoln Blvd.,
Room 480
Oklahoma City, OK 73105
(405) 521-3441

Employment Service and Job
Training:
Employment Security Commission
212 Will Rogers Memorial Office
Building
2401 N. Lincoln Blvd.
Oklahoma City, OK 73105
(405) 557-0200
(405) 557-7121
(405) 557-7255

Department of Labor
4001 N. Lincoln Blvd.
Oklahoma City, OK 73105
(405) 528-1500

## OREGON

FEPA:
Oregon Bureau of Labor and
Industries
Civil Rights Division
800 NE Oregon St., # 32
Portland, OR 97232
(503) 731-4873
(503) 229-6589 (TDD)

Employment Service:
Employment Division
875 Union St., NE
Salem, OR 97311
(503) 378-8420
(800) 237-3710 (TDD)

Job Training:
Economic Development
Department
Job Training Partnership Act
Administration
775 Summer Street NE
Salem, OR 97310
(503) 373-1995, Ext. 226
(503) 986-0123 (TDD)

Labor and Industrial Bureau
800 NE Oregon St., # 32
Portland, OR 97232
(503) 731-4070
(503) 731-4891 (Apprenticeship
and Training)

Commission for Women
Portland State University
Smith Center M-315
P.O. Box 751
Portland, OR 97207
(503) 292-8881

## PENNSYLVANIA

FEPA:
Pennsylvania Human Relations
Commission
101 South Second Street, Suite
300
P.O. Box 3145
Harrisburg, PA 17105-3145
(717) 787-4410
(717) 787-4087 (TDD)

Employment Service and Job
Training:
Department of Labor and Industry
1700 Labor and Industry Building
7th & Forester Streets
Harrisburg, PA 17120
(717) 787-3354
(717) 783-9308 (TDD)
(717) 787-5279 (Department of
Labor General Information)

## RHODE ISLAND

FEPA:
Rhode Island Human Rights
Commission
10 Abbott Park Place, 1st Floor
Providence, RI 02903-3768
(401) 277-2661
(401) 277-2664 (TDD)

Employment Service and Job
Training:
Department of Employment &
Training
101 Friendship St.
Providence, RI 02903-3740
(401) 277-3600
(401) 277-3718 (TDD)

Department of Labor
610 Manton Ave.
Providence, RI 02909
(401) 457-1800
(401) 457-1888 (TDD)

## SOUTH CAROLINA

FEPA:
South Carolina Human Affairs
Commission
2611 Forest Dr.
P.O. Box 4490
Columbia, SC 29240
(803) 253-6336
(803) 253-4125 (TDD)

Employment Service and Job
Training:
South Carolina Employment
Security Commission
P.O. Box 995
Colombia, SC 29202
(803) 737-2400
(800) 206-8035 (TDD)

Department of Labor
3600 Forest Drive, P.O. Box
11329
Columbia, SC 29211-1329
(803) 734-9600

Commission on Women
2221 Devine St., Suite 408
Columbia, SC 29205
(803) 734-9143

## SOUTH DAKOTA

FEPA:
South Dakota Division of Human
Rights
c/o Capitol Building
222 East Capitol St., Suite 11
Pierre, SD 57501-5070
(605) 773-4493

Employment Service and Job
Training:
South Dakota Department of
Labor
700 Governors Drive, Kneip
Building
Pierre, SD 57501-2291
(605) 773-3101

## TENNESSEE

FEPA:
Tennessee Human Rights
Commission
400 Cornerstone Square Bldg.
530 Church Street
Nashville, TN 37243-0745
(615) 741-4490
(615) 741-2491 (TDD)

Employment Service:
Tennessee Department of
Employment Security
Volunteer Plaza, 12th Floor
500 James Robertson Pkwy.
Nashville, TN 37254-0001
(615) 741-2257

Job Training:
Tennessee Department of Labor
710 James Robertson Parkway
Nashville, TN 37243-0655
(615) 741-1031

## TEXAS

FEPA:
Texas Commission on Human
Rights
8100 Cameron Rd., # 525
Austin, TX 78711
(512) 837-8534

Employment Service:
Texas Employment Commission
101 E. 15th St.
Austin, TX 78778
(512) 463-2661

Job Training:
Texas Department of Commerce
Work Force Development
Division
First City Centre, Suite 1200
816 Congress, P.O. Box 12728
Capitol Station
Austin, TX 78711
(512) 320-9806
(512) 320-9698 (TDD)

## UTAH

Utah Labor and Anti-
Discrimination Division
160 East 300 South, 3rd Floor
Salt Lake City, UT 84114-6600
(801) 530-6921
(801) 530-7685 (TDD)

Employment Service:
Utah Department of Employment
Security
P.O. Box 11249
140 East 300 South
Salt Lake City, UT 84147-0249
(801) 536-7401

Job Training:
Office of Job Training for
Economic Development
324 South State St., Suite 500
Salt Lake City, UT 84111
(801) 538-8750

Industrial Commission
160 East 300 South, 3rd Floor
P.O. Box 146600
Salt Lake City, UT 84114-6600
(801) 530-6800
(801) 530-7685 (TDD)

## VERMONT

FEPA:
Vermont Attorney General's
Office
Public Protection Division
Office of the Attorney General
109 State Street
Montpelier, VT 05609-1001
(802) 828-3171 (Voice of TDD)

Employment Service:
Employment and Training
Administration Department
P.O. Box 488
Montpelier, VT 05602
(802) 828-4000
(802) 828-4203 (TDD)

Job Training:
Office of Employment and
Training Programs
Five Green Mountain Drive
P.O. Box 488
Montpelier, VT 05602
(802) 828-4151
(802) 828-4203 (TDD)

Labor and Industry Department
Drawer 20
Montpelier, VT 05620-3401
(802) 828-2288

Governor's Commission on
Women
126 State St., Drawer 33
Montpelier, VT 05633-6801
(802) 828-2851

VIRGINIA

FEPA:
Office of Civil Rights
1503 Santa Rosa Road
Richmond, VA 23288
Human Rights Council
P.O. Box 717
Richmond, VA 23288
(804) 225-3294

Employment Service:
Virginia Employment Commission
703 East Main St.
Richmond, VA 23219
(804) 786-7097
(804) 371-8050 (TDD)

Job Training:
Governor's Employment and
Training Department
The Commonwealth Building
4615 West Broad St., 3rd. Floor
Richmond, VA 23230
(804) 367-9800
(804) 367-6283 (TDD)

Department of Labor and Industry
Powers-Taylor Building
13 S. 13th St.
Richmond, Va 23219
(804) 371-2327
(804) 786-2376 (TDD)

WASHINGTON

FEPA:
Washington State Human Rights
Commission
711 South Capitol Way, Suite 402
P.O. Box 42490
Olympia, WA 98504-2490
(206) 753-2987
(206) 753-6770 (TDD)

Employment Service:
Employment Security Department
212 Maple Park
Olympia, WA 98504-9046
(206) 438-4611
(206) 438-3167 (TDD)

Job Training:
Employment Security Department
Employment and Training
Division
605 Woodview Dr. SE
P.O. Box 9046, KG-6000
Olympia, WA 98507-9046
(206) 438-4611 (Voice or TDD)

Department of Labor and
Industries
P.O. Box 44000
Olympia, WA 98504-4000
(206) 956-5800

## WEST VIRGINIA

FEPA:
West Virginia Human Rights
Commission
1321 Plaza East
Charleston, WV 25301
(304) 558-2616

Employment Service:
West Virginia Bureau of
Employment Programs
112 California Ave.
Charleston, WV 25305-0112
(304) 558-9180

Job Training:
Bureau of Employment Programs
Job Training Programs Division
112 California Ave.
Charleston, WV 25305-0112
(304) 558-5920

Department of Labor
State Capitol Complex
Buiilding # 3, Room 319
1900 Kanawha Blvd. East
Charleston, WV 25305
(304) 558-7890

Women's Commission
State Capitol Complex
Bldg. 6, Room 637
Charleston, WV 25305
(304) 558-0070

## WISCONSIN

FEPA:
Department of Industry, Labor
and Human Relations
Wisconsin Equal Rights Division
P.O. Box 7946
Madison, WI 53707
(608) 266-0946

Employment Service and Job
Training:
Department of Industry, Labor
and Human Relations
P.O. Box 7946
Madison, WI 53707
(608) 266-2439

Employment Relations
Department
137 E. Wilson St.
P.O. Box 7855
Madison, WI 53707-7855
(608) 266-9820
(608) 267-1004 (TDD)

Women's Council
16 N. Carroll St., Suite 720
Madison, WI 53702
(608) 266-2219

Employment Relations
Commission
P.O. Box 7870
Madison, WI 53707-7870
(608) 266-1381

WYOMING

FEPA:
Wyoming Fair Employment
Commission
Herschler Bldg.
122 West 25th Street,
2nd Floor East
Cheyenne, WY 82002
(307) 777-7672

Employment Service and Job
Training:
Employment Resources Division
P.O. Box 2760
Casper, WY 82602
(307) 235-3200

Employment Department
Herschler Building
2nd Floor East
122 W. 25th St.
Cheyenne, WY 82002
(307) 777-7672

Women's Issues Council/Women's
Commission
820 Park St.
Worland, WY 82401
(307) 347-3836

TERRITORIES,
COMMONWEALTHS, AND
AMERICAN POSSESSIONS

*American Samoa:*
Government of American Samoa
Department of Human Resources
Pago Pago, AS 96799
(864) 633-4485

*Guam:*
Agency for Human Resources
Development
P.O. Box CQ
Agana, GU 96910
(672) 646-9341

Department of Labor
Government of Guam
ITC Building, 3rd. Floor
Box 9970
Tamuning, Guam 96911
(671) 646-9241

*Puerto Rico:*
FEPA:
Commonwealth of Puerto Rico
Department of Labor and Human
Resources
Anti-Discrimination Unit
505 Munoz Rivera Avenue
Hato Rey, PR 00918
(809) 754-2119

Employment Service:
Bureau of Employment Security
505 Munoz Rivera Avenue
Hato Rey, PR 00918
(809) 754-2119

Job Training:
Right to Employment
Administration
G.P.O. Box 4452
San Juan, PR 00936
(672) 646-9341

Civil Rights Commission
112 Juan B. Huyke Street
P.O. Box 2338
Hato Rey, PR 00919

*Commonwealth of the Northern Mariana Islands:*
Job Training:
Commonwealth of the Northern
Mariana Islands
JPTA Programs
Office of the Executive Director
Civic Center
Saipan, CM 96950

*Trust Territory of the Pacific Islands:*
Minister of Social Services
P.O. Box 1138
Majuro, Republic of the Marshall
Islands 96960
Private Industry Council
P.O. Box 100
Koror, Republic of Palua 96940
Government of the Federated
States of Micronesia
Office of Administrative Services
P.O. Box 490
Pohnpei, FM 96941

*Virgin Islands:*
FEPA:
Virgin Islands Department of
Labor
2131 Hospital Street
Christiansted,
St. Croix, VI 00820
(809) 773-1994

Employment Service:
Virgin Islands Department of
Labor
2131 Hospital Street
Christiansted,
St. Croix, VI 00820
(809) 773-1994

Job Training:
Virgin Islands Department of
Labor
Employment and Training
7 & 8 Queen St.,
Christiansred
St. Croix, VI 00820
(809) 773-1994

Civil Rights Commission
P.O. Box 6645
St. Thomas, 00804

# Private Organizations

The following organizations provide a wide range of publications. Some provide services to women and others who have suffered discrimination. Many of these organizations are general support groups that advocate women's rights. Most have state and local chapters nationwide. This type of support can be valuable in many ways. You can meet women dedicated to helping others, talk to women who have been through similar challenges, and sometimes get help with fund raising or other financial support.

Many professions also have women's groups at the national, state, or local level. Find out if yours does, or if other local groups exist that could give you support and ideas.

American Association of Retired
Persons (AARP)
601 E St. NW
Washington, DC 20049
(202) 434-2277

Membership in AARP is open to
anyone over the age of 50. AARP
has a legal services division that is
especially concerned with discrimination in which age is a factor.

American Bar Association (ABA)
Public Education Division
750 N. Lakeshore Dr.
Chicago, IL 60611

The ABA publishes a brochure
called *The American Lawyer:
When and How to Use One,*
which can help you locate and
choose a lawyer. It is available free
of charge by writing the ABA at
the address above.

American Federation of State,
County and Municipal Employees
(AFSCME)
1108 K St. NW, 2nd Floor
Washington, DC 20005
(202) 757-1756

Center for Law and Social Policy
1616 P St. NW, Suite 450
Washington, DC 20036
(202) 328-5140

The center is involved in various
civil rights issues, including
employment discrimination. Its
lawyers sometimes represent
clients in major cases.

Center for Law in the Public
Interest
5750 Wilshire Blvd., Suite 561
Los Angeles, CA 90036
(310) 470-3000

About half the work of this organization centers on employment
law. Its lawyers sometimes represent clients in major cases.

Coalition of Labor Union Women
(CLUW)
15 Union Square
New York, NY 10003
(212) 242-0700

CLUW unites women active in
various unions nationwide. It has
many local chapters that lobby
around issues concerning women
and promote union organizing
efforts, affirmative action, and
increased female leadership in
unions.

The Feminist Institute
Clearinghouse
P.O. Box 30563
Bethesda, MD 20814
(301) 951-9040

This organization publishes
low-cost books to help women
who become victims of sex discrimination and sexual harassment. Inquire about their
publication list.

Lawyers' Committee for Civil
Rights Under the Law
1400 Eye St., NW, Suite 400
Washington, DC 20005
(202) 371-1212

This group specializes in all types of discrimination law, with a special focus on the rights of black persons. It has numerous regional offices and makes referrals to qualified lawyers in private practice.

National Association for Female Executives (NAFE)
127 West 24 Street
New York, NY 10011
(800) 634-6233 or (212) 645-0770

NAFE is an organization that provides numerous support services for career women. It has local chapters in most major cities and publishes *Executive Female* magazine, as well as various brochures.

National Black Women's Health Project
1237 Ralph David Abernathy Blvd., SW
Atlanta, GA 30310
(404) 758-9590

National Committee for Pay Equity
1126 16th St., NW, Room 411
Washington, DC 20036
(202) 331-7343

This committee consists of united groups with the goal of promoting legislation and education toward equal pay for all women.

National Employment Law Project (NELP)
475 Riverside Dr., Suite 240
New York, NY 10115
(212) 870-2121

NELP assists employment lawsuits filed on behalf of low-income people by local legal service organizations across the nation, and makes referrals to such organizations.

National Employment Lawyers Association (NELA)
535 Pacific Ave.
San Francisco, CA 94133
(415) 397-6335

This association of lawyers working in employment law educates lawyers interested in the field, promotes greater use of alternative dispute resolution, establishes employment law clinics, and provides information and referrals to the public.

There are many local chapters of NELA. Write to the national headquarters to find out if there is one in your area. This would be a good place to find a qualified and dedicated attorney to counsel and/or represent you.

National Federation of Business and Professional Women's Clubs of the U.S.A.
2012 Massachusetts Ave.
Washington, DC 20036
(202) 293-1100

This group represents business and professional women in 300 occupations. Its purpose is to promote full participation, equal opportunity, and economic self-sufficiency of working women.

National Labor Law Center
2000 P St., NW
Washington, DC 20036

This branch of the National Lawyers Guild provides assistance to lawyers in the employment and labor law fields and can make referrals to lawyers practicing in these areas.

National Lawyers Guild (NLG)
55 Avenue of the Americas,
Suite 301
New York, NY 10013
(212) 966-5000

This nationwide organization of civil rights lawyers advocates all aspects of civil rights law, including employment law. It has many state and local chapters, and refers people to its members for representation.

National Organization for Women (NOW)
1000 16th St., NW, Suite 700
Washington, DC 20036
(202) 331-0066

National Women's Law Center
1616 P St., NW
Washington, DC 20036
(202) 328-5160

This group works to guarantee equal rights for women under the law and seeks protection and advancement of women's legal rights.

New Ways to Work
149 Ninth St.
San Francisco, CA 94103
(415) 552-1000

This organization promotes part-time work, especially through job sharing. It provides information and assistance on job sharing to employer, employees, and unions, and publishes information on job sharing.

Nine to Five National Association of Working Women
614 Superior Ave., NW,
Room 852
Cleveland, OH 44113
(216) 556-9308

This national association of female office workers supports better pay, equipment, advancement, working conditions, and the elimination of discrimination among clerical employees.

NOW Legal Defense and Education Fund
99 Hudson St., 12th Floor
New York, NY 10013
(212) 925-6635

This organization provides a variety of helpful publications for women who are victims of employment discrimination, including a Legal Resource Kit on sexual harassment. The kit includes a sample letter to a harasser and a copy of the publication *Sexual Harassment in the Workplace Litigation*, which is prepared for lawyers handling this type of case.

Tradeswomen, Inc.
P.O. Box 40664
San Francisco, CA 94104
(415) 821-7334

This group supports women in blue-collar work through a newsletter, information and referral system, and conferences.

Trial Lawyers for Public Justice
1625 Massachusetts Ave., NW,
Suite 100
Washington, DC 20036
(202) 797-8600

Women Employed
22 W. Monroe, Suite 1400
Chicago, IL 60603
(312) 728-3902

This national group of women works to solve problems, promote reform, and expand economic opportunities. Write for their list of publications.

Women's Legal Defense Fund
1875 Connecticut Ave., Suite 710
Washington, DC 20009
(202) 986-2600

This group works to secure equal rights for women through litigation, advocacy, information, and education. It publishes brochures, manuals, and handbooks.

Women's Occupational Health
Resource Center
N320 E. 43rd St
New York, NY 10017

Women's Rights Project of the
ACLU
c/o American Civil Liberties Union
132 W. 43rd St.
New York, NY 10036
(212) 944-8000

Founded by Supreme Court Justice Ruth Bader Ginsberg, this branch of the ACLU strives to end sex discrimination through education and litigation. Its lawyers represent clients in class actions and precedent-setting cases. It produces brochures and pamphlets for public education.

Young Women's Christian
Association of the U.S.A. (YWCA)
726 Broadway
New York, NY 10003
(212) 614-2700
(check for local office in many cities nationwide)

Many local YWCAs have career services centers sponsored by the United Way. The mission of these centers is to train displaced homemakers, single parents, and other women entering or reentering the workforce in job search skills. Your local YWCA may offer additional services as well.

## Organizations Promoting Alternative Dispute Resolution

American Arbitration Association
140 West 51st Street
New York, NY 10020
(212) 484-4000

This organization provides information on arbitration and other forms of ADR. It publishes a widely used program of rules and regulations for arbitration, and a directory of arbitrators and mediators with expertise in various fields. It also makes referrals to the various AAA offices throughout the country.

American Bar Association
Standing Committee on Dispute Resolution
1800 M St., NW
Washington, DC 20030
(202) 331-2258

This ABA committee provides information and referrals. It publishes the *Dispute Resolution Program Directory,* which lists local mediators and arbitrators with expertise in various fields, as well as local groups and organizations that provide or promote ADR.

National Institute for Dispute Resolution
1901 L St., NW, Suite 600
Washington, DC 20036
(202) 466-4764 (voice and TDD)

This organization makes referrals to local arbitrators and mediators and serves as a clearinghouse for information on various forms of ADR.

Council of Better Business Bureaus
4200 Wilson Blvd., Suite 800
Arlington, VA 22203
(703) 276-0100 (voice and TDD)

Many local Better Business Bureaus provide ADR services. This national organization provides training for the 177 local bureaus and makes referrals. The following organizations provide education, films, training materials, and consultation to employers to promote diversity and prevent discrimination and harassment in the workplace:

Anderson-Davis
1300 A 12th Ave.
San Francisco, CA 94122
(415) 661-4040
or
424 S. Newark Way
Aurora, CO 80012
(303) 360-6584

Bureau of National Affairs, Inc.,
Communications Center
9439 Key West Ave.
Rockville, MD 20850-3396
(800) 233-6067

Center for Women in Government
University at Albany
Draper Hall, Room 302
1400 Washington Ave.
Albany, NY 12222
(518) 442-3900

Coronet/MTI Film and Video
108 Wilmot Rd.
Deerfield, IL 60015
(800) 621-2131

Haimes Associates, Inc.
708 S. Washington Square
Philadelphia, PA 99106
(215) 922-1617
J. M. Glass, Inc.
P.O. Box 9999
Spokane, WA 99209-9985
(509) 326-4989

Learning International
Sexual Harassment Awareness
Program
200 First Stamford Pl.
P.O. Box 10211
Stamford, CT 06904
(203) 965-8400

NOW Legal Defense Fund
99 Hudson St., 12th Floor
New York, NY 10013
(212) 925-6635

Onolee Zwicke & Associates
3887 State Street, Suite 22
Santa Barbara, CA 93110
(805) 682-2523

Quality Education Development,
Inc. (QED)
41 Central Park W
New York, NY 10023
(212) 724-3335

E. I. DuPont DeNemours & Co.
1007 Market St.
Wilmington, DE 19898
(302) 774-1000

# TABLE OF CASES

# INDEX